Integrating Computers into the Curriculum
A Handbook for Special Educators

Integrating Computers into the Curriculum
A Handbook for Special Educators

Edited by

Michael M. Behrmann, Ed.D.

Associate Professor
Curriculum and Instruction
George Mason University
Fairfax, Virginia

A College-Hill Publication
Little, Brown and Company
Boston / Toronto / San Diego

Appendices: Robert S. Gall, Ph.D.

Photographs: Carl T. Cameron, Ph.D.

College-Hill Press
A Division of
Little, Brown and Company (Inc.)
34 Beacon Street
Boston, Massachusetts 02108

Library of Congress Cataloging in Publication Data
Main entry under title:

Integrating computers into the curriculum: a handbook for special
   educators / edited by Michael M. Behrmann.
         p.   cm.
      "A College-Hill publication."
      Bibliography.
      Includes index.
      1. Special education — United States — Computer-assisted
instruction.   I. Behrmann, Michael M.
LC3969.5.I58 1988
371.9'043 — dc19   88-9244
                                                                          CIP

ISBN 0-316-08755-6

Printed in the United States of America

Contents

Preface   vii

Introduction   ix

Contributors   xvi

Chapter 1   *How Computers Work*   1
     Michael M. Behrmann

Chapter 2   *Therapeutic Applications and Adaptive Devices*   29
     Elizabeth A. Lahm and Karen Greszco

Chapter 3   *The Computer in School and Classroom Testing*   59
     Wayne P. Thomas

Chapter 4   *Electronic Toys and Robots*   79
     Joel Mittler

Chapter 5   *Using Authoring to Individualize Instruction*   103
     Marion V. Panyan

Chapter 6   *Computer Assisted Instruction in Special Education*   145
     Dianne Tobin

Chapter 7   *Word Processing and Related Tool Applications*   179
     Jeffrey W. Hummel

Chapter 8   *Electronic Spreadsheets and Data Base Management*   205
     Carl T. Cameron, Kathy Hurley, and Kate Wholey

Chapter 9   *Keys to the World: Microcomputer Technology and Telecommunications*   231
     Robert S. Gall

Appendix A   *Glossary*   261

Appendix B   *Networks*   267

Subject Index   279

Preface

This book is designed to assist teachers, administrators, and related services personnel, in incorporating computer technology into school curriculum. It addresses practical and currently available methods of using technology in the curriculum, with generic examples relating to exceptional children where possible. Unlike its sister book, *Handbook of Microcomputers in Special Education,* (Behrmann, 1984) [1] which focused on the nature and needs of children with handicaps and the ways that computers can address those needs, this book deals with the computer as a tool for teachers, administrators, related services personnel, and most importantly, children. This book should be useful to teachers of children who are non-handicapped, as well.

There is a clear discrepancy between what computers are capable of doing in educational settings and what they are actually used for. This book provides an overview of current model applications that benefit children with handicaps and the persons serving them. Computer technology is capable of even more, but that is for the future. As computers get more powerful, new applications will be developed to meet the needs of children with handicaps. However, it is often easier to design and market powerful hardware than powerful software, particularly when the applications are so varied. To date, the most powerful applications have been generic, that is, application software designed as productivity tools (including word processing, data bases, and spreadsheets). These types of applications have been creatively applied to the needs of children and personnel in the schools.

Computer applications in educational settings are generally classified into three major categories: computer assisted management (CAM), computer managed instruction (CMI), and computer assisted instruction (CAI) (Behrmann, 1984). These three categories are still valid, but only categorize the computer as a tool for adult educators. When children are considered, a whole new perspective on computers in education needs to be evaluated. Thus, an additional and important category of application software in education and special education, computer assisted learning (CAL), needs to be added.

In order to utilize computer tools correctly, it is important to understand the applications, their limitations, how they work, and to have enough skill to use them. This book is designed to provide educators with the fundamental knowledge necessary to successfully integrate the computer into the educational curriculum. The first chapter will provide basic

---

[1] Behrmann, M. M. (1984). *Handbook of microcomputers in special education.* San Diego: College-Hill Press.

information on how computers work and the technical information necessary to implement different applications. The following eight chapters discuss important tool applications for teachers, administrators, related educational personnel, and children. The topical areas addressed include therapeutic applications, testing, play, instruction, word processing, data base management and spreadsheets, telecommunications, and information retrieval.

Introduction

Computers in educational settings need to have some of their mystique stripped away, and educators should begin to evaluate their usefulness. Computers, in the most basic sense, are just dumb tools, no different from a shovel. Just as a shovel has a specific job to assist a capable human being, computers have jobs that can assist people.

There are several general advantages of computers: speed, accuracy, capacity, precision, and versatility. They can perform many activities, including evaluating large amounts of data faster, more reliably, and more precisely than a human being. In educational settings, computers as tools show some distinct advantages. They may be used by groups or by individuals. They allow teachers to better provide children with errorless learning experiences and immediate feedback according to established learning principles. Students can work at their own pace, and the computer can be adapted to meet individual student needs. Computers can also accept and provide information in a variety of ways. They can collect and analyze a variety of data, from demographics and inventory to individual or group student performance data. The same computer that preschoolers use for learning in their classroom can be used by their teacher after school.

COMPUTERS AS EDUCATIONAL TOOLS

Educators can use computers as tools in a variety of areas. Traditionally identified categories of applications have been computer assisted management (CAM), computer managed instruction (CMI), and computer assisted instruction (CAI). Generally, administrators and central office personnel have been primarily involved with CAM, while teachers, diagnosticians, and other direct service personnel use CMI and CAI.

Computer Assisted Management

Administrators use computers for management purposes. Word processing makes efficient use of clerical time and provides individual communication with large numbers of parents as well as school board members. Spreadsheets enable administrators to predict variations of future budgets and to have better control over expenditures and income in current budgets. Data base management provides easily accessible information on demographics, test results, transportation, and related services. Current and accurate information can, in turn, result in better services to children. Telecommunications provide better communication between administrators and direct service personnel within districts using electronic mail, and better access to outside information sources regarding policy decisions and personnel recruitment. Administrators can also use the computer to conduct research within the school division, construct local test norms and conduct program evaluations. Thus, computers have had a significant impact on administrators, who, in turn, affect the teachers and children within their school system.

There is great potential for administrators to use this technology beneficially. One example is the option of removing categorical labels (e.g., *learning disabled*) from children. There has been a continuing controversy in special education concerning the stigma attached to labeling children (Hobbs, 1974).[2] There is currently a system-wide data base required in the Individualized Educational Program (IEP) regulations of Public Law 94-142. This data base includes evaluation and service provision data on current and past students that could be used to make decisions on direct services without labeling. Whereas changing from a "labeling system" for service provision to one that uses this new data base is no small task. It is possible that this tool will benefit students who are handicapped by removing some of the stigma of a handicap.

Computer-Managed Instruction

Microcomputer technology can also be a management tool for teachers and other related services providers. These individuals can use computers in a way that directly affects instruction. Word processing facilitates parent and teacher communication, assists in writing reports (including IEPs), makes test construction and assignments easier, and assists in such instructional applications as handouts and transparencies. Spreadsheets assist with classroom budgeting, making handouts that need a column-type format, and also with grading and test calculations. Data base managers provide access to materials housed elsewhere in the school, and assist with classroom inventory and classroom demographic information for reports. Telecommunications provide teachers with access to information and advice in and out of their school system. Electronic bulletin boards and mail may provide new ideas for instruction, a forum for exchanging views and information, a source for help for particular problems, and location of specific material. For example, a hard-to-find Braille text may be available from a teacher in another state. Information data bases for bibliographic information (e.g., ERIC), as well as specialized data bases for materials (e.g., ABELDATA), are also available.

---

[2] Hobbs, N. (1974). *The future of children.* San Francisco: Jossey–Bass.

Specific computer applications are also available for teachers to test and monitor student performance. The ability to precisely monitor students is perhaps the greatest potential benefit for teachers. While many instructional software packages have some student performance data collection capability, most data from software cannot be integrated into more generic evaluation software. Currently, teachers are limited to software that requires manual input of data (collected either by software or the teacher) before it can be analyzed. Teachers also have access to limited testing software, enabling them to put raw scores into the software package and have derived scores and very cursory analyses done. Optical scanners can also decrease turn-around time for standardized tests, making results more relevant to direct instruction. While test application software can be a time saver and can reduce errors, it still has far to go before it provides a truly effective tool for teachers. When integrated CMI systems become a reality, the teacher and other service providers will be able to view and analyze performance data, from initial testing through current performance in instruction. This will allow teachers to plan and change instructional interventions in a much more efficient way.

Computer-Assisted Instruction

CAI is also a useful tool for direct service providers. It is capable of introducing knowledge and skill (tutorial), developing fluency (drill and practice), and providing opportunities to apply or generalize knowledge and skill to realistic situations (simulation and problem solving). These three steps are the basic objectives of educating children, and *CAI is only one tool in a continuum of instructional tools for achieving basic educational goals.*

Software application packages for instruction are being introduced quite rapidly. CAI is not the much-criticized, poorly designed drill and practice software of the early 1980s. Most instructional software is more sophisticated now. Textbook manufacturers are even developing computer courseware as supplementary materials, including appropriate drill and practice programs. Teachers also have additional tools for CAI development in the form of authoring software programs. Many of the applications developed through course authoring packages enter the public domain, and then teachers can either develop their own software or adapt other applications to meet individual needs.

As a tool for teachers, the computer must be viewed just as any other intervention or instructional material. Just as a teacher asks, "Should I use a 'Language Master' with Bobby?," the same type of question should be asked about the computer. The advantages and disadvantages of using computers must be addressed to meet the needs of each child.

There are many advantages of using computer aided instruction: a computer can provide immediate feedback when a teacher is occupied elsewhere; it can collect and analyze large amounts of discrete data on student performance in a precise and reliable manner; software can create multimodal instruction using graphics, sound, and illustrations; a computer can provide cues and help to each student on demand; a computer does not get impatient, allowing students to work at their own pace in an errorless environment when desirable; it can accept input of information in a variety of formats (adaptive devices); computer use can motivate students.

There are also disadvantages to using CAI: computers cannot adjust to situations that are not preprogrammed; they cannot listen and respond to students' related problems; they cannot observe child's behavior other than computer input; software often has very limited scope and sequence; software may not be available or appropriate; software may be prohibitively expensive; software review may take an inordinate amount of time; documentation may be poor or nonexistent; and use of the computer may frustrate the student.

In order for teachers to use CAI as a tool, factors such as these and others must be evaluated. As the power (memory and speed of classroom computers grows and instructional software becomes more intelligent and powerful, computers may take over many of the routine daily instructional tasks of the teacher. Computers will never, however, be able to compete with human beings in terms of flexibility and ability to evaluate many of the subtleties of the learning process. Teachers should find that CAI can give them the freedom to improve the quality of education by focusing on the more important instructional tasks and allow them to avoid some of the time-consuming monitoring tasks that are related to one-to-one instruction in today's classrooms.

COMPUTERS AS TOOLS FOR CHILDREN WITH DISABILITIES

Today, computers can be a learning tool for children just as paper and pencils were for previous generations. Computers can help make the learning process more efficient and make individuals more productive in everyday living. Computer technology has great potential benefits for children and adults with disabilities. Its power rests in the application of the technology as a tool for *manipulation* of ideas and objects, and as a tool for *compensation,* to take the physical or cognitive handicap out of a disability.

Computer technology as tools for children fall into four general categories: (1) a learning (academic) tool, (2) a living tool, (3) a vocational tool, and (4) a recreational tool. The following sections will briefly discuss each of these areas.

Computers as Learning Tools

Computers can provide children with tools that are similar to those used by adults. Computer assisted learning (CAL) applications include word processing, spreadsheets, data base management, and even simple programming languages. These application software packages for children may be easier to learn and less powerful than those designed for adults, but they give children essentially the same ability to manipulate ideas, concepts, and information as do adult productivity tools.

Word processors can be used by students to manipulate text, edit, get clean copy, and check spelling and grammar. For children with severe handicaps, word processing can allow the manipulation of whole words and phrase tables using adapted keyboards or switches that assist in written communication. Using voice synthesis, text can be spoken, allowing students who are visually handicapped or those with severe reading deficits to use word processing. Programming using languages such as *Logo* allows children to explore mathematical geometric concepts, space, and environment. For example, children with physical handicaps who are unable to move about can control *Logo* robots to vicariously explore their physical environments. Spreadsheets and data bases can also be used by children with handicaps for such activities as understanding math concepts by manipulating and managing numbers and formulas.

Telecommunications can assist in information access and use, allowing children to learn from other children in distant geographical locations or by using information retrieval systems. These applications can also be used with adaptions to allow users who are disabled to have access to otherwise unavailable technology based resources.

Computers as Living Tools

Children are also able to use the computer in daily living. For children with multiple handicaps, the computer can be used to manipulate the environment, turning on televisions and other electrical appliances. Robots can even manipulate food and drink. Voice synthesizers and communication software packages allow children who are non-verbal to talk to teachers and peers. Children who are visually impaired can read books and other material with optical scanners and synthesizers. Children who are deaf and mildly handicapped can communicate with other children using telecommunications. Word processing, spreadsheets and data base productivity tools can assist in communication and in such activities as balancing checkbooks and retrieving recipes.

As a living tool, computer technology must be programmed to be flexible and allow access to standard computer applications to the greatest extent possible. For children with multiple handicaps, the capacity to perform multiple tasks, such as answer the phone while the word processor is being used, is important, or the person calling might hang up by the time work is saved on the word processor. This requires the development of integrated systems where multiple tasks and multiple functions are possible. Additionally, portability is an issue because a communication device may be needed in both the school and home. Newer and more powerful microcomputer technology is quickly making this a reality.

The Computer as a Vocational Tool

Computers are also being used extensively in vocational settings. Our society is changing from an industrial base to an information base. Cottage industries specializing in information manipulation are springing up throughout the United States. Additionally, the manufacturing industry is developing an increased technological base. Automated manufacturing is rapidly changing the face of industry.

Just as technology can be adapted to allow most children to manipulate words on a word processor, vocational applications can be adapted as well. Technology manufacturers such as Apple and IBM include design parameters in new equipment that ensure that standardized interfaces to office equipment allow use by many disabled persons. Robotic work stations have been developed at such companies as Boeing Industries to enable employees who are quadriplegic to work. For individuals who are difficult to integrate into the work setting, telecommunication offers an option of working at home or in a smaller cottage industry better suited to meet the needs of workers who are disabled. Services such as mailing lists and data bases can be maintained by workers who are disabled who have the capability of being productive yet need special medical or other assistance.

Computers as Recreation and Leisure Tools

Computers can provide expanded ability for children who are disabled to engage in appropriate recreational activities. For example, socialization is enhanced through telecommunications, where autodialers can easily contact friends. Prewritten messages can make electronic mail cost-efficient. Access to art is now available through graphics packages for drawing and color printers. This software can be used with adapted devices to allow children who cannot hold a crayon to express themselves by drawing. Synthesizers enable a child who cannot use a piano keyboard to explore music and sound. Access to video games is also possible. With adapted devices and electronic control over the speed of the computer, a child who is disabled can play such popular video games as "Space Invaders" or "Pac Man."

EMPOWERING CHILDREN THROUGH TECHNOLOGY

In order for children who are disabled to use these new and powerful tools, it is necessary to provide them with the appropriate training and easy access to technology. For people who are disabled particularly those with multiple handicaps and higher cognitively functioning, we need to emphasize *access* to systems, with the primary emphasis on allowing them to use commercially available computer hardware and software with as little adaptation as possible.

Contributors

Michael M. Behrmann, Ed.D.
Associate Professor
Curriculum and Instruction
George Mason University
Fairfax, Virginia

Carl T. Cameron, Ph.D.
Associate Professor
Curriculum and Instruction
George Mason University
Fairfax, Virginia

Robert S. Gall, Ph.D.
Professor of Education
University of Lethbridge
Alberta, Canada

Karen Greszco, O.T.R.
Occupational Therapist Consultant
Herndon, Virginia

Jeffrey W. Hummel, Ph.D.
Assistant Professor
The Johns Hopkins University
Research Associate
Center for Technology in Human
   Disabilities
Baltimore, Maryland

Kathy Hurley
Vice President
Mindscape Inc.
Northbrook, Illinois

Elizabeth A. Lahm, D.A.Ed.
Center for Special Education
   Technology
Center for Exceptional Children
Reston, Virginia

Joel Mittler, Ed.D.
Assistant Dean
C.W. Post Center of Long Island
   University
Brookville, New York

Marion V. Panyan, Ph.D.
Associate Professor
The Johns Hopkins University
Director
Center for Technology in Human
   Disabilities
Baltimore, Maryland

Wayne P. Thomas, Ph.D.
Associate Professor
Educational Leadership and Human
   Development
George Mason University
Fairfax, University

Dianne Tobin, Ph.D.
Assistant Professor
The Johns Hopkins University
Research Associate
Center for Technology in Human
   Disabilities
Baltimore, Maryland

Kate Wholey
Research Associate
MACRO Systems, Inc.
Silver Spring, Maryland

CHAPTER 1

How Computers Work

MICHAEL M. BEHRMANN

Microprocessor technology is beginning to permeate nearly every portion of society. Computerization is found in the grocery store, the bank, the telephone system, and even in the toys children play with. Although this technology is beginning to be used as everyday appliances are, the microcomputer found in most classroom environments is still considered a "magic black box" that is not to be touched or invaded by educational personnel. If an appliance does not work properly, most people only call the repairman after they have attempted some basic trouble-shooting in order to save time and, more importantly, money. It is embarrassing and aggravating to pay $85 for a television service call when all that needed to be done was to reset a circuit breaker, replace a 10-cent fuse, or make sure the cord is plugged in correctly.

This chapter is designed to remove some of the mystery from the "magic box" by discussing basic operations and terminology for using microcomputers and the devices that are associated with computers in educational settings. It will provide an overview of how computers work in order to establish a basis for understanding technical jargon and detail necessary for operation, to define software parameters for a telecommunication or instructional application, and to explain the basics of hardware and software documentation. More detail on computer basics can be found in other texts, such as Bitter's *Computers in Today's World* (1984).

TYPES OF COMPUTERS

In the world of education, there are three basic types of computers used: microcomputers, minicomputers, and mainframe or maxicomputers (there are also super computers, but these are not yet being applied to schoolage populations). The characteristics that distinguish these categories are generally determined by power consumption requirements, environmental requirements, power and speed, and perhaps most importantly, the trained personnel that operate the machines (see Behrmann, 1984). To some degree the lines of demarcation between these computers are getting fuzzy because of the miniaturization and power of desktop computers that can be operated with limited training.

Mainframe and minicomputers have traditionally been used by school administrators to assist with scheduling, demographics, data collection and analysis for reporting, test evaluation, and payroll. Even administrators have not generally used the computer directly, but have had full-time personnel operating it. These computers generally have environmental requirements such as clean, air conditioned, and specially designed rooms, equipped with special power service. They are also much larger than microcomputers, some taking up an entire room or floor of a building. Thus, they are usually physically isolated from primary users.

Microcomputers have changed traditional computer use dramatically. Nearly simultaneously, microcomputers began to be used by administrators in managing schools, and early desktop computers became popular with personnel in the classroom for their potential instructional use. In education, common computers include such brand names as Apple, Commodore, IBM, and Tandy. While desktop computing power is quickly approaching that of minicomputers, the primary characteristic of microcomputers directly affecting the school is *personal* use; that is, the teacher, administrator, and even children directly use the computer in everyday work and generally do not need to have immediate access to computer specialists. Recently, even smaller, battery operated "laptop" computers have been introduced into the schools. These computers can operate up to eight hours on rechargeable batteries and can be taken home, used on airplanes, or moved from class to class by a child. They often use liquid crystal display (LCD) screens or can be attached to a regular monitor. Most laptop computers have capabilities identical to their desktop cousins.

Personal computing in the school environment is providing efficiency to teachers and administrators. The efficiency, however, does not come without a price. That price is time — time to learn to use application software and make the computer and associated devices (e.g., printers) work correctly.

In order to achieve relative independence from expensive technicians, who are often not available in school environments, it is necessary for school personnel to learn the rudiments of setting up hardware and software and how to troubleshoot when problems occur. The next two sections discuss some of the standard terminology and knowledge of computer hardware and software needed to make desktop computers work.

COMPUTER HARDWARE

A microcomputer has two major components: the system unit, where most of the operations take place, and peripheral devices, which provide the computer with ability to accept information (input) and display or transmit information (output).

The System Unit

This is the main "box" that houses the circuitry of the computer. Its primary components are the Central Processing Unit (CPU) and the main computer storage. CPUs and memory are found as integrated circuits (ICs), which are microminiaturized electronic circuits printed on IC "chips." CPUs are identified by manufacturer numbers printed on the chip, usually one of the larger ICs in the system unit. Common CPUs in computers in educational settings include the 6502 (MOS) technology found in Apple II computers, the 8088 (Intel) series in IBM, the Z-80 (Zilog) found on early Radio Shack and Heath-Zenith computers, and the 68000 (Motorola) in Apple Macintosh and Commodore Amiga computers (see Figure 1–1). Within the CPU are the control unit and the arithmetic-logic unit (ALU). The control unit acts as a traffic officer, synchronizing the operations and flow of information to and from all parts of the computer, including the ALU, which performs the necessary operations and returns the processed information to the controller (Bitter, 1984).

The main computer memory is composed of read only memory (ROM) and random access memory (RAM). ROM is generally encoded on IC chips and contains the necessary instructions for the CPU to operate the com-

FIGURE 1–1. *Three central processing unit (CPU) integrated circuits (ICs), left to right: IBM-Intel 8008, Apple-MOS 6502, Zilog Z-80.*

puter without software when the computer is turned on or "booted up." ROM is nonvolatile memory, that is, it does not disappear when the electricity to the computer is turned off. In addition to the basic computer instructions encoded in ROM, some computers have applications software such as word processing in ROM, thus allowing certain applications software to be automatically available when the computer is booted.

RAM is volatile memory, which allows the computer to temporarily store computer instructions, called "programs" or "software," while the computer operates according to those instructions. This memory allows the computer to rapidly access those instructions as well as store information derived from the application until it can be permanently stored by other memory devices. RAM is commonly associated with terminology such as 64K or 640K, the number of kilobytes of information that the computer can temporarily store until the power is turned off. When the amount of memory reaches one million bytes, the terminology changes to increments called "megabytes" or "megs" of memory. Thus a 1.4 meg memory holds 1,400,000 characters in memory.

In addition to the CPU and main memory, the system unit often has other features, depending on the design of the computer. Most system units also include a power supply that transforms alternating current (AC) to direct current (DC) and a "mother board" that provides the circuitry to enable the computer to utilize peripheral devices. "Ports" or physical connectors where cables can be plugged into the system unit allow communication with external peripheral devices.

Internal Communication in the System Unit

Computers internally communicate in "machine language" rather than in English or even in programming language such as BASIC. This machine language generally uses binary mathematical representation of numbers. If one thinks of how a computer must operate in its most basic function, it is a device that controls electrical circuits. If a circuit is "on" (electricity is running through a specific circuit) the computer represents this as a "one." If a circuit is "off" the representation is "zero." Thus, every operation of a computer is represented by zeros and ones.

The mathematical binary system is the basic language of computers and all functions of the computer must be represented as a series of these two numbers. Each "zero" or "one" is called a "bit" of information. A "byte" of information is the string of bits that a computer can process at one time CPUs in microcomputers are designed to process information in 8, 16, 32, or 64 bytes of information simultaneously. A string of eight bits of information makes up one byte in an Apple II, 16 bits make a byte in an IBM, and 32 bits make a byte in a Macintosh or Commodore Amiga. Generally, computer memory is described in terms of bytes since each of these bytes of information can in turn represent a letter of the alphabet or digit, a concept that is easy for us to understand. However, unless the applications software is encoded in ROM, the software and text must share the space in RAM. For example, in a 640K computer, a word processing software program may require 128 kilobytes of memory, thus enabling the user to store and work on documents that have up to 512,000 characters in the document. If the average word length is 10 letters and spaces, this translates to approximately 50,000 words, quite a significant amount of text.

As one might guess, the larger the amount of information processed simultaneously by the CPU, the faster the machine. This also limits the amount of directly "addressable RAM" (how much memory the CPU can access at one time). Eight-bit machines can only access 64K, 16-bit machines can have 640K, and so forth. The size of RAM allows larger and generally more powerful application software to be developed and run. Less powerful computers such as the Apple IIe have been able to expand addressable memory by adding "banks" of memory. The Apple adds 64K memory banks but each bank must be separately addressed by the CPU.

Some computers such as the Apple II series (8 bit) and IBM PC (16 bit) have "open architecture." The system unit can be opened and the computer can have additional features (peripherals) added. Other computers, such as the older Apple Macintosh and many laptop computers, have a "closed architecture" whereby the devices must be included in the original computer design or must communicate with the computer through communication channels or "ports" in the system unit. Due to the nature and needs of the heterogeneous special education population, systems with open architecture have proven most popular. These systems generally have a series of "slots" on a "bus" where circuit boards that control peripheral devices can be installed (see Figure 1–2). The bus provides the highway through which information or commands controlled by the CPU must travel to and from these devices to the CPU and main memory. This highway uses different numbers of lanes or "traces" where information can travel in "parallel" down the bus. The number of traces is determined by whether the computer is an 8, 16, or 32 bit machine. Thus in an Apple, which is an 8-bit computer, eight bits of information can simultaneously travel down the bus and to other parts of the computer. Information traveling down the traces can be compared to a metrobus traveling on a highway. Each of the slots acts as a bus stop where information can get on or off in a single trip. As the number of bits simultaneously transmitted increases, the power and speed of the computer increase.

FIGURE 1-2. *A computer within a computer: A Microsoft Z-80 installed on the bus of an Apple mother board.*

Peripheral Devices

Peripheral devices allow for the input or output of information to and from the system unit. These devices can either be housed within the system unit using one of the slots on the bus, or they can be connected by cables through ports on the system units. It is even possible to have a "computer within a computer" by installing a specially designed peripheral card in a slot. For example, there are cards that allow IBM computers to run Apple software or allow Apples to run CP/M. These cards actually have most of the components of the other system's mother board on the peripheral card. These cards generally allow the "peripheral computer" to access drives, printers, and other devices through the host computer's input/output channels.

Terminology for sending information from one device to another is called "I/O" for input/output. Some devices perform both functions and generally are used for computer-to-computer transmission of information or data storage and retrieval of information. Computer-to-computer transmission of information is generally done through networks and uses modems and other special peripheral devices, which are briefly described in this chapter and in Chapter 9. Since data storage devices are commonly accessed by the CPU and information moved from nonvolatile storage media to volatile RAM, these devices will be discussed next.

Data Storage and Retrieval Devices

Peripheral I/O data storage devices include floppy disks, tape, hard, or "fixed" disks, and newer optical storage devices. Storage can be accessed either sequentially or randomly. Storage devices can store from thousands of characters to millions, depending on the specific technology used.

Disk drives are the most common storage devices that perform both input and output functions. These magnetic storage media come in three common sizes, 3.5 inch, 5.25 inch, and 8 inch versions. "Floppy diskettes," the magnetic storage media used in disk drives, are popular because of their low cost, the relatively large amounts of data they store, and the speed with which they can access information randomly (see Figure 1–3). They are very efficient in storing and retrieving information. Most applications software packages are available on floppy disk. Disks are blank when purchased and, assuming that they meet specifications of a computer manufacturer, they can be used with many different types of computers. Depending on the computer model and the way that computer formats the disk, storage can range from 160K (Apple II) to 1.4 megabytes (IBM PS/2) of memory.

Tape memory can also be used, but it has the disadvantage of "linear access," much like finding a specific music track on a cassette tape versus putting the needle down on the track of record album. Floppy disks use "random access." While early microcomputers often had cassette storage

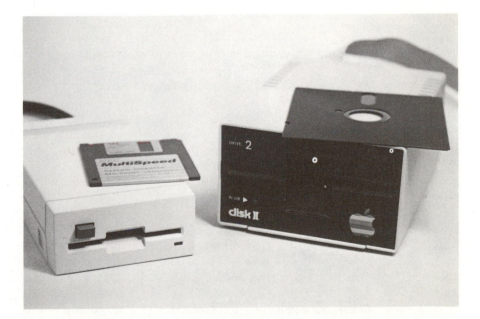

FIGURE 1–3. *3.5- and 5.25-inch disk drives and diskettes.*

capability and several early laptop computers used microcassettes, most tape storage today is used to back up or make a copy of large amounts of information held on hard or fixed disks.

Hard or fixed disks are very popular with individuals having large amount of information to store or a large number of software programs to access. Storage capacity ranges from 10 megabytes to 140 megs or more. These disks can rapidly access very large amounts of data and large numbers of applications quickly and reliably. For handicapped users who may have difficulty seeing or manipulating floppy disks, a hard disk system requires the user to merely turn the computer on in order to access any application available. Two notes of caution are necessary for hard disk users: good organization is necessary or you may have a hundred million characters of useless and inaccessible information, and backing up information stored on a hard disk on tape or floppy disk is necessary because these systems occasionally "crash" (fail to work).

Optical storage of data using laser technology is currently entering the microcomputer market. Compact Disk Read Only Memory (CDROM) and Write Once Read Only Memory (WOROM) are adding even larger amounts of data storage and retrieval for microcomputers to access (see Figure 1-4). CD drives provide as much as 600 megabytes of memory. For example, the entire Grollier Encyclopedia (20-plus volumes) is on a single 5-inch CD similar to the CD used in the music industry. The information on the Grol-

FIGURE 1-4. *Phillips CD-ROM drive with optical compact disk.*

lier Encyclopedia disk is accessible using a very sophisticated data base retrieval system that can search for words and phrases and even search for combinations in the same file, paragraph, or sentence. WOROM technology takes this one step further, allowing the user to actually determine the content of the disk and write to it once (current technology requires highly specialized and expensive equipement to write information on CDs). Using such technology, large data bases such as ERIC can be sent to individual users or libraries, avoiding "on-line" computer and telephone charges.

One final word on disk storage is needed. Some computers, including IBM and Apple, have software and hardware that will allow the user to take a portion of RAM and define an electronic disk drive. This can speed up software applications significantly because no mechanical access to information is necessary. However, the information stored in these electronic drives is volatile and disappears when electricity is interrupted, so caution should be exercised by saving data in magnetic storage.

Computer-to-Computer Input/Output Devices

Computers can talk to each other, providing and storing information for one another's use. Communication is achieved either through a hardwired network or the telephone system using a modem. A modem is a device that changes the zeros and ones of the binary machine language to auditory tones (e.g., a high frequency for a zero and a low frequency for a one) that can be discerned by a modem at the other end of the phone line. The term "modem" actually stands for *mo*dulating and *dem*odulating sounds. Modems can also be used to connect phone systems with worldwide telecommunications networks that use their own mainframe computers, satellite, and microwave communications (see Chapter 9 for more detail). Other network systems include Local Area Networks (LANs), which use wiring similar to cable television. These networks are usually found in a single facility because distances of over 500 feet need regular signal amplification. However, they are capable of simultaneously transmitting voice, data, and video with many thousands of devices communicating simultaneously. In a local environment such as a classroom or a suite of offices there are small networks using host computers with hard disks as network controllers or "servers." These use network systems such as IBM's Token Ring, or a UNIX system, which enable the host computer to provide access to software packages, electronic mail, and also allow the small group of networked computers to communicate with each other.

INPUT DEVICES. There are a number of mechanisms for putting information into the computer. Standard input devices found on many computers in educational settings include the keyboard, game paddles, joysticks, a "mouse," and even another computer. Additionally, there are touch-screens that allow selection by touching the monitor screen; touch-tablets that can be used for graphics input or electronically divided into multiple switches, pointing devices such as a mouse, light pens or infrared pointers that inter-act with a monitor or special pad; and optical readers such as those incor-porating bar codes. There are also many more sophisticated input devices as well as specially designed input devices adapted for handicapped users (see Figures 1–5 and 1–6). Adaptive devices range from single switches that can be connected through a game port to those that act as a keyboard emu-lator. More sophisticated input devices can evaluate eye movement or changes in reflectivity between the eye and the eyelid. Muscular sensing devices used in biofeedback can also be used as input devices, as can voice recognition, which allows an individual to speak into a microphone to con-trol the computer.

In general, input devices use one of three access methods: direct selec-tion of information desired for input, a software-controlled procedure, or a coding system. With direct selection, the user directly accesses the informa-tion that is desired as input. Pressing the letters or numbers on the key-board acts as a direct selection procedure, which results in that letter or number being input into the computer. Software-controlled selection pre-sents the user with an array of choices in a predetermined sequence with a "cursor" or video indicator moving from choice to choice. The user may

FIGURE 1–5. *Adapted input device: A chin switch.*

FIGURE 1-6. *Adapted keyboard as an input device: Muppet Learning Keys.*

press a single switch or an array of switches to provide input when prompted by the computer. This process is generally a much slower means of providing input into the computer, but may be necessary because of a physical or cognitive disability. (see Figure 1–7). Encoding requires the user to memorize certain shorthand "codes" for input that the computer can translate into action or text. Chapter 2 goes into greater detail on input as well as output devices and selection processes.

OUTPUT DEVICES. Just as there are a variety of peripheral input devices available for computers, there is a range of ways that computers can "output" information to the user. Standard peripheral output devices include monitors and printers. It is also possible to output information to another computer using a network connection or through a telephone. The most common output devices are a monitor or television and a printer that can produce text and graphics either in color or black-and-white. There is also a variety of more sophisticated output devices, including voice and music synthesis, environmental controllers such as those that operate electrical appliances and battery-operated toys, and even robots that manipulate objects in the environment. Specially designed adaptive output devices have also been developed, including commuication devices that can speak for non-verbal users, machines like the Kurtzweill Reader that reads different

FIGURE 1-7. *Adapted input and output: A battery-operated toy activated by a switch.*

type fonts, and braille printers to print material for visually handicapped individuals.

    Monitors are either color or monochrome and can be either standard or high resolution. Many older computers used standard televisions as monitors. Since these televisions were designed to convert radio signals to video, it was necessary for computers to send a radio signal to the television's receiver. Thus computer signals were sent through a radio frequency (RF) modulator. Most new computers use monitors rather than televisions and use a digital video signal. Standard monitors and televisions are generally limited to a few colors on the screen at one time (e.g., Apple II) and are characterized by jagged lines and circles. These monitors and televisions generally are not capable of producing readable text in more than 40 columns. High resolution monitors have more dots, or pixels, per inch and thus are easier to read, can produce 80 columns, and have the capability of providing more and crisper colors on the screen (see Figure 1-8). High resolution color monitors are called "RGB" monitors because they send separate red, green, and blue signals from the computer to the monitor rather than sending a single composite signal similar to that of a cable television. RGB monitors can display hundreds of colors at the same time. Thus different cables and interfaces or ports are necessary for RGB and composite monitors.

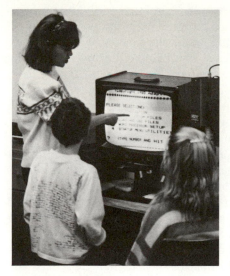

FIGURE 1-8. *A high resolution monitor that makes text easier to read.*

There are also other video output devices that are becoming popular in education. "Interactive Videodisc and Videotape" allows the computer to access laser and videotape technology in powerful instructional packages that make the once passive television accessible for interactive learning. Videodiscs use the same laser technology as CD ROM. A single side of a videodisc the size of an LP can hold 54,000 different pictures, which have a random access time of less than two seconds. Interactive videodisc and tape can present sequences of film, individual pictures, text, and even software for the computer to use. Additionally, computer graphics and text can be "overlayed" on the video, allowing highlighting or textual information to be added. The capability of this technology has yet to be fully explored in educational settings, but the instructional power has enormous potential.

Printers. There are six basic categories of printers: dot matrix, ink jet, thermal, daisywheel, laser printers, and plotters. The computer sends information to the printer either through a parallel or a serial communication line. A parallel printer gets information much faster because multiple wires send coded information simultaneously at generally faster transmission speeds. A serial printer has information sent as a string of characters, each letter being coded by a series of signals which the printer decodes and translates into text. Serial printers are most suitable for networks and mainframe communications because they can have long cables. Parallel printers need to be within 14 feet of the computer. When investigating a printer for purchase two factors that are especially important are the quality of the print and the speed of the printer. Speed is usually measured as characters per second (cps).

Dot matrix printers use a print head that combines individual pins to form letters much like the pixels on the monitor. Depending on the number of dots per character and the type font used, the quality of text can vary from barely legible to letter quality. They can print either by hammering the pins on a ribbon or by using heat to transfer the text onto special thermal paper. Dot matrix printers can also print graphics as easily as text because they are printing each dot on the page. Color dot matrix printers use multi-colored ribbons to print color graphics and text.

Thermal printers work much like dot matrix printers except they use heat to transfer characters to specially developed paper. They may or may not need a ribbon to make the transfer depending on the paper and printer used.

Ink jet printers spray ink directly onto specially prepared paper through a moving orifice that shapes each letter or graphic character. Ink jet printers are much quieter than dot matrix printers but require more care and maintenance because the ink can dry and plug the print orifice.

Daisywheel and thimble printers use metal or plastic print heads that have letters, numbers, and a limited number of special characters on them. These work much like a traditional typewriter: characters are hammered on a ribbon, one letter at a time, to produce the printed text. These printers generally produce high quality text, but they are slow and noisy and generally need more maintenance. Daisywheel printers also have a very limited ability to produce graphics.

Laser printers, on the other hand, are quiet and fast and can produce high quality text that approaches that produced by a typesetter. They are capable of producing fine graphics, and when combined with a digital scanner, they can even copy photographs and line drawings. They work much like a copy machine, with text and graphics sent to a memory "buffer," where an entire page is stored and then printed as an entire unit. Laser printers are extremely fast, printing eight or more pages per minute. By comparison, a letter quality dot matrix printer or a daisywheel printer may take two or three minutes to print a single page.

Plotters are generally used to produce graphics. Some are capable of working on much larger paper, up to poster size, than printers. Plotters use a series of different colored pens to make graphic drawings. They need specialized software to make the graphics, but the results are generally very high quality.

COMPUTER SOFTWARE

Computer software can be defined as the sequence of instructions that controls the operation of the computer's hardware. Software can be encoded permanently on ICs as ROM or on some storage medium (generally a floppy disk) that can be transferred into RAM. Software fits into three general categories: operating, programming, and applications software.

Operating System Software

Operating system software is the set of instructions that makes a particular brand or model of a computer function. Operating software contains the fundamental commands that the user must know in order to effectively use a specific computer. Such commands as "copy" and "save" files, "load" and "run" software programs, as well as other commands to access peripheral devices, are incorporated into operating software. Generally just enough instructions to allow the computer to use other operating software are encoded in ROM. With most of the computer's operating instructions on disk, manufacturers can upgrade operating software and expand and refine the system later. It is necessary to have basic operating software booted on the computer in order for any applications software to operate. Thus, many applications packages have directions for placing that operating software on the original disk or storage media using that software. While it is possible to first boot the operating software and then insert a disk with the applications software (for example, a math instructional package), it is much more convenient to just place the applications package in the disk drive and turn on the machine.

Many computers call their operating software "DOS," which stands for disk operating system. For example, MS-DOS is MicroSoft DOS and is the operating system for IBM compatible computers. Apple II computers use Apple DOS or PRO-DOS. Another common operating system for computers using Z-80 CPUs is called CP/M which is Control Programs for Microcomputers. CP/M was an early standard operating system for microcomputers and a large number of software applications packages was developed using CP/M. Due to the quantity of applications software available in CP/M, Z-80 cards (computers within computers) have been popular peripheral devices to add shortly after a new computer is marketed.

Programming Software

Programming languages provide the mechanism for computers to carry out instructions. These instructions must be written in a "language" that the computer can understand or there must be a translation to that language. Each of these languages has its own grammar and syntax. Since the computer is basically not very smart, each of these languages must precisely define what the computer is to do. The low-level language that computers understand is called "machine language." A second level of programming language (mid-level) is called "assembly language." The third level of programming (high-level) more closely resembles human language. Each higher level of language needs a greater amount of translation and takes more time for the computer to operate. Most computer users in education do not need to know much about low- and mid-level languages, other than to understand how the computer uses them to operate.

Low Level Languages

Computers use "binary" as their machine language. In an eight-bit computer, the CPU needs to use a series of eight binary digits in order to execute instructions. Just how language that humans understand is translated into the binary number language computers understand can be seen by explaining how the computer represents text and numbers using the American Standard Code for Information Interchange (ASCII). *ASCII* uses a seven bit code that uses binary signals to identify letters, numbers, and special control codes, non-graphic characters that control operations such as carriage returns, clear screen, and backspace. *ASCII* assigns each character a number from 0 to 128. For example, the capital letter "A" is assigned number 65. In binary, the number 65 is represented as 01000001. Briefly, this can be translated to the number 65 which represents "A" in *ASCII*. More information on *binary* can be found in Behrmann (1984) and Bitter (1984).

Mid-Level Languages

At this level of language, letters are often used to represent the machine language. *Assembler* and *HEX* (for hexadecimal) are used as a programmer's shorthand to binary. In *HEX,* for instance, a base of 16 rather than a base 2 binary language is used. The numbering system is the same as *binary* from 0–9, and then letters from A–F are represented by 10–16. In *HEX,* then, the coded number 65 representing the *ASCII* letter "A" would be 41 or 4×16 (64) plus one, equaling 65. The *HEX* representation of 366 would be AB, or $(10 \times 16) + (11 \times 16) = 160 + 176 = 366$. It should be noted that it is highly unlikely that any educational computer user will need to know mid-level programming.

High-Level Languages

High-level languages are much more like human languages. These languages can be all-purpose such as *BASIC* (Beginners All Purpose Symbolic Instructional Code) or developed for specific applications such as business *COBOL* (Common Business Oriented Language). Other high-level languages include *Pascal, C, Logo, Pilot, Forth,* and many others. Each language has advantages and disadvantages. Most are available on different brands of computers.

Educators in general have also not chosen to learn most high-level programming languages, nor do they really need to learn them. A few teachers and administrators who are the primary computer resource personnel or who are teaching computer science have learned languages such as *BASIC*, *Pascal* and *C*. More educators, however, are choosing to learn simple authoring programs and *Logo* because they can be directly applied to the classroom. *Logo* is a language that can be taught to young children to provide them with a tool to explore space and time with the computer. Authoring languages such as *Pilot* are used by teachers to develop instructional applications software. It is not the purpose of this text to teach even introductory use of any high-level programming language, but rather to make educators aware of their existence. Chapter 5 discusses authoring languages in detail.

Applications Software

Computers have become popular in our society because of their applications. Applications software provides educators and children with the ability to use computers effectively. Computers have become important tools, making life and learning easier and faster in the classroom, in vocational situations, in recreation, and finally in daily activities. Applications software includes programs popular with business, such as word processors, data base managers, and electronic spread sheets. It also includes tutorial and instructional software used in training in schools, homes, and the workplace. Recreational applications include games, music, art, and socialization through telecommunications. Finally, computer software applications include programs associated with everyday living, including writing, balancing a checkbook, dialing and answering the phone, and even having a computer read a newspaper story aloud using a voice synthesizer.

The primary requirement of applications software is that is is designed to provide access and use of the computer with as little technical knowledge as possible. In computer jargon, this is called being "user friendly." Readers should note, however, that as applications increase in complexity and power they often require that the user learn and remember more material. This learning may be directly related to the individual software package or it may require technical knowledge of the operating system and the hardware.

GETTING COMPUTERS TO COMMUNICATE WITH PERIPHERALS AND EACH OTHER

There are five major ports that a computer uses to access peripheral devices: game ports, video ports, audio ports, parallel ports, and serial ports.

Depending on the model, there may also be additional ports mounted on peripheral cards that are inserted in the slots on the mother board's bus allowing external disk drive access or other input and output devices such as a mouse or digitizing pad. However, many I/O devices are designed to take advantage of the standard access channels to the system unit.

Once these ports are connected by hardware, software parameters may need to be defined in order for the devices to communicate. These communication channels are particularly important for printers and modems that enable computers to communicate over telephone lines.

Hardware: Cables and Interfaces

The system unit must be able to identify peripheral devices as well as be configured to use them. This is accomplished through software and hardware. The permutations of these configurations are extensive, and manuals must be read to work with specific hardware. However, it is important to note that there may be "dip-switches" (see Figure 1–9) or "jumpers," either on the mother board, on peripheral cards, or in the peripheral devices that configure the computer for memory and number and types of storage devices (e.g., disk drives). They also allow other peripheral devices to be configured in order to communicate with each other.

FIGURE 1–9. *Dip switches in upper left corner of circuit board (labeled SW1 & SW2) make it possible to configure peripherals.*

Game Ports

Game ports allow the computer to primarily accept input devices. These may include joy sticks and paddles used to play computer games, or provide single-switch access to disabled individuals who are using adaptive software. Other input devices such as touch windows, light pens, mice, and digitizers have also been developed for the game port. Game port interfaces in newer microcomputers are generally nine pin "D" connectors (named after the shape of the plug). These are generally accessible on the outside of the system unit, either designed into the unit or available as peripheral cards that can be inserted in the bus slots. The old Apple II series computer also had a 16 pin connector located on the mother board of the computer (see Figure 1–10). These connectors were difficult to insert and remove without breaking, and a special tool called an IC remover was needed to take the connector out safely. A number of vendors introduced connector extensions outside the system unit that were easier to operate.

Video Ports

Video ports are used primarily for interfacing the monitor with the system unit. As noted previously, monitors can be standard or high resolution, monochrome or RGB, or a standard television can be used. There are three primary types of video signals used with computers: a radio frequency (RF) signal, a composite (single wire) signal, and a synchronized (multiple wire) signal. The radio frequency signal requires an RF modulator to transform the digital video signal into a radio wave signal that can be used by a standard television receiver. A digitized composite signal is transmitted through a single wire to the monitor using an "F" or "BNC" connector (much like that used in cable TV) or, more commonly, a standard phono (RCA) plug. A

FIGURE 1–10. *Joystick with a 16 pin connector.*

synchronized signal is required for high resolution RGB monitors, generally using a nine pin "D" connector like the game port interface. Although only three primary signals are used, there is an enormous variety of interface connectors (see Figures 1-11, 1-12, & 1-13), most of which have adapters to make it possible to get the right connector at the system unit end and the monitor end of the cable. Computers also use other video I/O devices. For example, enhanced graphics peripheral cards may be necessary for high resolution color monitors and computer controlled videodisc players may have their own interface card and associated cable connectors. These devices may also have cable connections through serial ports and audio ports simultaneously.

Audio Ports

Audio ports on computers are probably the simplest output devices, although audio via voice synthesis can be slightly more complicated. Most computers have their own audio speaker, but also have a port allowing audio to be played through the monitor or external speaker. Newer com-

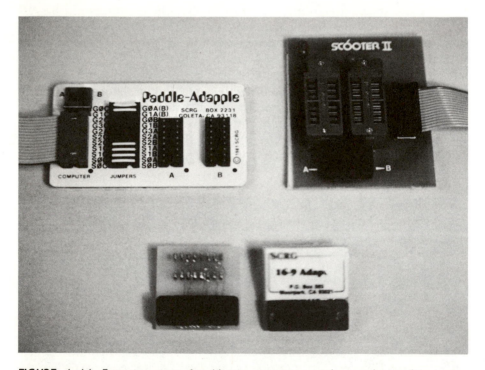

FIGURE 1-11. *Extension ports for 16 pin connector and an adapter for a nine pin "D" connector.*

FIGURE 1-12. *Radio frequency (RF) modulator with RCA connectors and nine pin RGB "D" male and female connectors.*

puters such as the Apple II GS, the IBM PS/2 and the Commodore Amiga have sophisticated sound synthesizers that can produce high quality mono and stereo sound (music or voice). These systems can be attached to a stereo amplifier or speaker. External ports for audio connectors most often use the RCA phono plug or a mini-plug. There are fewer variations in audio plugs than in video plugs, but still may be necessary to have adapted available (see Figures 1-14 & 1-15).

Parallel Ports

Parallel ports are primarily used as output channels to communicate with printers. However, since printers must also "talk to" computers, parallel ports have the capacity to be used for input. On the IBM, an adaptive

FIGURE 1-13. Composite video connectors and adapters, left to right: UHF plug (male) to RCA jack (female), BNC jack to F jack, BNC plug to UHF plug, RCA jack to BNC plug, UHF plug to F jack, and F plug to RCA jack.

FIGURE 1-14. Female audio and video connectors on the back of a TV/monitor, top left to bottom right: VHF and UHF antenna connectors, 75 ohm "F" connector, BNC video-in and video-out, BNC video-out and RCA audio-out, RCA audio-in and audio-out, and EIAJ eight pin synchronized video and audio.

FIGURE 1-15. *Audio connectors, left to right: Two subminiature (3/32") plug to jacks, mini (1/8") plug to RCA jack, subminiature jack split to two plugs, standard (1/4") to RCA jack, mini plug to standard jack, and RCA plug to mini jack.*

device called the PC A.I.D. (Don Johnson Developmental Equipment, Zurich, IL) acts as a keyboard input device that uses single switches.

As discussed earlier, the computer is able to use multiple channels of transmission simultaneously. If eight wires are used, then a complete byte of information can be sent at one time on an Apple II. A parallel interface for a 16 bit computer requires 16 wires for data transmission, and so forth. Many dot matrix and ink jet printers use a parallel interface with the computer. Thus they are commonly known as "parallel printers." The connecting cable generally uses eight wires and connections are often made using a "Centronics" type connector. Some computers, such as the IBM, require a different connector, a "DB-25" pin connector, at the system unit. Shaped like a capital "D," it has 25 separate wires attached to the interface (see Figure 1-16). The IBM does not send 16 bit parallel transmissions to the printer, but uses an eight bit interface and uses ASCII code to transmit textual material. Parallel printers are generally very fast, able to print as much as 300 lines per minute. High speed laser printers can use parallel information to print up to 20,000 lines per minute. The primary disadvantage of parallel transmission of information to printers is that the printer generally must be placed relatively close to the computer that is sending the data (computers can only reliably transmit parallel data over a short distance, up to 14 feet).

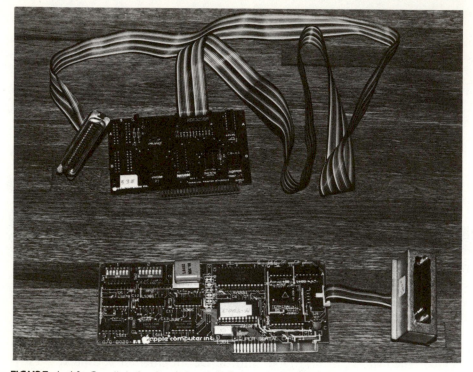

FIGURE 1-16. *Parallel (top) and serial (bottom) circuit boards and connectors. The parallel connector uses a Centronics connector and the serial card uses a "D" connector called a "DB-25."*

Serial Ports

Serial ports are generally used with printers and modems, although this port provides an easy interface between such devices as a mouse, voice synthesizers, and digitizers. Printers using a serial port are commonly called "serial" printers. Most daisywheel printers are serial printers, but dot matrix, ink jet, and laser printers can also use serial interfaces.

A serial port takes the information passing internally in the system unit and transmits data over a telephone (via modem) or other line bit by bit (in a binary "series" of zeros and ones). Thus only a free-standing single channel is required to transmit data (see Figure 1–16). The interface on a serial connector is typically an RS-232 connection. The cables generally use a DB-25 pin connector. In order to transmit serial data, it is necessary for the computer to add additional information so the peripheral device (e.g., a serial printer) knows when the information representing the character begins and ends. This is done through the setting of software parameters and through command signals sent through multiple wires (generally there are 3–7 connections) in the serial interface cable. With the appropriate amplification device, serial transmission is reliable over long distances.

Software: Communication Between Devices

While each computer and peripheral device has its own idiosyncrasies and it is *absolutely necessary to read the manual* in order to make devices work as specified, there are some general standards in data communication. Because there are many manufacturers of computers, printers and modems, these devices must be able to communicate effectively. Therefore, there are some standard procedures and standard terminology in the field. For example, in common terminology, "DCE" refers to data communication equipment, usually a computer or modem, but a device that is a source of data. "DTE" or data terminal equipment usually refers to a printer or "dumb" terminal with no source data. There are a number of features that need to be understood as they relate to data communications. These features or parameters must be set in such a manner that the devices can communicate without losing information. The following discuss the parameters that are primarily found in data communications.

AMERICAN STANDARD CODE FOR INFORMATION INTERCHANGE (ASCII). *ASCII* codes fit easily within the eight bit configuration of microcomputers and even more powerful computers use this standard code to communicate.

CHARACTER WIDTH. This parameter defines the number of data bits (either seven or eight) that make up each of the characters being transmitted.

PARITY. When information that is formatted in parallel is changed to a serial string of binary digits, it is necessary for an additional bit to be added to such information as the seven bit *ASCII* characters, to allow detection of errors. To achieve this the communication device counts the number of one's in the seven binary bits and adds a one or a zero in the open eight bit to make an odd or even number of ones. The printer or peripheral device has been instructed that all transmissions must be either odd or even. Following transmission, the receiving device counts the numbers to ensure that they are odd or even. Sometimes there is no parity specified and the computer looks for "none." However, data transmission mistakes are more likely if there is no parity.

STOP AND START BITS. In addition to knowing when there are transfer errors, the computer must be able to identify when characters or data transmissions begin and end. These are bits added to indicate the beginning and end of each character. At low transmission speeds two stop bits are often used; at higher speeds one is usually used.

TRANSMISSION SPEED. Baud rate is the terminology that indicates the number of bits transmitted per second. Generally baud rates are 110, 300, 1200, 2400, and 9600. A rate of 300 baud equals a data transmission rate of about 250–300 bits per second (bps), while 1200 baud means approximately 1200 bps. One baud is one change or modulation per second. A 300-baud transmission carries 25 to 30 characters per second, and 1200 baud carries 100 to 120 characters per second. It is not uncommon for modems to be 300–2400 baud and printers to run at 9600 baud.

LINE ENDS. Like a typewriter, the microcomputer uses a carriage return in internal files to indicate a move back to the left margin and a one-line paper advance. Some computers distinguish between a carriage return and a line feed, and require both. Communications software should add line feeds to carriage returns if necessary and strip incoming line feeds when accomplished by a carriage return. If these steps are not taken, double line feeds may be noted, or the receiving device may have lines write over previous lines.

FILTERS AND PAUSES. For some communications systems, certain characters must be deleted for the receiving device to function properly. Additionally, some receiving devices require a short pause at the end of each line to allow them to process the incoming information.

SYNCHRONOUS AND ASYNCHRONOUS COMMUNICATION. An important distinction is also made between synchronous and asynchronous communications. Asynchronous communications (usually with modems and printers) utilize a start/stop data transfer method that send digital signals one character at a time. The bit configuration of a standard *ASCII* character includes a start bit and one or more stop bits, seven binary information bits and a parity bit.

Synchronous communications (generally used for micro-mainframe communications) involves block mode data transfer, or characters that are transmitted as a group. A timing signal establishes the data transmission rate and special synchronization characters are sent before transmission to synchronize the transmitters and receivers. Synch characters maintain synchronization between blocks. Data is held in a buffer until a block has been transmitted. The "synchronous" designation comes from the use of synchronization characters that are put at the beginning and end of each data block, negating the need for asynchronous start and stop bits.

COMMUNICATION CHANNELS. There are three types of data communication channels. "Simplex" provides one-way communication only, as in television. "Half-duplex" is alternating two-way communication over a single channel or line (the peripheral must wait for computer at the other end to stop before sending). "Full-duplex" allow simultaneous two-way communication, as in telephone conversation. In full-duplex communication "Echoplex" is available to allow transmission quality to be monitored by watching transmitted characters simultaneously being shown on the screen of the sending computer. A common error occurs when full-duplex is chosen at one terminal and half-duplex is at the other terminal, resulting in two of "eeaacchh" letter appearing on the screen.

FILE TRANSFER PROTOCOLS. File transfer protocols are standardized processes that help two devices interact without error for transferring data. These allow two devices to "handshake," that is, provide a pre-determined manner by which the receiving device signals the sending computer to pause (these signals may be called XON/XOFF, clear to send [CTS], and none). If the two computers do not agree on the handshake, portions of long files will be lost. The primary types of protocol are stop/start, send lines, and error free.

Stop/start protocols utilize the commands Ctl-S (DC3) to stop and Ctl-Q (DC1) to start transmissions. A user of a modem may be able to tell the host computer to stop transmission when the screen is full by pushing the control and "S" characters on the keyboard. Control and "Q" likewise restart the transmission after the screen has been read by the user. Communication software sends the same signals when the computer needs time to process or save information.

Send lines protocols process lines of text or data one at a time, not in bulk, like transmissions from a computer bulletin board. This type of protocol uses prompt characters to start and stop single line transmissions.

With error free transmission, both sender and receiver must use same software protocol such as Hayes Verification Protocol or X-MODEM. These protocols are particularly important when transferring program, code files, or data when bit loss is undetectable or may create significant problems later on. Note that textual transmission allow readers to see the characters or blocks of information are missing because data does not then make contextual sense. Strings of numbers and letters do not have that same contextual sense, and errors can easily be overlooked.

SUMMARY

Computers are not really difficult to understand or use, although nearly every user has wished at one time or another to pitch the machine out the window and go back to a simpler way of life. It was the intent of this chapter to take the mystery out of some of the computer's internal workings and provide some basic operational knowledge. The remaining chapters will address most of the ways in which computers are being most effectively used in the schools. The technology has much to offer, but we as educators still have a long way to go before the computer is as friendly as our television and microwave oven.

REFERENCES

Behrmann, M. M. (1984). *Handbook of microcomputers in special education.* San Diego: College-Hill Press.
Bitter, G. G. (1984). *Computers in today's world.* New York: John Wiley & Sons.
Hobbs, N. (1974). *The future of children.* San Francisco: Jossey-Bass.

CHAPTER 2

Therapeutic Applications and Adaptive Devices

ELIZABETH A. LAHM
KAREN GRESZCO

Since the introduction of microcomputers into education in the mid-1970s, the number of systems available to children has increased many-fold. The utility of the microcomputer as a tool for instruction and learning is now being realized, but for special populations, the utility extends far beyond that of regular education. Through its versatility, this new technology is allowing handicapped individuals access to a broad range of information and materials at a relatively low cost.

The physically disabled and sensory impaired populations typically require hardware-intensive, and therefore expensive, modifications to equipment and materials to gain access to information necessary for education. Because the microcomputer processes all information alike (i.e., as binary information), adaptive devices designed to perform one application are capable of performing other types of applications as well. Consequently, various applications capable of accessing vast quantities of information can be made available with one adaptive device.

To illustrate the need for access to information, consider the visually impaired individual who wants to read the morning newspaper and balance the checkbook before going to work in the morning. The newspaper is not available without the assistance of a sighted reader and special writing equipment is necessary to work on the checkbook. The microcomputer can access both types of information and the user would only need one set of adaptive devices. The newspaper can be obtained electronically and read either through synthesized voice or transferred to a braille hard copy. The checkbook information stays on a disk and can be read through the same media as the newspaper. Thus the technology, through its versatility, allows access to more information through fewer adaptive devices.

The physically disabled, like the sensory impaired, also have improved access to information through the use of a computer. With this population the versatility of input methods for computer access is the major advantage, although alternative outputs such as voice synthesis or electronic control devices may also be beneficial. Minimal motor movement is all that is required to feed information into a computer when appropriate software and hardware adaptations are made. The computer does not care if the user sends information from a keyboard, a keyboard emulator, or a single switch as long as it receives the appropriate *ASCII* code for the desired information. In other words, if the computer is looking for a RETURN, whose *ASCII* code is hexidecimal number 0D, and it receives the *ASCII* code of HEX 0D from an adaptive keyboard emulator such as the Express 3 from Prentke Romich Co., the computer will not know the difference. The individual using Express 3 may have been using a single switch to select the command RETURN from the adaptive keyboard, and have absolutely no ability to use a standard keyboard. The *ASCII* code of HEX 0D may also be generated through specifically written software, without the assistance of sophisticated hardware. In short, the computer does not care where the code comes from and the standard keyboard is only one alternative to provide that code.

Communication disordered and learning handicapped individuals require varying degrees of hardware and software adaptations to benefit educationally from the use of computers. Typically the communication disordered individual will require more hardware adaptations if voice assistance is desired. Learning problems, whether in language, cognition, or perception will require more software adaptations.

There are two major factors that govern the amount of adaptation made to a computer system to meet individual needs: user goals, and abilities. Within education the goals may range from supplemental learning opportunities, to motor training in physical or occupational therapy, to individual systems for communication. Abilities range from mildly learning handicapped, to sensory impaired, to severely physically disabled. With these broad ranges, potential computer system configurations are numerous. Two additional factors that must be considered for therapeutic and adaptive applications of computers are the owner of the system and additional users. School computers may need to serve a number of individuals. Dedicated individual computer systems for personal communication that require highly specialized software and hardware in order to meet personal and educational goals may not be feasible. Thus, the dollars spent must maximize access for the greatest number of people at the expense of maximizing access for one individual. The computer in a therapy setting may have similar group needs but also might require very specialized equipment for a number of functions.

ADAPTIVE DEVICES

Standard hardware components of microcomputer systems include the computer, keyboard, disk drive, monitor, printer, and other peripherals such as joysticks and paddles. These are known as hardware because they are mechanical and electrical devices with physical reality. Hardware may be broken down into two categories: input and output. Input relates to information entering the computer and output relates to information coming out of the computer. There are many alternative input and output devices available that allow users access to the microcomputer. Many can be mounted in a variety of locations to meet individual needs, and usually do not interfere with normal keyboard use. Most devices require special software for operation.

Input Devices

The standard input method is through the computer's keyboard. Alternative methods include switches, videopointing devices, keyboard emulators, and voice recognition devices.

Switches

The first alternative to inputting information into the microcomputer is by the use of switches. Switch types include pressure, mercury, myoelectric, infrared, and optical, and they can be operated using various types of movement patterns, depending on the individual's ability (see Figure 2–1). Virtually any small muscle group with voluntary control can activate a switch. The Words+, Inc. infrared switch works with as little as an eye blink or merely eye movement. The P-Switch from Prentke Romich Company detects muscle movement and translates it into a switch closure. Sensitivity of the switch can be adjusted to detect either small movements or larger deliberate movements while ignoring unintentional ones. Burkhart (1985a, 1985b) has published two excellent books illustrating many inexpensive, easily constructed switches that can be used for computer access. ComputAbility Corporation, Don Johnston Developmental Equipment, Steven Kanor, Ph.D., Inc., Prentke Romich Company, and Zygo Industries all supply commercially made switches.

FIGURE 2-1. *The Unicorn Expanded Keyboard set up as two switches.*

Switches must be attached to the computer using a switch interface input box (available from almost all switch distributors). There are two types of switch interfaces: nontransparent and transparent. With a nontransparent interface, the user needs to purchase application software which has been specifically written to read the switch. This is called a nontransparent application because the switch can only be used with special software. The other interface method, called transparent, also uses special input boxes or peripheral cards. These interfaces allow the user to run off-the-shelf software by providing a switch-accessible keyboard display or Morse code. Those currently available include the Adaptive Firmware Card (Adaptive Peripherals) for the Apple, the PC-AID (DADA) for the IBM/PC/XT/AT and compatibles, and the TetraScan (Zygo), which can also act as a portable communication device. The interface is called transparent because the computer does not realize that input is not coming from the keyboard or joystick inputs. Users can set a number of parameters, including speed, selection method, and scanning array format, to meet their individual needs.

Video Pointing Devices

Video pointing devices include joysticks, light pens, trackballs, paddles, the mouse, digitizing tablets, and touch-sensitive pads or screens. While some of these devices require significant motor coordination, others only require a single touch. The mouse, paddes, trackballs, and joystick require eye-hand coordination for the user to manipulate a remote object in the appropriate dimension. Light pens require the user to touch the video screen with a special stylus. Touch-sensitive devices are activated by hand or object contact with the surface.

Like switches, many of these devices require software written specifically for them. Some are relatively new and consequently applications software is not readily available. However, they have good potential application to the handicapped population. Some commercial software publishers are writing their programs so that a variety of input devices can be used while some hardware manufacturers are developing programming tool kits to allow the nonprofessional programmer to more easily program them in *BASIC*. These initiatives by the software and hardware industries are making these devices more readily available to handicapped users.

The Power Pad from Dunamis, Inc. has a 12 by 12 inch working surface area and uses overlays that may be customized. A variety of programs is available from Macomb Projects, the LAUSD/UCLA Computer Team, and Dunamis, Inc. The TouchWindow (Personal Touch Corp.) may be attached to the microcomputer monitor screen or may be placed in front of the user on the table. Software programs using the TouchWindow are currently available from Laureate Learning Systems, Inc., Sunburst Communications, Broderbund, Personal Touch Corporation, Baudville, Koala Technologies, and Penguin Software. The Muppet Learning Keys (Sunburst) is a specially designed keyboard for young children featuring number and letter keys in sequential order, and eight color keys. The PEAL programs (Meyers, 1983a, 1983b) of *Exploratory Play and Representational Play* make use of the Muppet Learning Keys with a speech synthesizer, and are designed for young children. Softkey Systems, Inc. has adapted the Koala Pad as an adapted keyboard for those with limited hand movement. The keys are extremely small about a half-inch by a quarter-inch, but the order may be customized.

Keyboard Emulators

The emulator is transparent in that it makes the computer think that the keyboard is being used as the input device. Two types are alternative keyboards and stand-alone personal communication devices that can also be used as keyboard emulators. A number of the alternative keyboards work with the Adaptive Firmware Card. These keyboards are specially designed for the physically handicapped user. The Unicorn Expanded Keyboard (Unicorn Engineering Company) is a thin, flat, plastic panel with 112 touch-sensitive keys that can be customized according to the user's needs. This may include an enlarged standard keyboard array with special keys or limited input arrays such as picture matrices for communication. The King Keyboard (TASH) has keys that are separate, enlarged, and recessed. Each key requires 200 grams of force and provides feedback through a slight click. The Mini Keyboard (TASH) is a small sized keyboard (7½ × 4½ inches) that is activated by touching the pen-sized key areas with the conductive tip of a probe.

Many manufacturers of electronic communication devices are now upgrading them to interface with microcomputers and serve as keyboard emulators. Individuals who own these personal communication devices are now able to interface with computers and use their devices to communicate with the computer (input information). The Touch Talker and Light Talker (Prentke Romich Company), ScanWriter and TetraScan (Zygo), SpeechPac (Adaptive Communication Systems, Inc.), and Trine (Words+, Inc.) are all examples of communication devices that may be used independently or as an interface to access a microcomputer.

Voice Recognition Devices

Human voice or sound sequences can be interpreted by a microcomputer and used as input information. This requires users to "train" the computer to recognize their voices by giving it repeated voice samples. Intelligible speech is not essential, but the user must be able to produce *consistent* sounds that the computer can recognize. Special equipment is used to recognize and differentiate the various sound patterns. This type of device is particularly useful for quadriplegics with good verbal abilities. Four of these devices are the Voice Input Module (VIM) from Voice Machine Communications, Inc.; Shadow/VET from Scott Instruments Corporation; Waldo from Artra Inc.; and Intro Voice II from ComputAbility. Voice input is improving, but environmental sounds as well as factors such as a common cold may reduce the efficiency of the voice recognition system.

Output Devices

Many of the output devices normally used with microcomputers are not appropriate for individuals with special needs. As with input devices, there are a number of alternative output devices that can enable an individual to gain access to information that comes out of a computer. Output devices can be divided into five categories: video, print, audio, telecommunications, and radio frequencies.

Video Screens

It is difficult for someone with visual impairment to read text on a standard video screen because of the size and contrast of the letters. Letters are displayed as a series of dots that, because of their proximity to one another, appear to be connected (dot matrix format). On some monitors the quality of the display is better because the resolution is higher, with more dots per square inch, producing crisper, more solid letters.

Adaptations can be made by enlarging the size of the print on the video display through the use of software or special devices. The PC Lens by Nationwide Computer Products is a software program that enhances the standard IBM PC screen image. The characters are enlarged, spread apart, and colored. The program allows large print access to almost all commercially available software for the IBM PC.

Two simple hardware adaptations that may increase screen visibility are positioning the monitor for better visibility by using a monitor stand or mounting bracket, and mounting an anti-glare filter on the front of the screen. The DP-10 from Visualtek enlarges letters 2–16 times their original size. Letters can be displayed black on white or white on black, and the user is able to scroll through the screen with the use of a joystick. The system consists of a 19-inch display screen and processor, and a user control panel. The DP-10 plugs into the Apple and works with almost all Apple software (except those that use graphics). The DP-11 is compatible with the IBM PC and works in a similar manner.

Printers

Using special software and a graphics printer, print can be enlarged to provide large text hard copy. This is quite useful for the teacher who needs to develop large-print materials for the classroom. An alternative to printed text output is braille, both hard copy and refreshable. The Romeo Brailler from Maryland Computer Services, Inc. can be used in conjunction with a computer to produce braille hard copy. It can be easily and quickly interfaced with almost any computer system. The VersaBrailler can also be interfaced with a number of computers to produce refreshable braille. Raised Dot Computing publishes a number of programs that allow visually handicapped users to convert text into braille, edit in braille, and output it to either hard copy or refreshable braille.

Audio Systems

Voice and sound outputs are two ways of presenting auditory information to the user. The addition of voice output can be valuable to visually handicapped, speech or language impaired, and low-level or nonreading individuals. There are two kinds of speech: synthesized and digitized. Synthesized speech sounds robotic, but pitch and speed can be controlled, producing a wide variety of speech quality. Synthesis by rule systems (linear predictive coding) and synthesis by analysis (synthesized speech using text-to-speech algorithms) are two methods of producing speech. The Echo/Cricket (Street Electronics), Ufonic Voice (Josten Corporation), and Digitalker (National Semiconductor) are examples of speech synthesizers that use linear predictive coding. The Mockingboard (Sweet Micro Systems), Sweettalker II (The Micromint, Inc.), and Intex Talker (Votrax) are examples of synthesized speech using the analysis method.

Digitized speech sounds more natural than synthesized speech; however, it is more expensive and uses a great deal of computer memory. The Supertalker (Mountain Computer) is an example of a digitized speech system (Wilson & Fox, 1985). Although there are a number of inexpensive brands of speech synthesizers on the market, the Echo seems to be the most widely used in special education, rehabilitation, and hospitals.

There are four ways to achieve voice output in a computer system. The first is by purchasing complete computer systems that have a primary goal of voice output. The VP (Maryland Computer Service, Inc.) is a speech system that is used with the IBM PC and allows the user to hear what is on the video screen. A similar system, Total Talk II (Maryland Computer Services), creates a talking Hewlett-Packard computer terminal. Information appearing on the video screen or entered through the keyboard is spoken. It is designed to be used with a mainframe computer, although it can be connected to microcomputers. With a very specific goal, the ULTRA (Universal Laboratory Training and Research Aid) is a portable talking laboratory that is easily connected to a variety of measurement instruments and sensors commonly found in science laboratories. ULTRA converts the data to speech or some other form of auditory input. It can be used as a talking computer terminal and a personal computer.

The second method of incorporating speech into computer systems is through external voice synthesizers that interface with the computer. Some examples are the Votrax Type 'N Talk, Intex Talker, and Echo GP. These devices communicate with the computer through the serial port and need their own power supply. The advantages are that they can be used with any computer through the serial port and they have fairly high-quality voice. The disadvantages are that they require extra space, and are relatively expensive.

The third method of including speech in a computer system is through accessory expansion cards, which are placed inside the computer. These cards require special software to produce speech output. Some examples are the Echo II+ and the Mockingboard. This method is less expensive than the first two, but these synthesizers are not compatible with computers other than the ones for which they were developed.

Recently Apple instroduced the Apple IIgs and IBM released the Person System 2 (PS/2), both of which have a high quality speech synthesizer resident in the computer. This is the fourth method for applying speech to the computer system. To date, only a limited number of software programs use these synthesizers, but their high quality has tremendous potential for handicapped users. It is the cheapest method because it is not an extra peripheral.

Sound output, other than music, is most frequently used to enhance a program. Sound reinforcements are often incorporated into educational software. Used strategically, it can present important cues and feedback to the user. For example, a small click when a key is pressed may be important information for indicating that an input was received. This feature may be especially useful when no immediate visual feedback is provided, as occurs in some single switch communication programs when alternating between row and column scanning. Sound generators are typically resident in every computer, but auxiliary sound systems can be added. One example is Waldo (Artra, Inc.), which provides a stereo sound system.

Telecommunications

Through the use of modems, electronic information can be transmitted to another computer through the telephone wires. This practice is becoming more and more commonplace as the number of data bases and bulletin boards increases. For handicapped users, telecommunications may be the most efficient means of communicating with other handicapped users or the nonhandicapped world. It offers a wide variety of business, recreational, and communication options. Electronic mail and bulletin board services are available through a number of telecommunication services such as CompuServe, The Source, and SpecialNet (see Chapter 9).

Other Output Devices

The last group of computer outputs is neither auditory nor visual, at least not to humans. They include radio, infrared, and ultrasonic signals, and are frequently used to control external devices. Radio signals can be transmitted through electrical wires or through the air to activate electrical devices in the environment. The PC-1 Powerline (Bi-Comm Systems, Inc.) is an example of a device that sends computer-generated radio signals directly through power lines. Prentke Romich Company transmits radio data through space with its Wireless Data Transmission System. When used in conjunction with keyboard emulators or communication devices such as the Express 3, the signal becomes a computer input rather than output. Infrared light is also used to remotely control external devices. Zygo Industries has an optional ultrasonic/infrared link that allows computer control of its scan-WRITER. Waldo (Artra, Inc.) uses ultrasonic signals to provide a wireless link between the computer and a wire-based radio signal system for controlling electrical devices.

VIGNETTE 2-1
Selecting an Adaptive Device: Simple Can Be Better

Early one August morning, a telephone call came in to the Special Education Technology Lab at George Mason University. It was from a teacher requesting technical assistance to help her provide an adapted computer for a child scheduled to be in her first grade class in September. She reported that the child was of normal intelligence, but had a congenital double amputation of both arms at the shoulder and had only "flippers" that were not really functional.

She had done some research on adaptive devices and found that the Adaptive Firmware Card would enable him to use the computer effectively. She was aware that GMU had a variety of devices and wanted to make an appointment to see the Firmware Card and discuss appropriate educational software applications. She had even gone as far as getting a budget item approved to order the equipment.

Before making the appointment, the GMU staff member investigated what computer-related activities the child had engaged in during his preschool class. His teacher said that he had been using a computer and an electric typewriter by typing with his feet and toes on the keyboard.

The GMU staff member then suggested that rather than using an expensive adaptive device that would only hinder the child's ability to use the computer, the teacher could simply place the computer on the floor with the monitor situated so that the student could enter data while viewing the screen. He also suggested that if the computer needed to be moved one location to another, it could be placed on a scooter board or a small cart that the child could push.

Other Adaptive Devices

Sometimes simple adaptations can make a computer more accessible to the handicapped (see Vignette 2-1). A simple adaptation is to use a keyguard, which is attached to or placed over the keyboard. The keyguard prevents inadvertent striking of a key. The keys are accessed through key-sized holes with fingers or pointing devices such as hand-held sticks, head sticks, or mouth sticks. Keyguards may be purchased from such companies as ComputAbility, Don Johnston Developmental Equipment, Prentke Romich Company, and TASH. Fully figured or custom keyguards with only specific keys open for particular software needs are available from Adaptive Technology, Inc. A moisture guard that attaches to the keyboard with double faced tape and protects it from moisture or drooling, which are often problems, is available from Don Johnston Developmental Equipment.

Another simple adaptation is to change the work station. When using the computer in a school or institution, there will be many individuals who use the same computer, and it is often difficult to appropriately position the computer, monitor, or adaptive input devices. This problem can be solved by using adjustable or hyrdraulic tables. A tilt table that allows the angle of the keyboard to be adjusted to give increased visibility and accessibility can be easily constructed or purchased commercially (Don Johnston Developmental Equipment).

INTEGRATING COMPUTERS INTO THE CURRICULUM

Early applications of the microcomputer with special populations in the schools were borrowed without modification from those used with the nonhandicapped population. Since that time, computer use in special education has paralleled the regular classroom in types of applications, but with increasingly specialized software. These applications can be grouped into three categories: computer-assisted instruction (CAI), computer-managed instruction (CMI), and use of computers as a tools for living and learning.

Computer-assisted instruction can be a highly interactive method of learning that is accessible to the student at any time (Rushakoff, 1984b). The flexibility of the microcomputer as a medium for instruction leads to the potential matching of CAI and specific learner characteristics. With careful software design, instructions can be delivered to facilitate efficient learning. Unfortunately, very few teachers currently have the opportunity to assist in the design of instructional software, so the match between learner characteristics and the curriculum must be addressed through software selection and utilization in the classroom. The *teacher, therapist, and clinician bring knowledge* of the child's strengths and weaknesses and in-depth knowledge of development and intervention strategies *to the software selection process.* This expertise is necessary for appropriate selection and integration of computers into the curriculum (Graham, 1984; Panyan, 1984).

Beyond traditional academic instruction, the computer can be used to supplement instruction in communication, visual perception, fine and gross motor skills, auditory perception, recreation, and daily living skills (see Table 2–1). Instruction in all areas spans the transdisciplinary team typically involved in the delivery of services.

Computer-managed instruction programs provide direct service personnel a means for meeting the individualized instruction mandate of keeping detailed records of student learning. CMI programs offer the teacher and therapist a vehicle for consistent and efficient assessment, systematic record keeping, charting and analysis of data, and determination of teaching objectives (Graham, 1984; Rushakoff, 1984a). With the assistance of CMI, learning progress and intervention strategies can be more efficiently linked to facilitate better educational planning.

Direct instruction can be achieved through the use of CAI. Further instruction can be facilitated through the use of CMI. The computer can also be used as a tool for learning. It can play an important role in enabling

TABLE 2-1. *Areas for integrating computers into the curriculum.*

Curriculum Area	Occupational Therapy	Physical Therapy	Speech Therapy	Classroom	Vision
Language development			X	X	
Concept development	X	X	X	X	X
Communication					
oral			X	X	
written	X	X	X	X	
Visual-perception					
discrimination	X		X	X	X
figure ground	X		X	X	X
memory	X		X	X	
sequencing	X		X	X	X
Motor (gross or fine)					
accuracy	X	X		X	X
coordination	X	X		X	X
timing	X	X		X	
sequencing	X	X		X	
Auditory perception			X	X	
Math operations				X	
Reading				X	
Attention & concentration	X		X	X	
Memory					
visual	X		X	X	X
auditory			X	X	
Creative/logical thinking				X	
Leisure-recreational					
skills	X			X	
Assist with independent					
living	X			X	
Biofeedback	X	X			
Vocational skills	X		X	X	X

the handicapped to participate in classroom activities such as writing, speaking, independent reading, and creative expression.

Voice synthesizers and word processors, coupled with adaptive input devices when necessary, provide many individuals access to educational information that was previously not possible. Vanderheiden (1983a) stated "of crucial importance to any physically handicapped child with near or above normal intelligence is the ability to write. No normal child could receive adequate education if he or she did not do any written exercises, homework or independent work as a part of the educational program" (p. 9). Word processors provide motorically handicapped individuals a means for writing with minimum effort. The nature of word processors also encourages creativity, organization, and self-critiquing.

Participation in class through speech is a new opportunity for many nonverbal individuals. Voice synthesizers allow active participation in class discussions and the ability to raise questions in real time, giving the nonverbal individual greater access to learning opportunities.

Voice synthesizers can also be used in conjunction with some CAI programs and electronic information. This ability allows nonreaders or visually handicapped persons the chance to participate independently at learning stations.

THERAPEUTIC APPLICATIONS OF COMPUTERS

Computers are most frequently used by therapists as management tools, with evaluation being one of the top uses. As seen in Table 2-1, the areas of instruction are many and overlap with all therapists as well as the classroom teacher. Few instructional uses of the computer are reported in the special education literature because very little software that meets the specific needs of therapists exists.

Evaluation Applications

The computer can be used as an evaluation tool in a number of ways but the individual's ability to access the computer must first be assessed and an appropriate system designed. The transdisciplinary model is the most effective approach to assessing computer access. All professionals providing services to an individual can provide valuable information regarding abilities and limitations to help determine instructional strategies and recommend potential computer adaptations. The classroom teacher provides information on cognitive abilities, the speech therapist on speech and language abilities, and the occupational and physical therapists on motor abilities or limitations.

Prior to computer use, it is important to have the occupational and physical therapists evaluate the individual's motor skills, including range of motion, muscle strength, muscle tone, movement patterns, endurance, and visual-motor perception. Determination of the most desirable sitting position for computer use is important too, and it may be necessary to recommend adaptive devices to position the individual appropriately during computer use. Once positioning is determined and all evaluation data is available, the transdisciplinary team can make recommendations for adaptive equipment. It is advantageous for the team to be familiar with a wide variety of adaptive hardware and software (see Figure 2-2).

Speech–language pathologists and occupational and physical therapists have used computers as evaluation tools in four ways: to administer tests, for diagnosis, to teach specific skills, and to collect observational data.

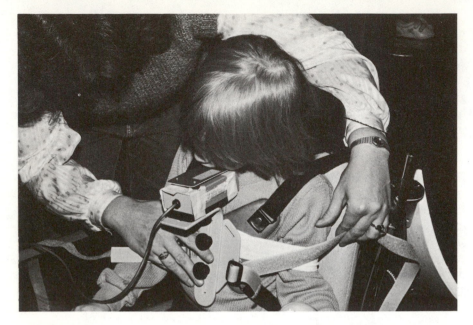

FIGURE 2-2. *Therapist adjusting chin mount for a switch during an evaluation.*

Speech and Language Assessments

Three types of software programs are available to augment assessment by the speech–language pathologist: evaluation of phonological processes, assessment of language performance, and determination of hearing aid prescriptions (Schwartz, 1984). Stoker (1983) uses CAST (Computer Assisted Speech Tool) to diagnose phonetic and phonological speech skills of deaf individuals and to generate a personalized skill profile to be used in deciding speech intervention strategies. A program titled Articulation Error Analysis (Southern Micro Systems) objectively analyzes articulation errors using standard articulation instruments, and prints a report for the clinician within seven minutes. In the area of language development, Harlan, Larimore, and Smith (1984) use a computer to analyze SICD (Sequenced Inventory of Communication Development) data. Their method of coding test data and other pertinent information (e.g., etiologies and demographics) provides the clinician with fast, accurate, and quality information for a large population of preschool language-delayed children. In a similar manner, Bishop (1984) uses an automated LARSP (Language Assessment, Remediation and Screening Procedure) to provide clinicians with a complete grammatical profile of a client's language. Some tests are now designed to be administered directly on the computer, for example, the Screening Test of Syntactic

Abilities (Rushakoff, 1984a). Here the computer is used to present the test item as well as analyze the data and generate the report.

Physical and Occupational Therapy Evaluations

The computer has made an impact on the fields of physical and occupational therapy in the area of evaluation. It is now possible to interface single instruments with a microcomputer and software to allow therapists to use biofeedback and physiological monitoring in client evaluation and treatment. The physiological monitors that can be used during client exercise or activity may detect, amplify, and record information that is not available by direct clinical observation. A variety of physiological responses can be measured by electromyography, electroencephalography, thermal, RP interval, galvanic skin response, and electrocardiography and monitored by computers (Sidler, 1986). Through biofeedback and monitoring, the therapist can measure the effectiveness of treatment techniques and can assist in developing more efficient or effective treatment strategies. More documentation of the use of biofeedback and monitoring is available in the field of physical therapy. At the Mayo Clinic (Gronley & Perry, 1984) and Rancho Los Amigos Gait Laboratories (Laughman et al., 1984), physical therapists have interfaced instruments with computers in order to provide automated gait analysis. Madeiros (1984) reported the use of automated measurement systems for the clinical analysis of motion by monitoring muscle function, energy expenditure, and postural equilibrium. Comput-Ability has a computerized Unex II Exercise System which may be valuable to therapists. This system is integrated with an IBM PC and contains a computerized ergometer, incentive spirometer, heart rate monitor, hand dynamometer, sphygmomanometer, restorator II, and fat caliper.

Software is being developed in the field of occupational therapy to augment traditional assessment techniques. Often, programs used in the evaluation process can be used in treatment too. For example, the *Visual Perceptual Diagnostic Testing and Training* programs (Greenberg & Chamoff, 1986) were developed with the aid of an occupational therapist and are designed to assist in the diagnosis and treatment of many visual-perceptual problems associated with brain injury. The programs are appropriate for kindergarten through college age levels and assess the following areas: visual field, figure ground, visual memory, visual discrimination, dot patterns, visual scanning, and maze negotiation. Programs that have been developed for educational or recreational purposes can be used to augment traditional assessments of visual perception and fine motor skills. One area in which software is frequently borrowed is in the occupational therapist's evaluation of fine motor abilities needed to use adaptive hardware to access the computer.

CURRICULUM AREAS

Motor Training

Many young or severely involved individuals have not developed suffi-cient understanding of cause and effect relationships for computer use. The occupational therapist, in addition to the classroom teacher, is often involved in training these individuals in the use of adaptive input devices before the computer can be considered as a functional tool for education, communication, or recreation.

Several programs are available for training in the area of cause and effect relationships and use of the input device selected. The Omnibox from Expert Systems Software, Inc. interfaces with adapted battery operated devices, such as toys or recorders, an Apple IIe or II+ computer, and up to four switches. Omnibox software includes *Switchmaster*, which monitors the number of times and how long the switch is activated, and the number of trainer prompts needed; *Toy Assessor*, which collects data on the student's use of two different switches and allows the trainer to compare the effectiveness of each switch; and *Toy Scanner*, which is designed to bridge the gap between computer pro-grams that require a timed response and switch use with battery operated toys. The *Single Switch Assessment* (Rushakoff & Hansen, 1981) can be used to determine the most efficient switch type and location. This program requires higher cognitive skills than the previous three because it uses text prompts. A limited number of software programs is available for developing increased motor control. *Motor Training Games* (Schwejda & McDonald, 1979) has a number of game-type activities in which the trainer can customize the scan-ning speed or rate of presentation according to individual needs. Many com-mercial programs designed for the normal population can also be used to increase motor control. For example, any program that uses a scanning method of choice selection can be used to increase motor timing.

Another application of switch training is to try to increase the individual's movement skills. When the individual has developed some skill in using a switch that has been placed in a consistent location, the switch can be moved to another location in order to elicit increased move-ment or increased range. This may be useful in teaching the individual to use two switches at the same time.

Language Development

Language development and augmentative communication are two intervention areas that generally overlap with classroom objectives. Speech therapists often use CAI to supplement clinical work in language devel-opment. For vocabulary development, programs such as *First Words* and *First Categories* (Laureate Learning Systems, Inc.) are available

able for the young child. A set of six programs designed specifically for the special needs of aphasic students is available from ComputAbility (1986a). The set includes *Noun Association, Opposites and Similarities, Categories, Reading Comprehension, Sentence Construction,* and *Vocabulary Development.* Other areas of language intervention with the computer include grammar, word recognition, and reading comprehension (Rushakoff, 1984a).

Programs for Early Acquisition of Language (PEAL) (Meyers, 1984) are designed to encourage language development and communication with very young children. These programs, *Exploratory Play* and *Representational Play,* allow the child to experiment with language through play with familiar objects. Using real objects, customized picture overlays on the Muppet Learning Keys, and speech synthesis, the child is able to talk about the objects or give commands relating to the objects. Words can be combined to form two-word utterances.

Communication Training

Communication training falls under many disciplines. Switch training is often done by physical and occupational therapists, whereas content may be the responsibility of classroom teachers and speech therapists. No matter whose responsibility, communication is a required skill for interacting in the classroom environment. Before electronic and computer technologies, written and oral communication of the severely handicapped were most often limited to techniques such as pointing, head shaking, and eye gazing coupled with various encoding techniques. Interpreters would express in their own words what they thought the handicapped individual intended. Now computers enable nonverbal individuals to more clearly express their thoughts through written and spoken language.

A variety of computer programs matching a broad range of skills is available for word processing. On the introductory end of the range, two programs from Spinnaker combine pictures and text to introduce creation of stories, *Story Machine* and *Kidwriter. KidWord* (Seeds, 1984) has been successfully used to teach children to type one screen of text, move the cursor, clear the screen, and print what has been written. *Magic Slate* (Stranger, Kulzer, Elseth, & Lie, 1986) takes word processing one step further and offers a large print screen in a 20-column display that incorporates the full editing features of a word processor. *Bank Street Writer* (Kusmiak & Riggs, 1984) completes the spectrum of easy to use word processors.

Other specialty word processors that incorporate speech synthesizers are available, one at each end of the abilities spectrum. *Keytalk* (Meyers, 1985) voices letters, words, and sentences as they are entered on the keyboard. The objective of the program is to teach keyboarding along with early reading and writing skills through discovery learning techniques.

Talking Screen Textwriter (Rosegrant & Cooper, 1983) and *Listening to Learn* are more complete word processors that use the voice synthesizer to provide spoken review of the text on the screen. The primary objective is to provide auditory feedback during the writing process. *Dr. Peet's Talkwriter* (Hartley) introduces similar techniques for young children, but also adds a program called *Double Touch* that encourages visually handicapped students to explore the keyboard and write text.

Programs designed to augment verbal communication are available for virtually all computers and ability levels. These range from very limited to unlimited vocabularies with pictures or text. Some have sophisticated presentation techniques such as nested menus or leveling, others try to replicate the concept of a book with sequential "paging" techniques.

The most common screen presentations include menus and matrices. The menu method presents a limited list of options, with each option branching to further options. Sometimes the level of nesting of the menus can be quite complex. Precautions must be taken to limit the number of entries required of the user to get the desired result. One example of a nested menu communication program is *Talking Wheelchair* (Bennin, 1984).

The matrix method of presentation displays a grid of options in the row–column formant. Generally the user can "page" through a number of these matrices to access additional vocabulary (see Figure 2–3). An example of this presentation method is *Picture Communication* (Cohn, 1982) distributed by ComputAbility, Inc.

Pictures, symbols, and words can all be incorporated into menu or matrix systems. Pictures range from near-photographic quality to rebuses that represent concrete and abstract items. The more abstract the picture the closer it gets to a symbol. Symbols, like pictures, represent meanings but do not necessarily attempt to visually represent the object (McDonald, 1975). Blissymbolics is a good example of a very complete symbol system.

Three selection techniques are used with communication programs: scanning, encoding, and direct selection (Vanderheiden, 1975; see Figure 2–3). In scanning, a cursor or indicator moves and the user waits for the cursor to be positioned with the desired item before selecting. Two types of scanning are available: one where the cursor moves automatically and the user stops the movement with the switch; the second is by stepping, in which the user moves the cursor one position at a time each time the switch is activated. Selection occurs when the cursor is allowed to stay at one position for a preset length of time. Both selection techniques are available in the *Picture Communication* program (Cohn, 1982).

Stepping and scanning are two of the most common selection techniques used in communication software, and these techniques are frequently incorporated into instructional software. Difficulties in using the techniques were noted, and so a number of training programs have started to

FIGURE 2-3. *The Touch Talker (Prentke-Romich) allows either direct selection or encoding to be used during communication.*

emerge. On a very early cognitive level, *Choice Maker II* (Lahm, 1985) teaches scanning using a two picture screen. *Rabbit Scanner* (Rettig & Greenlee, 1985) teaches scanning in a five position horizontal format.

Encoding requires the user to either memorize codes or use a separate chart of codes for items available to be entered into a system. One example of the encoding selection technique is the *Talking BlissApple* program (Vanderheiden & Kelso, 1982). The user enters numeric codes for Blissymbols into the computer to construct a sentence or phrase.

Direct select is the easiest selection technique to learn because no intermediate memory or visual tracing tasks are required. The user directly enters the desired item. The keyboard is the most commonly used direct select input device. On a more simple scale, programs that use input tables such as the PowerPad or the Unicorn Board are examples of direct select, in which the select options are placed on the board and the user touches the item to select it. For example, *SimpleCom I* (Tanner & Satterfield, 1985) uses the PowerPad divided into halves with "yes" and "no" displayed on each side, to teach yes–no response communication. The user simply touches the correct side. The *TouchWindow* (Personal Touch, 1985) is a relatively new input device that is ideal for the direct select technique because it can be mounted on the screen, removing a level of abstraction by allowing the child to interact directly with the stimulus rather than a remote switch. All direct select input devices require a certain level of physical competence, and thus the technique cannot be used by everyone.

Computer-based communication programs are available in pictures, symbols, and words. To date there is not an abundance of research to support one method or another. When considering buying or developing a communication program for an individual, it is necessary to be aware of the design options available, to assess the potential user's abilities to determine the best type of program, and to have the individual try out whatever programs are available.

Vocational Training

Microcomputers are entering the vocational training curriculum both in schools and in rehabilitation centers because they benefit handicapped individuals in three major ways: bringing assistance to individuals for less cost, allowing access to information available to nonhandicapped peers that was previously not available to them, and developing intelligent prostheses that help offset the information-processing problems of the handicapped (Vanderheiden, 1983). An example of improved access via computers is the use of speech recognition features. While many handicapped adults have some keyboard skills through use of single fingers or head pointers, the process is long, tiresome, and difficult when the user is required to execute simultaneous key presses such as shift-A for capitalization. Transparent speech recognition systems allow concurrent keyboard and voice entry for virtually all software programs, giving individuals with severe motor impairment vocal access to all software and available electronic information.

Within the rehabilitation setting, four approaches to job training are in use: computer learning for information access and general office job skills, specialized environments for computer programmers, specialized equipment used as sensory aids, and software-based assessment and training. The first approach is used by Holleman (1986) to train disabled college students on standard computer software for personal and job use. A Computer Learning Center has been established through continuing education that has adopted an open entry and exit policy. This allows the students to learn at their own pace and on a schedule that meets their needs. Assistants are always available as well as a variety of adaptive equipment (e.g., braillers, voice synthesizers) and sign interpreters to make the technology accessible. Skills learned can be transferred directly to a number of jobs and will provide a means for the students to continue accessing new information through the computer.

The University of Maine at Orono has established a Rehabilitation Project in Data Processing to train disabled students to become business applications computer programmers (White & Cormier, 1986). To achieve their goal, they have simulated a business-like environment in which to conduct their training. Although the costs are high, they have found the project to be cost-effective.

Off-the-shelf adaptive devices such as those used in the Holleman training project are not always adequate to meet the needs of some individuals and some job situations. Specialized environments may not be enough either. The Sensory Aids Foundation has developed a number of equipment prototypes for computer-related jobs to meet some very specialized needs (Phillips & Russell, 1980). These include a Traffic Service Position System for long distance operators, an Optacon tracking guide for CRT displays, a digital indexing system for cassette audio recorders, a speech annunciator for providing speech output for digital laboratory instruments, large-print video terminals, and talking information management systems for speech output of visual displays while using business applications software. A caution is raised when considering training on these specialized devices. The skills learned often do not transfer to new devices, and technology is changing too rapidly to invest significant time on training when the skills may soon be obsolete.

For those who do not have severe motor disabilities, software has been developed to assess individual potential for different career areas and to provide training through simulations and CAI. Two companies that lead the field in this area are The Conover Company, Ltd. and MCE Inc. The Conover Company has a number of assessment packages that utilize the computer for delivering task directions and collecting data and hands-on materials for performing specific tasks. Both Conover and MCE have a variety of training programs available, ranging from nuts and bolts assembly to job survival skills such as work and personal habits on the job. Most of these programs require a fair amount of reading skill, but some can be used with a cassette control device to assist low and non-readers.

Recreational Uses

Recreational uses of computers include art, music, games, and environmental control. There have been areas of the curriculum in which the handicapped have been unable to participate. In the area of art, graphics programs such as *Print Shop* (Broderbund, 1984), *Stickybear Printer* (Hefter & Lusby, 1985), or *Paint with Words* (MECC, 1984) can be used to design and paint pictures. Free-hand drawing programs are available that use alternative input devices such as the Koala Pad, TouchWindow, joysticks or mouse. One program available to the severely physially disabled individual is *Pic-Man* (Lee et al., 1985) which allows the user to draw using a single switch.

The Adaptive Firmware Card brings many music and game programs to the physically handicapped user (see Figure 2–4). The majority of games use

FIGURE 2-4. *Three children taking turns playing a computerized board game.*

paddles or joysticks. Specially designed input devices can easily be constructed to emulate these peripherals, making a large library of recreational programs available.

Environmental control is an area of recreation not previously available to severely handicapped individuals. Electrical and battery operated device controllers such as the X-10 controller and the Omnibox add new meaning to recreation. Radios, televisions, stereos, and other leisure applicances are now accessible. Battery operated toys can also be made available to very young populations to promote free play activities at a very early age.

Daily Living Skills Instruction

It is easy to understand the application of the computer in the special education curriculum in academics and communication, but not as easy to visualize its place in the daily living skills curriculum. As in vocational education, software is emerging that addresses community living skills such as money management, survival words, and home safety. MCE Inc. and The Conover Company are two publishers of this type of software.

In addition to instruction in daily living skills, the computer can be used to directly assist in tasks within the home, school, job setting, and community. Two types of assistance are available: environmental control and environmental manipulation. Through special devices such as the BSR X-10 controller and the Omnibox, both electrical and battery operated devices can be controlled through the computer. The BSR X-10 controller, or similar controllers, can be installed in computers as single function boards or they can be incorporated into multi-function boards or devices. One example of a multifunction board is Waldo, a voice-activated home controller with speech output, clock and calendar, and specialized sound generators. Through appropriate software, individuals can gain control over electronic and other devices. Training for environmental control can begin at an early age (Lahm, 1987). Environmental control includes security and communication aspects, allowing individuals who otherwise would be dependent to live more independently. Of course, much of every environment is inanimate and not controlled by electricity or other power sources. For some severely disabled individuals, these objects will never be controlled without the help of another person. Eating utensils are a good example. Research is being conducted at a few rehabilitation facilities to explore the use of robots to assist individuals in a number of daily living tasks. One voice controlled robot is being used for feeding, manipulating the spoon, glass, and oven for the user (Leifer, 1983). A second study incorporates a robotic arm into a work station for controlling the telephone, turning pages, and performing other "office" tasks (Seamone, 1983). At Carnegie Mellon University, K. G. Englehardt is heading a team that is also exploring the use of robots to assist disabled and elderly clients.

While these applications are far from availability for the classroom, primarily due to cost, it is helpful to know that someday these capabilities will be available and affordable.

Therapeutic Applications

Speech–language pathologists have probably incorporated the microcomputer into their curriculum more than any other professionals who work with handicapped children. In addition to assessment, speech–language pathologists frequently use the microcomputer in direct therapy. Voice and articulation therapy is a unique application because it relies on sophisticated external instruments and voice recognition technologies. Instruments designed to measure and map voice patterns in terms of frequency, intensity, nasalization, vocal onset, respiration, and perturbation are linked with microcomputers to assist in analysis and to provide visual feedback to the speaker (Bull & Rushakoff, 1987). One such system that uses an Apple II computer is Visi-Pitch (Kay Elemetrics). Users attempt to match their voice pattern with that of a model. This application is especially useful with hearing-impaired persons who have difficulty hearing speech samples.

In another area of voice therapy, Rubow and Swift (1985) have developed a microcomputer-based biofeedback device that is worn by a client and continually gives feedback on voice intensity. It has been used to treat

Parkinsonian dysarthria and facilitates generalization of voice control from the clinical setting to the mainstream.

Physical therapists have used biofeedback and physiological monitoring in treatment. Applications are similar to those used in evaluation and are especially useful in gait training (Gronley & Perry, 1984; Laughman et al., 1984), monitoring exercise and activities, and in developing better treatment techniques. Occupational therapists are using the computer to assist with treatment of traditional therapy goals and objectives in the areas of cognitive rehabilitation, visual–perceptual training, and visual–motor training (Dunford, 1986; Gordon, 1984; Sidler, 1986; Wall, 1984; Wicks, 1986). Many therapists are finding that the computer is a more accepted modality for treatment than traditional visual–perceptual training tasks, and that clients' motivation to perform these tasks is increased by using the computer (Benkin, 1984). A number of programs have been designed specifically for cognitive rehabilitation (Sidler, 1986). One of these, *Programs for Cognitive Rehabilitation* (Bracy, 1984), has been used by Wambolt (1986) for the treatment of hemianopsia (visual field deficit) and neglect. The comprehensive *Visual Perceptual Diagnostic Testing and Training* programs (Wicks, 1986) use a drill and practice technique to assist in the treatment of perceptual deficits, eye-hand coordination and concentration. In addition to specific programs, many programs that are labeled educational can be used by occupational therapists to work on treatment goals.

HARDWARE RESOURCE DATA BASES

Specialists and teachers can also use the computer as a means for accessing information. Through the use of modems, data bases such as ABLEDATA, SCAN, NIS, and Paperchase are able to quickly provide information on a variety of topics, including equipment and resource lists of services. Access to information services has proven successful at the Bryn Mawr Rehabilitation Hospital (Christie, 1986). A team of specialists uses ABLEDATA to obtain information on commercially available products designed to provide assistance in independent living. The team is using the data base to find the most appropriate pieces of equipment for clients. The specialist and the educator can also develop and maintain valuable professional networks and exchange ideas and information from bulletin boards or forums such as the Disabilities Forum and Handicapped Users' Data Base on CompuServe. KendallNET is a communications network that links schools and programs for the deaf. Through the use of a bulletin board system and personal mail, KendallNET allows students, parents, and educators to exchange ideas about computers in the education of hearing-impaired individuals (Mackall, 1985). Gallaudet College is using a unique networking system. Personal computers are being used in the classroom as a means of learning how to use written English as communication through dialogues between teachers and students on computers (Batson, 1985).

INSTITUTIONAL VERSUS INDIVIDUAL OWNERSHIP OF COMPUTER SYSTEMS

The list of specialized hardware available for the disabled population is impressive and continually growing. After reviewing a description of devices available to assist disabled persons, it is easy to get very enthusiastic about developing a system for an individual or group of children. But, there is a tremendous difference between what is desirable and what is affordable and feasible. A major factor in selecting a system is whether it will be purchased by an individual or by an institution or agency (see Table 2-2).

Most handicapped individuals will be introduced to microcomputers in publicly funded settings such as schools or rehabilitation centers. They may also interact with computers in the mainstream community. The nature of the institution as well as the specific application of the computer will often dictate the degree to which efforts will be made to either purchase special

TABLE 2-2. *Microcomputer applications with institutionally owned versus individually owned systems.*

Environment	Application	Institution	Individual
School	Therapies: OT, PT, Behavior, Speech–language	X	
	CAI	X	X
	CMI	X	
	CAM	X	
	Access	X	X
	Communication		X
Rehabilitation	Therapies: OT, PT, Behavior, Speech–language	X	
	Job training	X	
	Communication		X
Community/vocational	Recreation/leisure	X	X
	Job access		X
	Community access	X	X
Home	Environmental control		X
	Communication		X
	Daily living		X
Recreation/leisure			X
Education — access			X

computers or make modifications to hardware or software. Computers found in the mainstream community often have few, if any, modifications for handicapped users because they are designed to meet the needs of a large group of people in the most cost-effective way. Computer systems in schools serve fewer individuals and must consider both group and individual needs of a very diverse population. Computers used in rehabilitation centers or in therapy settings serve a still smaller number of individuals, and often must be adapted to very specific individual needs related to job training. The more specific the purpose of the computer and the more individual training provided, the more specific the hardware adaptations must be. Thus, institutionally owned systems must be very versatile.

Individuals who decide to purchase computers usually have very specific applications in mind, such as supplementing education using computer assisted instruction (CAI) or providing basic communication. The specificity of the goal and the availability of funds are the governing factors in this system design. There will be no concern about other users. The goal is to optimize functioning of the individual, so any piece of hardware or software has potential for incorporation into the system.

SUMMARY

To successfully integrate computers into special education and therapy curricula, three major areas must be addressed. First, what capabilities should the system have? The wide variety of adaptive devices now available make the range of capabilities almost endless. Second, in which curriculum areas will the system be used? The range of possible applications include basics such as motor training and language development, and more specialized areas such as daily living skills, vocational education, and recreation. Highly specific uses often fall within the therapy curriculum. Each application determines the hardware and software required for the computer system. Third, who will purchase the system? This impacts tremendously on the capabilities of the system. School or institutional systems often must meet group needs at the expense of meeting the needs of specific users, whereas the privately purchased computer system can meet specific needs.

REFERENCES AND SUGGESTED READINGS

Barton, L. E., & Zuckerman, R. A. (1986). *DATA* [Computer software]. Kent, OH: Kent State University.
Batson, T. (1985). Networking in the classroom with deaf students. In M. Gergen (Ed.), *Computer technology for the handicapped — Applications '85 selected proceedings of the 1985 Closing the Gap conference* (pp. 185–191). Hutchinson, MN: Crow River Press.

Behrmann, M. M., & Lahm, E. (1984). Using computers with children with sensory and physical impairments. In M. Behrmann (Ed.), *Handbook of microcomputers in special education* (pp. 103–137). San Diego: College-Hill Press.

Bennin, J. (1984, January). The talking wheelchair. Paper presented at the Technology and Special Education Conference, Reno, Nevada.

Betourne, C., & Flinn, G. (1986, July 9). Switch to switches. *Occupational Therapy Form*, pp. 1–2.

Bishop, D. M. V. (1984). Automated LARSP: Computer-assisted grammatical analysis. *British Journal of Disorders of Communication, 19*(1), 78–87.

Blaschke, C. L. (1986). Technology for special education: A national strategy. *T.H.E. Journal, 13*(6), 77–82.

Bracy, O. L. (1984). *Cognitive rehabilitation* [Computer program]. Indianapolis, IN: Psychological Software Services.

Broderbund Software, Inc. (1984). *Print shop* [Computer program]. San Rafael, CA: Broderbund.

Bull, G. L., & Rushakoff, G. E. (1987). Computer and speech and language disordered individuals. In J. D. Lindsey (Ed.), *Computers and exceptional individuals* (pp. 83–104). Columbus, OH: Charles E. Merrill.

Burkhart, L. J. (1985a). *More homemade battery operated devices for severely handicapped children with suggested activities.*(rev. ed.). College Park, MD: Author.

Burkhart, L. J. (1985b). *Homemade battery powered toys and educational devices for severely handicapped children* (3rd ed.). College Park, MD: Author.

Burns, W. H. VI. (1985). *Microelectric aids and handicapped children: An interfuture project studying applications of microelectronic aids in the communication and education of severely physically and communicatively handicapped children.* (ERIC Document Reproduction Service No. ED 258 405)

Campbell, P. H., & Esposito, L. (1987). Computers and severely and physically handicapped individuals. In J. D. Lindsey (Ed.), *Computers and exceptional individuals* (pp. 105–124). Columbus, OH: Charles E. Merrill.

Chial, M. R. (1984). Evaluating microcomputer hardware. In A. H. Schwartz (Ed.), *Handbook of microcomputer applications in communication disorders* (pp. 79–123). San Diego: College-Hill Press.

Christie, S. (1986, July 2). Rehabilitation engineering: Technology for independence. *Physical Therapy Forum*, pp. 1, 3.

Cohn, J. T. (1982). *Picture communication* [Computer software]. Pine Brook, NJ: ComputAbility.

ComputAbility. (1986a). *Aphasic six* [Computer software]. Pine Brook, NJ: Author.

ComputAbility. (1986b). *Unex II exercise program* [Computer program]. Pine Brook, NJ: Author.

Cooper, R. J. (1986). *Point to pictures* [Microcomputer software]. Lake Zurich, IL: Don Johnston Developmental Equipment.

Dunford, M. E. L. (1986, November 5). The use of microcomputers and microswitch technology in occupational therapy. *Occupational Therapy Forum*, pp. 1, 3–4.

Expert Systems Software, Inc. *The OMNIBOX* [Operating manual]. Nashville, TN: Author.

Fitzgerald, G. E. (1985, October). *Development of an interactive videodisc training package in classroom observation skills.* Paper presented at Computer Technology for the Handicapped conference, Minneapolis, MN.

Fox, B., & Wilson, M. (1982–1983). *First words, First categories* [Computer software]. Burlington, VT: Laureatte Learning.

Goodrich, G. L. (1984). Applications of microcomputers by visually impaired persons. *Journal of Visual Impairment and Blindness, 78*(9), 408–414.

Gordon, R. E. (1984). Use of technical aids in occupational therapy treatment. *Developmental Disabilities Special Interest Section Newsletter, 7,* 1.

Graham, L. P. (1984). Use of microcomputers for the remediation of learning problems in children with communication disorders. *Journal of Childhood Communication Disorders, 8*(1), 79–88.

Greenberg, H., & Chamoff, C. (1986). *Visual perceptual diagnostic testing and training* [Computer program]. Wantagh, NY: Educational Electronic Techniques.

Gronley, J. K., & Perry, J. (1984). Gait analysis techniques: Rancho Los Amigos Hospital Gait Laboratory. *Physical Therapy, 64*(12), 1831–1838.

Harlan, D. E., Larimore, H. W., & Smith, M. A. (1984). Computer processing of SICD data. *ASHA, 26*(5), 23–25.

Hartley Courseware, Inc. (no date). *Dr. Peet's Talkwriter* [computer software]. Dimondale, MI: author.

Hasselbring, T., & Hamlett, C. (1983). *Aimstar* [Computer software]. Portland, OR: ASIEP Education Co.

Hefter, R., & Lusby, D. (1985). *Stickybear printer* [Computer program]. Middletown, CT: Xerox Education Publications/Weekly Reader.

Holleman, J. J. (1986). Expanding opportunities: Disabled students and microcomputer instruction at Berkeley's Vista College. *T.H.E. Journal, 13*(6), 68–71.

Horsman, L. (1983). Disabled individuals can talk to their computers. *Rehabilitation Literature, 44*(3–4), 71–75, 85.

Kay Elemetrics Corporation. (no date). *Visi-Pitch* [Computer software]. Pine Brook, NJ: Author.

Kneedler, R. B. (1984). *Special education for today.* Englewood Cliffs, NJ: Prentice-Hall.

Kusmiak, G., & Riggs, G. (1984). *Bank street writer* [Computer program]. San Rafael, CA: Broderbund Software.

Lahm, E. A. (1985). *Choice maker I* [Microcomputer software]. Fairfax, VA: Microcomputer Systems for the Handicapped.

Lahm, E. A. (1987). *Software designed to teach young multiply handicapped children to use the computer for controlling their environment: A validation study.* Unpublished doctoral dissertation, George Mason University, Fairfax, Virginia.

Lasky, E. Z. (1984). Introduction to microcomputers for specialists in communication disorders. In A. H. Schwartz (Ed.), *Handbook of microcomputer applications in communication disorders* (pp. 1–15). San Diego, CA: College-Hill Press.

Laughman, R. K., Askew, L. J., Bleimeyer, R. R., & Chao, E. Y. (1984). Objective clinical evaluation of function: Gait analysis. *Physical Therapy, 64*(12), 1839–1845.

Leifer, L. (1983). Interactive robotic manipulation for the disabled. In *IEEE Computer Society-Digest of Papers,* 1983 COMPCON, pp. 46–49.

Mackall, P. (1985). KendallNET — Computers helping deaf educators and students communicate. In M. Gergen (Ed.), *Computer technology for the handicapped — Applications '85 Selected proceedings of Closing The Gap's 1985 conference* (pp. 177–181). Hutchinson, MN: Crow River Press.

Madeiros, J. (1984). Automated measurement systems for clinical motion analysis. *Physical Therapy, 64*(12), 1846–1850.

McDonald, E. T. (1975). Design and application of communication boards. In G. C. Vanderheiden & K. Grilley (Eds.), *Nonvocal communication techniques and aides for the severely physically handicapped* (pp. 105–119). Baltimore: University Park Press.

MECC. (no date). *Blissymbolics bliss drills* [Computer software]. St. Paul, MN: Author.

MECC. (1984). *Paint with words* [Computer program]. St. Paul, MN: Author.

Meyers, L. F. (1984). Unique contributions of microcomputers to language intervention with handicapped children. *Seminars in Speech and Language, 5*(1), 23–33.

Meyers, L. F. (1983a). *PEAL exploratory play* [Computer program]. Santa Monica, CA: PEAL Software.

Meyers, L. F. (1983b). *PEAL representational play* [Computer program]. Santa Monica, CA: PEAL Software.

Meyers, L. F. (1985). *Keytalk* [Computer program]. Santa Monica, CA: PEAL Software.

Morrison, R. C., & Lunney, D. (1984). The microcomputer as a laboratory aid for visually impaired science students. *Journal of Visual Impairment and Blindness, 78*(9), 418–425.

Morrissette, D. L. (1984). Large-print computers: An evaluation of their features. *Journal of Visual Impairment and Blindness, 8*(9), 428–434.

Nolley, D., & Nolley, B. (1984). Microcomputer data analysis at the clinical mental retardation site. *Mental Retardation, 22*(2), 85–89.

Panyan, M. V. (1984). Computer technology for autistic students. *Journal of Autism and Development Disorders, 14*(4), 375–382.

Personal Touch. (1985). *TouchWindow* [Computer program]. San Jose, CA: Author.

Petrofsky, J. S., Heaton, H. III, & Phillips, C. A. (1983). Outdoor bicycle for exercise in paraplegics and quadriplegics. *Journal of Biomedical Engineeringt, 5*(4), 292–296.

Phillips, S. H., & Russell, Y. S. (1980). Development of prototype equipment of innovative employment of blind and partially sighted persons. *Journal of Medical Systems, 4*(2), 215–226.

Rettig, M., & Greenlee, R. (1985). *Rabbit scanner* [Microcomputer software]. Kansas City, MO: Sherwood Center for the Exceptional Child.

Rosegrant, T. J., & Cooper, R. A. (1983). *Talking screen textwriter* [Computer program]. Phoenix, AZ: Computing Adventures.

Rubow, R., & Swift, E. (1985). A microcomputer-based wearable biofeedback device to improve transfer of treatment in Parkinsonian dysarthria. *Journal of Speech and Hearing Disorders, 50,* 178–185.

Rushakoff, G. E. (1984a). Clinical applications in communication disorders. In A. H. Schwartz (Ed.), *Handbook of microcomputer applications in communication disorders* (pp. 147–171). San Diego: College-Hill Press.

Rushakoff, G. E. (1985b). Microcomputer assisted instruction in communication disorders. *Journal of Childhood Communication Disorders, 8*(1), 51–61.

Rushakoff, G. E., & Hansen, K. (1981). *Single switch assessment program* [Computer program]. (Available from G. E. Rushakoff, Clinical Microcomputer Laboratory, Box 3W, Department of Speech, New Mexico State University, Las Cruces, NM).

Schwartz, A. H. (1984). Microcomputer applications: Facts, functions, fads, and fallacies. *Journal of Childhood Communication Disorders, 8*(1), 89–111.

Schwejda, P., & McDonald, J. (1979). *Motor training games* [Computer program]. Seattle, WA: Washington Research Foundation.

Seamone, W. (1983). The application of robotics to the patient with high spinal cord

injury (quadriplegia): The robotic arm/work table. Paper presented at the NATO
Advanced Study Institute on Robotics and Artificial Intelligence, Pisa, Italy.

Seeds, M. A. (1984, October). KidWord. *Cider,* pp. 31–32.

Sidler, M. R. (1986). Impact of technology on rehabilitation. *Occupational Therapy in Health Care, 3*(3–4), 55–84.

Southern Micro Systems. (no date). *Articulation error analysis* [Computer software]. Burlington, NC: Author.

Spinnaker. (no date). *Kidwriter* [Computer program]. Cambridge, MA: Author.

Spinnaker. (no date). *Story machine* [Computer program]. Cambridge, MA: Author.

Stranger, D., Kulzer, J., Elseth, P., & Lie, S. (1986). *Magic slate* [Computer program]. Pleasantville, NY: Sunburst Communications.

Stoker, R. G. (1983). A computer-assisted diagnostic and prescriptive tool for use in teaching speech to the deaf. *American Annals of the Deaf, 128*(5), 625–630.

Tanner, S., & Satterfield, B. (1985). *SimpleCom I: Yes/no communication* [Computer program]. Duluth, GA: Dunamis.

Vanderheiden, G. C. (1983a). Non-conversational communication technology needs of individuals with handicaps. *Rehabilitation World, 7*(2), 8–12.

Vanderheiden, G. C. (1983b). The practical use of microcomputers in rehabilitation. *Rehabilitation Literature, 44*(3–4), 66–70.

Vanderheiden, G. C., & Kelso, D. (1982). *The talking Blissapple.* Madison, WI: Trace Research and Development Center.

Wall, N. (1984, June). Microcomputer activities and occupational therapy. *The Exceptional Parent,* pp. 25–28.

Wamboldt, J. J. (1986). Computer-assisted therapy for treatment of hemianopsia and neglect. In E. N. Clark (Ed.), *Microcomputers: Clinical applications* (pp. 25–36). Thorofare, NJ: Slack.

White, R. C., & Cormier, R. J. (1986). The Rehabilitation Project in Data Processing: A prototpye demonstration project of university, state government, and industrial cooperation. *T.H.E. Journal, 13*(6), 72–76.

Wicks, S. (1986). Software for visual perception deficits: A review. In E. N. Clark (Ed.), *Microcomputers: Clinical applications* (pp. 57–60). Thorofare, NJ: Slack.

Wilson, M. S., & Fox, B. J. (1985, June). *Trends in integrating speech into software.* Paper presented at the Special Education Software Conference, Arlington, VA.

Young, M. E. (1984). Constraints on microcomputer access for visually impaired persons. *Journal of Visual Impairment and Blindness, 78*(9), 426–427.

CHAPTER 3

The Computer in School and Classroom Testing

WAYNE P. THOMAS

W hile much has been written (and done) about computer use in instruction and in support of instruction, the topic of computer use in testing and test processing has received substantial attention only from a few measurement specialists and still fewer software writers. Much of the software which does exist tends to be greatly limited in its speed, in its versatility, and in the degree that it facilitates performance of the functions of testing in the classroom and the school system.

Perhaps this is fortunate, because few educators are adequately prepared to deal with testing and the use of computers in testing at a more than cursory level. Courses that prepare future teachers to evaluate, construct, and interpret testing information are rarely popular with teacher trainees, and the testing activities of a school system are frequently in the hands of a few specialists at the central office level. These specialists process test scores (or more frequently, contract with distant companies to process them) in ways that produce summary reports useful for end-of-the-year administrative decision-making. However, reports of instructional utility typically arrive too late to substantially influence instruction, even if the classroom teacher were interested in using them.

TEACHER USE OF TEST INFORMATION

Many teachers receive information from two primary types of testing activities: those that compare the student's performance to that of other similar students on standard sets of items (norm referenced tests), and those that compare the student's performance to pre-set standards on items keyed to the local curriculum (criterion referenced tests). Some tests combine those two basic intents for use of testing information by allowing the teacher to specify a set of items that are relevant to the local curriculum and to local specifications (an item domain), and then providing norm referenced as well as criterion referenced interpretations of this set of relevant items (domain referenced testing).

Although teachers need to know about norm referenced test information (e.g., national percentile scores in reading) for making placement or selection decisions, most prefer criterion referenced information, which provides information on the degree of student mastery or non-mastery of specific skills. This preference is understandable because criterion referenced tests purport to provide information on skill mastery, which can guide directly the teacher's efforts in instruction. For example, Johnny's lack of mastery of the test objective "student can add two-digit numbers" might lead to the teacher's emphasis of those skills in the next instructional session.

However, at least two problems with teacher over-reliance on criterion referenced testing should be pointed out here. First, Johnny may master all the skills at some level but still remain low in overall score when compared to other similar students because his mastery is minimal, or deteriorates without constant reinforcement and retesting, or is merely recollection of items from the previous test or just lucky guesswork. Second, defining minute sections of the curriculum — each of which is to be tested by means of a few test items — may lead to curriculular fragmentation and a teacher's emphasizing one set of skills after another without maintaining instructional coherence. Teachers may be so concerned with measuring "mastery" of small curricular areas as assessed by test items that are easily influenced by guessing and other measurement uncertainty that they lose sight of the overall patterns of student competence, especially in skills not easily measured by the typical criterion referenced or norm referenced test.

IS MICROCOMPUTER USE ADVANTAGEOUS IN TESTING?

An important point is that typical teacher uses of test information may not be improved by the introduction of computers to the classroom testing environment. In fact, the use of computers may well produce information from ineffective testing even faster and with more errors of interpretation than was possible manually. Since well-intentioned teachers do not want to automate any confusion resulting from testing practices with which they don't feel comfortable, it behooves educators to work on the problem of test usage and interpretation before and as computers are introduced into classroom testing.

Despite the potential drawbacks, there are advantages to computer use that should lead to their natural use in testing activities in the schools. Some of these are the same computer advantages that educators learn about in their first computer literacy course. For example, the advantages of fast processing of data, the ability to store and retrieve large amounts of information, and the ability to perform computations and other data processing tasks accurately would appear to lend themselves very well to the testing administered by the average teacher or administrator. Yet several types of testing tasks routinely performed by educators, such as test construction, scoring, processing, administration, and record-keeping, continue to be performed either manually by the educator or by another person away from the site of testing and test usage.

Goals of Classroom Testing

Most classroom testing can be thought of as an indirect way to examine and estimate the levels of a student's true achievement or potential for achievement. Testing is indirect in that it usually poses a hypothetical task or situation under circumstances that are removed from "real world" performance. The purpose of testing is to arrive at the best possible measurement of a student's performance using methods that are most practical for the tester and student in terms of time, resources, and instrusiveness. In classical testing theory, "best measurement" means that the observed score should be as close to the true score as possible (reliability of measurement) and that the test should measure what it is intended to measure (validity of measurement). Thus, reliability, validity, and practicality of measurement are three major goals of well-designed testing activities. When these are combined, they should ideally result in testing activities that are not overly burdensome for the student or the teacher, are not too costly in time and resources, and offer worthwhile, accurate, and useful information to the teacher and parents.

Effects of Computer Use in Testing

Most testing uses of computers have focused on practicality, by offering ways to speed up the collection of student responses to posed questions, improving the speed and accuracy of the scoring and analysis of student responses, and storing and retrieving large amounts of student data in order to reduce teachers' record-keeping work load. This focus has occurred because speed of operation and capacity of information storage are areas in which computers may out-perform humans. However, the effect of introducing computers into the testing situation in order to improve practicality has led, in some situations, to degradations of the reliability of testing and decreases in the value of test results. In addition, the limitations of computers regarding input of information (e.g., the use of machine-scored answer sheets) has led to further removal of the student's test taking from the student's performance in a real life situation.

The use of computers in the name of practicality and efficiency also has had an effect on the types of items that tend to appear on computer-processed tests. Forced choice items, especially the ubiquitous multiple choice item, have become the mainstay of test constructors, with a de-emphasis on short essay, fill-in-the-blanks and other types that require the student to produce the correct answer rather than only recognize it. A related problem is that multiple choice items, which require more cognitive demands than mere rote memory of knowledge, are difficult to write. In addition, it is easy for test constructors writing multiple choice items to focus on fragmentary factual parts of the curriculum rather than on the major issues or trends that may represent more important knowledge.

In summary, an answer to the question, "Is microcomputer use advantageous in testing?" might be that most testing applications simply automate operations that were previously performed manually. Some features of testing are more readily performed using a computer (e.g., item analysis), but overall, testing has probably not been vastly improved or substantially damaged by computer use because few really innovative testing practices have emerged. Many testing practices have been made more efficient, but at a substantial cost in staff training and in the loss of flexibility of testing practices. Test development as well as scoring and processing remain largely out of the control of teachers and, in many cases, out of the direct control of administrators.

COMPUTERIZED TESTING APPLICATIONS

There have been some developments in computerized testing applications in recent years, for example, the use of graphics on microcomputers to present testing information. But most testing uses of computers that appear in schools today are merely revisions of earlier software that was written for minicomputer and mainframe computers in the late 1960s and 1970s. before the common availability of microcomputers in education. In fact, much testing software today is minicomputer software developed in a timesharing environment, which has been transferred to a microcomputer. The author wrote such programs as a graduate student in the early 1970s and has transferred many of them to the more powerful of today's micro-computers. While these programs work successfully with some modifica-tions, they are usually slower in execution than software written expressly for modern micros in micro-oriented languages. In addition, these programs betray their age through their test-processing strategies (processing informa-tion in batches rather than smaller, more interactive transactions), the lack of graphics (which were possible in limited forms only with very high-powered computers), and their orientation toward the testing specialist rather than the teacher or school administrator in the character of their reports and requested inputs.

Where We Are Now

At present, there are several major ways in which computers may be used in testing activities. The computer hardware and at least some rudimentary software are available, but these applications may not be entirely free of undesirable features at present. These roles for computers in testing are as a test data collector, scorer, and reporter of data from norm referenced and criterion referenced tests; as a test developer and administrator; and as a storer, retriever, and presenter of test information for instructional decision-making.

The advent of desktop optical scanners (see Figure 3-1) and powerful microcomputers in the early to mid-1980s has led to the possibility that computer use in testing can break away from some of the limitations of the microcomputers first used in computer assisted instruction. In the past, the typical classroom microcomputer contained too little memory, had too little disk storage on floppy disks, and accessed disk storage and executed programming instructions too slowly to be of substantial use to the teacher in test processing of any large amount or complexity. The microcomputer, which may work well in computer assisted instruction, is frequently overwhelmed by the requirements posed by test processing activities.

In addition, it has been necessary to enter much, if not all, of the testing information into the computer by hand. This operation was time consuming and led to errors of data entry that required correction and consumed more time. After manually entering information, correcting errors, and then waiting for the computer to produce reports that may not be just what the teacher needs, the teacher may discover as many disadvantages as advantages to computer use in testing.

Administrators, who require more computer power and capabilities from the beginning and have fewer computers to buy, have generally acquired more powerful and more expensive microcomputers, comparable to those used in a small business, while teachers acquired classroom computers more comparable to home computers. This dichotomy has led to much of the current popularity in educational circles of IBM and IBM-clone microcomputers for administrative applications and Apple, Commodore, or other small computers for instructional applications. This basic difference between the hardware and software needs for a few, more powerful machines for administrative use, and the budgetary necessity for large numbers of cheaper (and consequently, less capable) computers for classroom use will be seen in several of the testing applications to be reviewed.

Figure 3-1. A small desktop scanning machine, the NCR Sentry 3000, is inexpensive and can be easily housed in a school office.

The Computer as Test Data Collector, Scorer, and Reporter

Computer software to process testing data is available in a variety of categories. Two of the largest categories are represented by software designed to score and report classroom tests and that designed to optically scan, score, and report tests for a school or school system. These two major categories differ primarily in the following areas:

- Method of input of test responses. The choices are usually manual data entry for classroom software versus optically scanned data entry for school and school system software.
- Type of testing reports desired. Summaries of individual student performance are available for instructional use by classroom teachers, possibly with instructional remediation suggestions, while administrative summaries primarily for use in program and curricular monitoring and evaluation are provided by school system software.
- Amount of test data to be processed, including size of test and number of students. A classroom test of 50 items administered to 30 students represents a simpler task than a 500 item test administered to 10,000 students.
- Whether test results can be stored in a data base and updated.
- Whether the scoring system can be customized by the user to work with any type of test (i.e., criterion referenced, norm referenced) rather than just with one test.

■ Supported hardware features such as use of fixed disk storage, capability of use with different printers or other peripheral devices.

Hsu and Nitko (1983), Nelson (1984) and others have discussed computer test scoring software designed for classroom instructional needs. However, few authors have discussed the design and specifications for a test scoring center within a school or a school system. This author and Brzezinski (1984), among others, have called for a unified and integrated test scoring system that is capable of meeting classroom instructional needs as well as the administrative and program evaluative needs of the school principal, the curriculum specialist, and the instructional leaders of a school system.

Centralized Data Analysis

Until recently, the teacher or evaluator working in a school setting frequently has depended on large-scale computers and statistical software for data analysis purposes. Typically such tasks as test scoring are accomplished using either the school system's central computer and large optical scanners or the computer equipment of an external scoring service. Many school systems have acquired statistical analysis packages such as the Statistical Package for the Social Sciences (Nie et al, 1975) in order to analyze testing or survey data. Some school systems have bought computer time and access to such software from local university or commercial vendors, but the type and level of training needed to operate such packages generally rule out their direct use by teachers.

However, many educators have found that centralized data analysis using large mainframes leaves something to be desired in several ways. First, the data and its analysis may not be under the control of the researcher or evaluator, and it is certainly not under the control of the teacher. This is especially true in the case of externally scored tests. Thus, the school evaluator gives up control over the accuracy of data to persons outside of the school system. Samplings of externally scored tests have revealed that a disturbingly high percentage of students scored may have at least one error in their testing reports (Johnson & Thomas, 1979).

A second characteristic of school evaluation data produced by existing methods is that the time interval between instrument administration and report receipt may be distressingly long, frequently as much as eight weeks. Even if evaluative data are processed on the school system's equipment, the analysis usually receives a lower priority than payroll or other important administrative data processing functions, contributing to delayed reports and thus to reduced impact of testing results on instruction.

Third, evaluators have contended with the factor of "take-what-you-can-get" analysis and reports, which may not well fit the evaluative or research questions of local interest. For example, company X's testing reports may not allow teachers to directly address local needs for evaluative information without further manual or computer analysis. Also, the large scale statistical analysis packages may not offer much control over the format of the output, necessitating a restructuring and retyping of the analysis reports before they can be given to local teachers, administrators, or school board members.

A fourth characteristic of contemporary evaluative data analysis is that it is costly in terms of required equipment (whether locally owned or not), support staff for the periodic high intensity analyses, and money spent to acquire optional reports to fully meet local needs. Thus, the per-student cost for such analyses is quite high when costs from all sources are considered, whether the data are processed by school system staff or by data processing or scoring services.

In addition, new software for test and survey scanning and scoring represents an important new capability for powerful modern microcomputers. At least one company now offers software that allows the user to scan, score, and print reports for virtually any norm or criterion referenced test (MicroScan Inc., 1987). In addition, statistical analysis packages, which formerly were limited to large mainframes, are now available for the new powerful microcomputer systems. Also, packages that were written expressly for micro use allow, in some cases, for even more interactivity and user control of data than do the batch-oriented packages with a mainframe heritage.

Even now, the new micros have smaller memories, slower execution speeds, and slower peripheral devices (e.g., printers) than do large mainframe computers. However, it is also true that the new micro systems are much cheaper and easier to use, with software that is much more "user-friendly" than in the mainframe case. This trade-off of some power and speed for increased flexibility and dramatically reduced cost can lead to very attractive possibilities for high-cost analysis needs such as test scoring. For example, a hardware plus software combination for test scoring might cost from one to ten percent of the cost of a large computer system to accomplish the same purpose.

Decentralized Data Analysis

For the first time, these new hardware and software developments make it possible to design and operate a practical distributed data collection and analysis system for use in the schools. Since test scoring is probably the most expensive and high volume part of a school system's evaluative data collection activities, the microcomputer-based decentralized data collection and analysis system might be especially worthy of consideration.

In the typical centralized model, test data collection occurs in classrooms and schools, and the source documents (i.e., test answer sheets) are sent to a central location such as the data processing center for either scanning or shipping to a scoring service. In this model, the source docu-

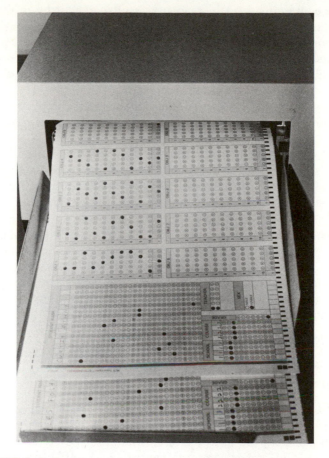

FIGURE 3-2. *Student response sheets being read by the scanner.*

ments are processed away from the site of test administration and the reports are sent back to the schools at a later date.

However, a decentralized mode of school-based data processing using microcomputers is now possible. In this model, each school or regional center would be equipped with a powerful microcomputer hardware and software system that could be used to scan and process tests on optical scanner sheets *on site* (see Figure 3-2). This would allow for quick turnaround of testing reports because the answer sheets would never leave the site of test administration. It might even be possible for teachers to scan and score their own students' answer sheets on a scheduled or walk-in basis and have the reports back in a few days rather than in weeks.

After the student reports were returned quickly to teachers for instructional use, the data could be sent to the central office either by mailing the diskettes containing student responses and scores, or by transmitting the data directly to a central computer by means of modems and available communications software. In either case, the data would be available more immediately for instructional needs in the schools and would be available to the central office staff without the shipping and handling of large quantities of answer sheets and printed reports.

Among the many reasons to consider the microcomputer-based, decentralized method of test scoring in a school system are the following.

FASTER TURNAROUND TIME FOR REPORTS. One microcomputer-based system can scan, score, and report on tests of several thousand students per week. The use of multiple systems on a regional or school-by-school basis could result in the processing of a entire testing program in one week.

POTENTIAL FOR IMPROVED ERROR RATE. Using a locally installed and controlled scoring system can allow the error rate associated with centralized scoring to be substantially reduced. In fact, using the test scoring software to print out and check student responses and scores can effectively reduce the error rate in direct proportion to the care and attention given to the scoring process.

NO SHIPPING OF ANSWER SHEETS. The answer sheets never leave the school system and, at local option, they may not leave the school where the test was given.

VERY COST EFFECTIVE. A microcomputer-based, decentralized scoring system (or even several of these systems) is much cheaper than larger computers. In addition, the use of several micro-based systems can reduce the peak demands on central computer facilities and staff, capabilities that may go idle during non-testing periods. Typically, the test scoring workload can be spread over existing clerks and instructional personnel in the schools with no need for new staff. This is true because each test user becomes responsible for his or her own small group of students only, and the normal workload associated with gathering and shipping answer sheets is reduced or eliminated.

INTERACTIVE, EASY-TO-USE SOFTWARE. The typical scoring system running on a central, large computer is a production-oriented, batch-processing system written for and by data processing specialists. Such software typically is not accessible directly to school evaluators and reseachers but must be used via computer professionals. The micro-based system, however, is designed for use by educators who are knowledgeable about evaluation and testing but who may not be computer experts. These individuals can set up the system and train the teachers in a school to use it advantageously.

TEST INFORMATION IS STORED ON DISKS. Schools can receive their own data on disk as well as their own reports for in-school use by building administrators and instructional personnel. Using these disks, local school personnel could write programs in *BASIC* or *PASCAL* to produce reports and analyses of interest to them. In addition, (1) less paper is required because multiple printed copies of each student's reports no longer may be necessary, and information can be accessed and displayed on a computer screen when needed; (2) the test data already will be machine-readable form and need not be rekeyed into a computer for use with other microcomputer software (e.g., a data management package); and (3) copies of the data and reports require much less space for storage than if printed output were used exclusively.

TEST ANALYSIS IS CLOSER TO THE POINT OF TEST ADMINISTRATION. Because the tests need not be sent out of the school system and turnaround time probably will be faster, test administrators such as teachers and counselors may take greater interest in error detection, in producing unbattered answer sheets, and especially in using the test reports the software produces.

THE TEST SCORING SOFTWARE MAY ALLOW FOR CUSTOMIZATION. The test scoring software may be able to produce different derived scores for teachers than for school board members, and may allow for different reports to be produced for diagnostic instructional needs than for summary administrative needs. Most importantly, the user may be able to control or at least change the format of the reports as well as select or reject subtests for particular uses of the information. In other words, the user may be able to customize the contents and the appearance of the test report to a considerable degree. In addition, the user could print as many copies of the reports as desired at little additional cost.

FURTHER ANALYSES POSSIBLE WITH INTERFACING SOFTWARE. A test scoring package producing standard *ASCII* data files could be used to produce data that other computer software can read. For example, a data base manager such as *dBASE III* or a statistical package such as *micro-SPSS* could read test data directly for further analyses.

TIMELY RESPONSES TO SPECIAL REQUESTS. A simple program written in *BASIC* and run using the data disks produced by the test scoring software could produce most specially requested reports fairly quickly.

In summary, a microcomputer-based test scanning and scoring system located in school, area, or district-wide centers, could form the heart of a very capable system for collecting and analyzing test and other evaluative data. This system could supplement any existing large computer facilities by enabling analysis at the point of data collection. Any data needed at a central location could then be sent there for storage or for further analysis if desired.

Guidelines for Evaluating Test Scoring Software

Microcomputer software that is capable of meeting schools' needs for test scoring is available in several forms from different software companies. Many testing companies now offer some form of microcomputer scoring of a limited nature for one or more tests that they sell. Some are designed only for teacher-made tests administered in conjunction with a given textbook curriculum. There are a few software packages, however, that will meet the schools' needs for scoring more than one test and for flexibility in report production and data analysis. There are certain general characteristics of the software that may determine how capably it will scan and score tests. The more characteristics, the more powerful and useful the software may be. Software characteristics to look for include the following.

GENERIC. The software should be capable of scoring virtually any test, whether norm referenced or criterion referenced. This allows the school system to use different tests and different types of tests for various groups of students. Thus, the school system does not become locked in to a particular test or testing company unless this is desired.

USER CUSTOMIZED. The software should allow the user to create composite scores, skip certain subtests, decide the format of reports, score parts of a test only, create local norms, and in every reasonable way, control the process of scanning and scoring so that local needs are exactly met.

CAPABILITIES BEYOND SIMPLE SCORING AND PRINTING. The software should provide data base capabilities for storage and retrieval of student responses and scores. In addition, features such as the capability to select student scores that meet certain criteria (e.g., reading scores lower than 50th percentile) should be offered.

USER FRIENDLINESS. The software should be easy enough to learn and use so that a clerk who had been provided with a manual can run the system after one day's training. There should be enough on-screen documentation so that the user who is familiar with the manual contents can run the system without constant reference to the manual. However, there should not be so much on-screen documentation that the system's performance is substantially slowed down.

INTEGRATED SOFTWARE. The software should allow the user to score some or all of the items of a norm referenced test (NRT) as if it were a criterion referenced test (CRT) without rescanning the answer sheets. This would allow for objectives mastery and domain mastery reports from the items of a norm referenced test. In addition, the software should be capable of producing a norm referenced analysis of the items from a criterion referenced test without re-scanning the answer sheets. This should be possible using local norms produced by the software or by using externally supplied regional, state, or national norms.

UPLOADABLE DATA. It should be possible to easily upload the contents of student response and score files to a larger computer or to another microcomputer using commonly available communications software.

USER-SELECTABLE REPORT FEATURES. The user should be able to determine which substests and derived scores are to be printed as well as the order in which they should be printed for each student. This feature allows for the production of different reports for different audiences.

USER-MODIFIABLE DATA. It should be possible to edit student identification information, responses, and scores after the answer sheets are scanned and the responses and scores have been written onto a disk. In this way, the correct data for students who are absent at the time of testing, have incorrectly filled out name and other identification information, and have not taken all subtests can be added later. If the student is re-tested, it should be possible to replace the student's old responses and scores with the new ones by either re-scanning or by manually entering the information onto the disk.

USER-CONTROLLED LEVEL OF INTERACTIVITY. The user should be able to control the degree to which the software runs as a production-oriented batch system as opposed to an interactive transactional system. In other words, the software should provide options that allow the user to scan, score, and report large numbers of students at one time without stopping; in addition, the software should allow for one student's answer sheet to be scanned, scored, reported and edited before moving on to the next student to repeat this process.

ENABLING OF TEST DEVELOPMENT. The software should provide reports that might be used by the local school system to investigate the characteristics of test items (e.g., an item analysis report) as well as the characteristics of score distributions from the test (e.g., a frequency distribution report with descriptive statistics).

ACCESS TO DATA FOR CLASSES AND INDIVIDUALS. It should be possible for a user to see on the computer screen both individual student testing information and class information. It should also be possible to print out this information.

SUPPORT FOR SPECIAL FEATURES. The software should allow for the production of anticipated achievement scores, the scoring of ability and achievement tests together, the production of local norms, the use of special composite scores, and other such functions associated with test scoring that local school systems may find useful.

While the list of suggested characteristics of worthwhile microcomputer test scoring software may seem to consist mostly of wishful thinking, it is important to note that software does exist now that can accomplish most of those functions. Since the software available from several companies is currently being improved, it is reasonable to assume that one or more microcomputer test scoring packages will soon be capable of all the suggested characteristics (see Vignette 3–1).

The Computer as Test Developer and Administrator

For many years, students have been presented test items via computer as a part of computer managed instruction software. Typically, such tests appeared at the end of an instructional module and provided information on the student's performance on that module. The same items were usually presented to each student, the student selected an answer to each item, and a raw score for each student was calculated at the end of the test. In other words, a test very similar to one that formerly had been administered using pencil and paper was now being administered at much greater cost using a computer.

In the 1960s, latent trait theory (now called item response theory) became a focus of discussion among testing experts such as Lord (Crocker & Algina, 1986). While mathematically sophisticated, this theory in several forms suggested that it should be possible to define underlying traits which account for student performance on a set of test items. The theory models how examinees who are of different ability levels should respond to a given item on a test.

Computer Adaptive Testing

In computer adaptive testing, a set of items has previously been defined as constituting a continuum of performance on an underlying trait of interest to the tester. Items ranging from very easy to quite difficult are available for presentation to the student. The student first answers easy items and proceed to successively more difficult items, all measuring the skill continuum of interest. At some point along the continuum of items of increasing difficulty, the student will begin to miss items and will then consistently miss items. At some point, items that are slightly easier can be administered until the "floor" and the "ceiling" of the student's range of

VIGNETTE 3-1
Test Scoring for Classroom Teachers — The Walk-In Scoring Center

On Monday afternoon, Mrs. Brown gave a test to her class of seventh graders. The students took the test on optically scannable forms. The questions took the forms of multiple choice, true-false, matching, and a form that allows students to indicate their approval or disapproval of sentence structure by marking a answer sheet grid.

Now, after class, Mrs. Brown enters the teacher workroom and drops her student's answer sheets into the optical scanner's automatic feeder. The scanner, a desktop model, is capable of reading the marks students made and transmitting them to the powerful microcomputer sitting on the same desk.

The computer's screen presents Mrs. Brown with a large menu of types of tests and items that it can scan, score, and report. Mrs. Brown selects the choices that describe the test features and then is shown a list of answer sheets the optical scanner is capable of reading. She selects the choice that describes the answer sheet her students used and inserts her answer key sheet on which the correct answers have been marked into the optical scanner. At this point, approximately three minutes have elapsed since Mrs. Brown entered the room.

Mrs. Brown then inserts her thirty students' answer sheets into the scanner, presses the start button, and watches as the sheets are scanned and the data is transmitted to the computer. This process requires about one minute.

After the scanning is complete, Mrs Brown selects "class summary" from the list of report choices offered by the computer on the screen. The computer then scores each student's test responses using Mrs. Brown's answer key, and prints out a list of student names and the number of correct answers each student attained on one sheet of paper. Another minute has elapsed.

Mrs. Brown decides that some students scores are lower than she expected and asks for an item analysis report. The computer prints out an item-by-item summary including number of correct responses to each item, item difficulty coefficient, item discrimination coefficient, and an overall measure of test reliability. Since Mrs. Brown has received in-service training in the interpretation of this information, she can use it to assess the quality of her test items. Another minute has passed.

Finally, Mrs. Brown asks for a "student profile" report. This report furnishes each student's responses, indicates whether that response was correct, and allows Mrs. Brown to visually scan all items for a given student or across all students for a given item so that she can see patterns of individual or class performance on test items of interest to her.

After fewer than ten minutes, Mrs. Brown now has all the information she needs to use her student test data to make good instructional decisions for each student. She finishes her work by inserting a floppy diskette into the computer so that each student's scores and responses can be recorded. She will take the diskette back to her classroom and read it into her classroom computer, which will

(continued)

VIGNETTE 3-1 (continued)

update the student's instructional data base records maintained since the beginning of the school year.

As she enters her classroom, she pauses briefly to remember the "good old days" of manual scoring of tests. She also recalls the first computer testing systems, which were incompatible with each other, made it necessary for her to keep voluminous written records in addition to her computerized records, and were slow in operation and required her to enter all student responses by hand. As she leaves school for the day, she is glad that the power of the computer was finally brought to the classroom in ways that improved her professional productivity rather than causing her more work. She only regrets that it took a lot longer to really do this than everyone had expected in the 1970s and early 1980s.

---

performance on that skill continuum have been explored. Thus, the student's performance relative to other students can be determined precisely without presenting all possible items to the student. The easier items that the student would always answer correctly may be skipped and the really difficult items that the student might find beyond his or her skill level, and therefore frustrating, would never be reached. The items that would be emphasized would be those representing the range of the student's ability to perform.

The result of this testing strategy would probably be that the student would be required to handle fewer items with no loss in the precision of his or her test scores. Thus, testing time could be substantially reduced. In addition, there would be reduced testing frustration, and opportunities to explore the peculiarities and depth of the student's mastery of the subject using slightly different items of equivalent difficulty. These factors could result in improved testing information.

A computer that could access an item bank of hundreds or thousands of items whose difficulties and other characteristics were well known could be used advantageously in this system. The computer could present the items and then branch to easier or more difficult items depending on the student's response. After presenting enough items to the student, the computer could furnish a score comparing the student's responses to those of other students, and could furnish a diagnostic summary of the student's patterns of mistakes in the set of skills being measured. In this scenario, the computer operates as a test constructor, test scorer, and source of diagnostic information for the teacher regarding strengths and weaknesses.

Concern about the expense and complexities of setting up a computer adaptive system probably will lead to its development only by large testing companies and very large school systems. These agencies have access to the large amounts of student data necessary to make the development techniques work properly, whereas most school systems do not. Moreover, if school systems use these item domains from other sources, there may be, to some degree, a mismatch between the local curriculum and the test items just as there is now in the case of many norm referenced tests used in school systems. A final problem area is that the underlying assumptions of the techniques used call for the trait measured to be unidimensional. This may not be the case in many typical school system tests. The use of computer adaptive testing may be limited to large school systems in specific areas of curriculum.

The Computer as Storer and Retriever of Test Information for Instructional Decision-Making

Computer software that presents instructionally diagnostic items to students, processes student responses, and stores this information in a student data base for retrieval and analysis is a valuable commodity to the teacher with huge amounts of information to organize and use in decision-making. Software in this category includes computer managed instruction (CMI) software as well as some computer assisted instruction (CAI) software, which probes student skills in teacher-selected areas and provides reports useful for computer-based decision-making in the classroom. In its simplest form, CMI software provides a summary of past student performance in a particular curricular area, and comparison of past performance to present performance. When specified mastery criteria have been met for a given have been met for a given skill area, new skills may be introduced by the teacher. The computer is used as a means of collecting and managing student performance data and as a source of summary reports on each student's progress.

Several researchers have been advocates of using computers to assist in observational data collection and analysis (Fitzgerald, 1985; Hasselbring, 1985). One example of a program to let teachers directly record observational data is the *DATA* program in which users create a coding system and use the keyboard as the recording device instead of a pencil and paper (Zuckerman, 1986). Data not entered directly into the computer from these types of tests or observational systems can be entered and analyzed through a generic data analysis program such as *Aimstar* (Hasselbring & Hamlett, 1983) or a custom designed program for a specific setting, such as the one used in the Oakdale Regional Center (Nolley & Nolley, 1984). Fitzgerald (1985) has developed an interactive videodisc training package to provide the needed practice time to become proficient at using a behavior coding system.

It is also possible to go further using software that is capable of applying decision rules to help the teacher determine the characteristics of the instructional plan for each student. A successful instructional decision of this type depends on the teacher knowing when to change the instructional plan as well as knowing what type of change is called for (Hasselbring & Hamlett, 1984). Thus, the worthwhile CMI software package provides data collection service and the appropriate data analysis service so the teacher can have a systematic record of the child's past performance as well as displays of present performance, applying decision rules to indicate appropriate instructional change required.

An example of data management software that provides useful information to special education teachers is *Aimstar*. Its use allows the teacher to manage student performance data that is entered periodically as the teacher delivers instruction following the student's individual plan, and to produce graphs and flowcharts of the student's progress without the time-consuming paper-and-pencil tedium. For each skill worked on with the student, the teacher enters data describing the number of correct and incorrect responses along with the time necessary for the student to produce these responses. After the data entry step, *Aimstar* can apply predetermined decision rules to produce graphs of performance in relation to time (in days) so that levels and trends of performance can be established.

A significant advantage of this approach over manual graphs is that the decision rules can be changed and the software can be used to quickly re-analyze student performance according to the revised parameters. This allows the teacher greater flexibility in analyzing student performance and saves significant amounts of time. If the teacher changes the instructional strategy, the software's plots of performance can follow the student's progress toward a level that meets the specified criterion.

The use of this type of software does not eliminate the need for teacher judgment, but does provide empirical data against which the teacher can apply professional judgment in order to improve instructional decision-making. The teacher is in control of the decisions at all times. The computer software simply informs the teacher as to ramifications and implications of the instructional decisions made.

SUMMARY

Properly used, computers can help educators meet three goals of classroom testing: reliability, validity, and practicality of measurement. While computer use in school and classroom testing can substantially improve its practicality (especially efficiency), precautions must be taken to avoid damaging the test's reliability and validity. With the proper planning microcomputer use in school and classroom testing can be quite advantageous for educators to the benefit of students.

There are several specific niches for successful use of computers in school and classroom testing. These include the computer as test scorer, the computer as test developer and administrator, and the computer as storer and record-keeper for testing information needed by educators. In each of these areas, the previously unrealized claims and promises of the 1970s are finally being met by modern computer hardware and software. Although the use of computers in school-based testing is still not without pitfalls, educators who carefully compare the advantages and the disadvantages of computer use in testing may well decide that the time has come to try it.

REFERENCES AND SUGGESTED READINGS

Brzezinski, E. J. (1984). Microcomputers and testing: Where are we and how did we get there? *Educational Measurement: Issues and Practice, 3*(2), 7–10.

Crocker, L., & Algina, J. (1986). *Introduction to classical and modern test theory.* New York: Holt, Rinehart, and Winston.

Fitzgerald, G. E. (1985, October 31–November 2). Development of an interactive videodisc training package in classroom observation. Paper presented at the Computer Technology for the Handicapped Conference, Minneapolis, MN.

Green, B. F., Bock, R. D., Humphreys, L. G., Linn, R. L., & Reckase, M. D. (1984). Technical guidelines for assessing computerized adaptive tests. *Journal of Educational Measurement, 21*(4), 347–360.

Hasselbring, T. (1985) Microcomputer applications in instruction. In E. A. Polloway, J. S. Payne, J. R. Patton, & R. A. Payne (Eds.), *Strategies for teaching retarded students* (3rd ed., pp. 154–175). Columbus, OH: Charles E. Merrill.

Hasselbring, T., & Hamlett, C. (1983). *Aimstar* [Computer software]. Portland, OR: ASIEP Education.

Hasselbring, T. S., & Hamlett, C. L. (1984). Planning and managing instruction: Computer-based decision making. *Teaching Exceptional Children, 16*(4), 248–252.

Hiscox, M. D. (1984). A planning guide for microcomputers in educational measurement. *Educational Measurement: Issues and Practices, 3*(2), 28–34.

Hsu, T., & Nitko, A. J. (1985). Microcomputer testing software teachers can use. *Educational Measurement: Issues and Practice, 2*(4), 15–27.

Johnson, R. T., & Thomas, W. P. (1979, April). *User experiences in implementing the RMC Title I models.* A paper presented at the annual meeting of the American Educational Research Association, San Francisco, CA.

MicroScan, Inc. (1987). *User's guide to the Domain Referenced Scoring System (DRSS).* Reston, VA: Author.

Nelson, L. R. (1984). Using microcomputers to assess achievement and instruction. *Educational Measurement: Issues and Practices, 3*(2), 22–26.

Nie, N. H., Hull, C. H., Jenkins, J. G., Steinbrenner, K., & Bent, D. H. (1975). *SPSS:*

Statistical package for the social sciences. New York: McGraw-Hill.

Nitko, A. J., & Hsu, T. (1984). A comprehensive microcomputer system for classroom testing. *Journal of Educational Measurement, 21*(4), 377–390.

Nolley, D., & Nolley, B. (1984). Microcomputer data analysis at the clinical mental retardation site. *Mental Retardation, 22*(2), 85–89.

Thomas, W. P. (1985, April). *Microcomputer use in testing and school evaluation.* A paper presented at the annual meeting of the American Educational Research Association, Chicago, IL.

Thomas, W. P. (1986, April). *Improving school evaluation using microcomputer-based domain referenced test scoring at the local level.* A paper presented at the annual meeting of the American Educational Research Association, San Francisco, CA.

Weiss, D. J., & Kingsbury, G. G. (1984). Application of computerized adaptive testing to educational problems. *Journal of Educational Measurement, 21*(4), 361–375.

Zuckerman, R. (1986). DATA [software program]. Kent State University.

CHAPTER 4

Electronic Toys and Robots

JOEL MITTLER

P lay, according the the values of our society, has a place in the lives of us all. Old or young, rich or poor, we choose our activities, obtain our play equipment, and find the time to engage in our chosen play. Educators have long recognized the value of play in the development of children. Play, it is believed, encourages intellectual, physical, and social growth among all. Play represents the opportunity to learn by doing, a principle long valued by educators. Summarizing a symposium on play and development with contributions by noted theorists including Piaget, Spitz, Lorenz, and Erikson, Piers (1972) commented that, "Play is a Must of the first order for individuals . . . and for mankind" (p. 172).

If the value of play has been accepted and demonstrated as an important variable in the lives of all children, then any interference with such activities should prove detrimental. Such is clearly the case with the exceptional learner, with the uniqueness of each child providing interference in the process of play. For example, it is obvious that the child with severe physical limitations is precluded from participation in many play activities, unless the activities or the play equipment are modified. Similarly, youngsters with cognitive impairments may be unable to engage in typical opportunities for play.

Adaptations of the activity, specific skill training, modification of the environment, and more have been suggested to enhance the leisure and recreational activities of exceptional children (Haring, 1985; Murphy, Carr, & Callias, 1986; Nietupski, Hamre-Nietupski, & Ayres, 1984). It is apparent, however, that current advances in technology may also assist youngsters with special needs to participate in recreational activities. Such advances include the use of communication enhancement devices, prosthetic devices, and electronic toys and robots. This chapter will investigate the latter area and suggest applications for exceptional learners.

ELECTRONIC TOYS

Although robots, which will be discussed in the next section, have been the most interesting of the microcomputer based toys available, there have been several other applications that are of equal, if not greater value to the special education student.

Educational Toys

For several years, Texas Instruments and other corporations have created microcomputer based learning toys that permit students to interact with a "toy" in an educational endeavor. Such toys include *Electronic Musical Soft Tunes* (Child Guidance Corp.), which provides cause-effect stimulation for children as young as three months. *Touch and Tell* (Texas Instruments) uses voice synthesis to provide young non-readers with learning activities using labeling. *Magic Wand Speaking Reader* (Texas Instruments) provides a bar code reader and a voice synthesizer to provide early readers with opportunities to "read their storybooks." This particular device has been adapted by Tiger Communication System, Inc. of Rochester, New York as an augmentative communication aid for handicapped children. Other Texas Instruments educational toys include *Speak and Spell* and *Read and Spell*.

Whether these toys are designed for the practice of cause-effect, pre-reading activities, reading, spelling, basic math skills, or other skills, they permit the child to input some response and get immediate feedback that can either reinforce the correct response or indicate an error. Similar to more costly computer programs and available in an simpler delivery system, these games often contain some sort of keyboard for entry of a response, a voice synthesized mode of response or a small screen that can provide the stimuli and record the input.

Considering the impact that electronic technology is having upon our entire society, it is not surprising that a similar effect is seen in the use of toys. Electronic toys abound on retailers' shelves, not only in toy stores but at electronic supply distributors as well. Toy catalogs are filled with the latest technological applications. Each successive year appears to produce a new application of technology, from hand-held video games to various educational devices that ask questions and give answers, and then talking animals and laser weapons. Despite this surge of innovative applications of technology, traditional favorites among electronic toys such as train sets, remote-controlled vehicles, and others, continue to be popular.

Can the youngster with special needs enjoy the pleasures of these electronic devices? Among the characteristics of many youngsters with handicapping conditions is the inability to initiate an action or to effect a change in the environment. In some cases, this is a direct result of physical or cognitive limitations. Thus, a youngster may be physically unable to start a toy in motion. In other situations, a child's inability to use a toy may reflect learned psychosocial response patterns that limit initiative on the child's part. Thus, it is common to see handicapped learners who are overly dependent on their caregivers to initiate actions.

Toys Enabling Active Interaction

Although electronic toys have other obvious uses, their ability to perform many actions with power or initiation supplied by a source other than the child's motor input permits handicapped children the opportunity to play. For example, once an electric train begins to move around the tracks, its continued motion is provided by its electric motor. Similarly, a dancing teddy bear will continue as long as it is left in the "on" position and its batteries supply power.

However, the difficulty often experienced by the child with handicaps is getting the toy to begin its action. One of the most creative solutions to this need of handicapped children, especially those with severe or multiple disabilities, has been the design of toys to enable active participation (Burkhart, 1980, 1982). Others have adapted off-the-shelf toys for use (Coker, Jr., 1984; Hughes, 1981; Jefcoate, 1977; Wright & Nomura, 1985). Steven Kanor of Hastings-on-Hudson, New York is an engineer who has spent many years adapting commercially available toys to meet the operating needs of handicapped children. His adaptations are based on the movement capabilities of each youngster, which are then matched with electromechanical switches. By identifying the movement that is most appropriate for the youngster, Kanor designs a switch that can be used to control a variety of adapted toys or other electronic devices. Available switches include those that are controlled by touch, light, voice, movement, position, and other stimuli. Several versions of each switch with differing sensitivities or type of stimuli required are available.

Among the most familiar electronic toys that can be useful with special needs children are remote-controlled devices. These toys permit a youngster with limited movement or cognitive ability the opportunity to exert some control over the device. Often by simply moving a switch, which can be adapted if necessary, the toy can be controlled from a wheelchair, a bed, or a desk. In addition, the remote-controlled device often can permit the toy to perform a relatively difficult movement such as flying or moving at great speed. The remote unit empowers the child who is often otherwise unable to exert such control over objects in the environment. Remote-control devices that use signals from television programs to activate toys in the home have also been introduced and marketed. This is supposed to encourage active rather than passive interaction with the television.

Many of the newer electronic toys are based on recent advances in computerization. Recent advances in technology led to the miniaturization of the computer chip, allowing a personal computer to fit on a student's desk and be available at an acceptable cost. The same technology is being applied to the toys and games today's children are playing with. While some are concerned about this change in children's toys and games (Smith, 1981), it is possible that computerization can enhance the functioning of children with special needs. One of the major applications of computer technology to toys is through the use of robots.

ROBOTS

Evolution of Robots

Although the field of personal service robots began with great promise, recent events have demonstrated the difficulties involved in bringing such technological wonders to the stage of practical use by disabled children and adults. While research continues on programming, reliability, vision, manipulation, mobility, and other critical aspects of robot development, the availability of these devices for popular or educational use is limited. The earlier generation of robots that were available in many retail stores have not been replaced with newer models. While consumers await the next generation of personal service robots, another branch of the evolutionary tree of robotics has appeared.

Robotic Toys

It is clear that some of the early developers of robots have shifted their interest to the creation of advanced robotic toys. Perhaps while they awaited the creation of a market in the field of education and new advances that address some of the limitations of earlier robots, they applied their knowledge to what they believe is a more dynamic and profitable area: the sale of advanced robotic toys. Most of these newer toy robots have combined the lure of stuffed animals with the natural attraction that children of all ages have for pets. Thus, they have endeavored to create life-like stuffed animal robots that emulate many characteristics of living animals.

Perhaps the most advanced robotic toy currently available is a stuffed animal. Phonetica One, Inc. (Colorado, City, CO) has created a large, very life-like dog. Fred (there will also be a Spuds McKenzie), that can actually move about the room in a very realistic manner that closely resembles a real dog. This generation of robotic pets accepts voice commands to move around and has synthesized speech to add to the realism of the toy. Coleco has introduced new *Cabbage Patch Talking Kids,* which carry on conversations with children, and even each other. Their mouths move when they speak and they have sensors in their hands and bodies so they will respond to their environment. Whether these advanced microelectronic toys respond through the use of "dog talk" or human-like voices, they add the communicative connection that real pets and most toys lack. In addition, these "voices" are usually evoked by having the user speak to the robotic toys, creating a limited, but imaginative, conversation.

Toy Robots

Robots have emerged as one of the most popular toys over the past few years. Although the idea of an automated man was generated centuries ago, and mechanical representations of animals and man were actually created years ago, the past few years have seen an explosion of interest in robots. The popularity of the "Star Wars" movie and its sequels, coupled with our country's adventures in space and the advances in inexpensive microcomputer technology undoubtedly led to the current interest in robots as toys for children. Various versions of robots suddenly appeared in toy stores, ranging in size from a few inches high to several feet tall and in price from a few dollars to several hundred.

Although it is difficult to determine the exact definition of a toy robot, this chapter focuses primarily on those toys that are electronically driven by battery, can be controlled through a microprocessor, and can retain commands until turned off. Many toy robots have human characteristics and therefore appear to have "body parts." In addition to these robots, which do possess some form of microprocessor, there are significant numbers of other toy robots and robot-like playthings that can be used for fantasy play and in other creative ways. These may be made of hard or bendable plastics, may be converted into other forms, or may even roll much like a toy car. The discussion to follow, however, will concentrate on the more advanced, computer-like robots, including some that exceed the traditional notion of toys.

Use of Toy Robots in the Classroom

The application of robots with exceptional individuals begins with their use in the classroom. Clearly, we are not at a point where the advanced robots that appear in science fiction or the movies will be seen in schools, although some advanced prototypes are beginning to emerge. The range of devices that falls under the term "robot" is quite large, and it is difficult to generalize from one example to another. The capabilities of one class of robots may be quite dissimilar from those of others. In general, however, the robots that have been used in schools are usually characterized by their ability to be programmed and to move in response to the program. In some ways, these robots can be conceptualized as mobile computers, but, as mentioned, with great variety of form and function.

Numerous applications of robotics to all aspects of elementary and secondary education have been described. Just a few years ago, enthusiasts were predicting that the educational robot would be as common a classroom tool as the microcomputer (Marsh & Spain, 1984) as students enjoy programming them to move, talk, and perform tasks (Howe, 1984). Robotic activities have been described for elementary school children (Friedman, 1986), although greater emphasis has been on uses at the secondary level, especially as part of an industrial arts curriculum (Decker & Krajewski, 1986; Heckard, 1986; Sheets, 1984; Whittaker, 1985).

Functions of Robots

Lahm (1984) and Kimbler (1984) described two functions of robots within special education: as an aid to education and as an extension of the self. In discussing the use of a robot in the instructional process, Mittler (1984) discussed six uses of robots in special education for both teachers and students:

1. Development of programming skills with immediate and *concrete* feedback.
2. Demonstration of behaviors to be modeled by the student.
3. Introduction of robot technology through the design, assembly, and programming of robots.
4. As a motivator for other academic and social skills development.
5. Demonstration of the complexity of human movement by programming similar movement in a robot.
6. Task analysis of a motor skill.

As an extension of the self, Mittler (1984) suggested the following four uses for disabled individuals:

1. To provide movement, sight, hearing, etc.
2. To control the environment.
3. To "speak for the individual.
4. As a "companion."

Some of these uses are possible with currently available robots, while others represent potential applications. Robots are still quite limited and, as the following discussion will demonstrate, are unable to fulfill all of the aforementioned uses. However, it is postulated that although the technology exists to permit robots to perform many of these skills, additional development in the application of this technology must still occur.

Classroom Activities

Numerous classroom activities can emantate from toy robots. Because robots generate excitement in most children, they usually provide motivation for participation in these activities. Classroom activities can include:

- Developing ideas for the use of robots
- Writing stories about robots
- Naming the robot
- Writing about what you would do if you had a robot of your own
- Design your own robot
- Dress up like a robot
- Design a city where a robot works
- Act like a robot
- Give commands to another student who plays robot.

Types of Toy Robots

The robot and robot-like devices that are currently available include toy robots with built-in microprocessors, robot kits, robotic arms for education, personal robots, and robotic arms for prosthetic uses. Each type of robot has its own characteristics and applications for exceptional individuals (see Vignette 4–1). Similarly, each type is unique in its operation, cost, and requirements for use.

Although there are numerous toy robots available, many are quite similar in their functioning and are limited in their usefulness within the special education classroom. These include the numerous robots that can be transformed from one shape to another, bend into different shapes, move forward when turned on, fire a missile, or even grow when placed in a bowl of water. Although these robots do not contain microprocessors, they, like most other robots, can be used to stimulate creative thinking or as a reinforcement for some desirable behavior.

More technologically advanced robots have touch sensors that detect when contact is made with objects, or sound sensors that detect a preprogrammed voice or claps of the hands, and respond by moving in a certain direction. Others have a built-in cassette tape player that can be

VIGNETTE 4-1
Teaching with a Toy Robot

Tommy is a 7-year old boy with mild learning problems. His second grade teacher notices that he still has some difficulties organizing his thinking and actions, and he still get confused when asked to give you his right hand or move to his left. Also, he doesn't have many friends in class.

Tommy's teacher has just introduced a new toy to the class. It is a six-inch robot called Compurobot. Tommy likes it already. At first he was a bit confused by all the buttons on top, but he soon learned which were the most important and which would make it move. Tommy's teacher asks him to put Compurobot on top of the big work table and make it go forward. Tommy is pleased that he can control this robot with the touch of a few buttons. Now, Tommy is asked to make it go forward the same distance and make it turn to the right. When Tommy presses the buttons that he previously pushed and then adds some new commands to make it turn, he finds that the robot goes forward twice as far before it turns. His teacher explains that until the robot is turned off, its memory repeats the previous steps. Tommy practices this new knowledge for a bit and then also learns that he can tell the robot to forget by clearing its memory.

Tommy is again asked to teach the robot to go forward and turn to the right. An experienced robot master, he does that with ease. His teacher then makes sure that Tommy can also make it turn to the left. He is shown how to control how far it goes forward and backwards as well as how far it will turn. After a good deal of practice on these skills, Tommy's teacher has him take Compurobot to the empty floor space in the corner of the room. There, he sees a course with turns mapped out on the floor. Tommy is asked to teach the robot to move through the course. He must estimate the distances he must input into the robot; estimate the amount he must tell it to turn; be careful to erase any mistakes he has made in the directions; remember that the robot will remember everything he tells it; and he must plan his solution one step at a time.

Tommy feels great each time the robot completes a different course that is on the floor. Over the next few days, Tommy gets to work with other children to tackle similar courses. They get to plan their program on paper before they work with the robot. They have timed races between teams of students. They even get to plan their own courses and some for other children to try. Tommy is having a great time and working on some of those other skills that were giving him a hard time.

programmed to deliver a taped message. Some are remote-controlled whereas others can be programmed up to a week ahead of time to perform some task. Some have a tray to carry materials; others have usable but relatively weak arms. All of these robots are designed as toys and are most impressive when seen as such.

Some of the more exciting and advanced "toy" robots have a built-in microprocessor that permits the robots to be programmed to perform a variety of steps. One of the first robot devices to permit this interaction was "Big Trak," a toy army tank that was programmable through a keyboard on top of the unit. Big Trak was made available in toy stores several years ago and presented educators with an opportunity to introduce robotics into their curriculum through the use of a toy that required few technical skills (Keller & Shanahan, 1983). Despite the technological opportunities available with Big Trak, some teachers were reluctant to adopt this new robot because of its representation of an army tank, which some felt was inappropriate for classroom use, especially with younger children. A newer toy, similar in functioning to Big Trak, is Compurobot, a programmable toy robot about six inches high that is powered by batteries. Compurobot can be programmed to move forward, backward, in a circle, turn left or right, make noises, adjust speed, control distance, and more. Both of these toys were available for less than $50 through regular toy outlets. They, and other similar toy robots, provide an excellent opportunity to introduce robots into the curriculum and augment instruction in other areas (see Table 4-1).

Another type of toy robot with direct implications for classroom use is a "Tasman Turtle," a small, mobile hemispherical robot (see Figure 4-1). Attached to a computer by a flat ribbon cable, the turtle is programmable through the computer in *Logo*, and can move in a concrete representation of the turtle that appears on the screen while putting its own pen down to

TABLE 4-1. *Activities with toy robots.*

- Establish equivalent distances for keyboard commands in inches, feet, centimeters. For example, Forward 2 = 2 inches, etc. Make a chart of these equivalents.
- Establish a similar chart for turning. For example, Right 2 = half rotation.
- Trace designs that are first drawn in chalk on the floor.
- Discuss and plan a system for noting each step in the program. Practice writing each step down.
- Draw squares, triangles, circles on the floor. Draw letters, numbers, etc.
- Discuss the estimation of distances based on equivalents. For example, how many forwards will it take to get to the mark?
- Have races with several robots moving through identical courses.
- Discuss pre-planning of steps versus trial and error programming.
- Let teams of children solve a problem (program the robot) together.
- Relate to the use of *Logo*.
- Turn upside down and watch how the wheels turn for forward, backward, right turn, left turn, or combinations of movements. Predict movement based on programmed steps.

Figure 4-1. *Teaching cause-effect with adapted switches made by Steven Kanor.*

draw on the surface. The robot is also programmable in BASIC and is most applicable where such programming is being taught. A much simpler type of turtle is available in a kit format. This robot, named "WAO," can be programmed with a small on-board keyboard or via an RS-232 port communicating with a personal computer. Lange (1985) has described the application of a turtle using *Logo* with hearing impaired children between the ages of 7 and 9. Lange found the turtle to be an excellent motivator, capable of linking abstract ideas to concrete actions, introducing children to programming, and more.

Robot Kits

It is currently believed that robots will play a significant role in industry in the near future. Several large corporations already employ robots to perform tasks that are either unhealthy, such as spray-painting cars; repetitive, such as spot welding or loading small objects; or difficult, such as moving heavy parts of machinery. Other, more exotic industrial applications of robots such as watch assembly, sheep shearing, fruit and vegetable picking, and even sushi making, have already been reported (Mittler, 1984). Therefore, secondary students with mild learning handicaps should be introduced to the characteristics of robots so that they will be prepared to enter the work force. In the process, they may extend their knowledge of electronics, industrial arts, and mechanics.

Robot kits are available that can demonstrate some of the simple characteristics found on more sophisticated robotic devices. These kits can demonstrate the fundamentals of robots and robot sensors by permitting students, individually or in cooperative groups, to assemble simple kits in a few hours. Other, more sophisticated kits create multi-functioning robotic devices that permit the student or teacher to build various projects that also demonstrate applications of computers, robotics, and engineering. Few, if any, of these kits have been designed specifically for the exceptional student, but many may be adapted for appropriate usage. Often these kits come with teachers' lesson plans, reading material, and quizzes. Although the kits are designed to be made by students, it may be most appropriate for the teacher to assemble the robot, which then can be controlled by the students through noises, claps, switches, touch, or other sensing devices. Some of the simple kits ranging in price from $25 to $50 include:

- *Peppy,* a three-wheel robot that responds to both sound and solid objects in its path.

  Medusa, a four-legged robot that responds to sound.

  Piper Mouse, a three-wheel robot that can be programmed to move in different directions by whistle commands.

- *Avoider,* a six-legged robot that uses an infrared beam to detect objects in its path.

- *Memocon Crawler,* a three-wheel robot that can be controlled through a computer or with a special keyboard that comes with the kit.

  Monkey, a sound-sensitive robot that climbs along a horizontal rope.

  Turn Backer, a robot that emits an infrared beam and avoids a wall when told to do so.

  Line Tracer II, a robot that traces any black line drawn on white paper.

  Mr. Bootsman, a six-legged, two-speed robot that moves in different directions, including a circle.

- *Circular,* a remote-controlled robot that moves on two large wheels in different directions.

- *Navius,* a robot that can be controlled by making pencil marks on a desk. It can repeat the movements it just made.

  S-Cargo, a robot that is controlled by sound and, when activated, follows preprogrammed movements included in a printed circuit board.

In addition to these simple kits, other, more complex computer and robot educational kits are available. Multibotics, Inc., has designed a series of workshops for the demonstration of sensors, motors, and robotics. These projects can often be interfaced with a personal computer. Another similar product that permits the assembling of robots that are controlled by computers is made by Fishertechnik. LEGO, the maker of popular children's building blocks, has recently introduced a new LEGO Educational System, LEGO TC Logo, which combines the programming language *Logo* on an Apple computer with computer-controlled LOGO building blocks. Using simple sensors and stepper motors, children can build and control an unlimited number of devices. Although the above were not designed specifically for the youngster with special needs, creative applications are possible.

In addition to these relatively simple robot kits, which are adaptable for use with students from elementary school onward, a more advanced application of robotics, with implications for vocational usage, can be taught through robot educational programs such as those designed by Rhino Robots. Rhino manufactures and distributes robotic devices, along with courseware, manuals, and hardware to introduce industrial robotics to secondary school students. A typical kit includes a robotic arm along with various motors, attachments for the arm, and software so that the various industrial applications of robotics can be demonstrated. Thus, students can be shown and can work with a robotic arm similar to those being used in industry. Systems such as Rhino encourage experimentation with novel applications that may be useful for individuals with handicapping conditions. Current and future engineers are adapting robotic arms like Rhino to be functionally useful to individuals with disabilities.

Personal Service Robots

One of the most exciting areas of recent technological development is that of employing the robot as a personal aide. The advanced technology for this use is emanating primarily from the application of robots in industry. There, robots are used to perform tasks such as assembly of several component parts into a whole unit, movement of materials around a factory floor, sorting of similar looking but different items, lifting of heavy materials, and painting or welding products. As industry continues to support research into the functional aspects of such robots (i.e., vision, movement, touch, manipulation), such information can be used to support the development of robots for use with disabled children and adults.

Personal robots (now included in the field of service robots), which combine some of the most advanced capabilities of robots with supposed ease of use, suggest that the science fiction notion of a robot may be at hand. Many exciting and innovative applications of this new technology may be postulated. Special education teachers could probably create a long list of uses for an "R2D2"-like friend to assist them in the classroom. Similarly, consumers of special education, representing all of the various handicapping conditions, could probably find even more uses for a personal service robot in school as well as at home. Many of these fantasized applications may not be possible for several years, yet several service robots are available for some uses now.

Availability

The availability of service robots for consumer use is dependent upon the manufacturers of these devices. These producers, in turn, require a ready market to buy their product. Unfortunately, due to several factors, including the complexity of programming a service robot for everyday use, many of the robots that have been available over the past five years have not been financial successes. Thus, this new and developing field of interest has been quite volatile for the past few years. Some of the service robots that were available are no longer in production, whereas others are still under development in engineers' workshops and laboratories. Most developers are quite familiar with the history of the Apple computer and its beginnings in a garage workshop. Today's inventors of service robots are hopeful of replicating the Apple success story. It is believed that as the field matures, programming requirements will be eased and useful applications will be demonstrated. These advances will lead to more exceptional individuals employing service robots at school and at home.

Characteristics

Although it is difficult to precisely define a personal service robot, it is possible to describe some of the characteristics commonly associated with these devices. Most stand between 18 inches and a few feet in height and are typically powered by an on-board system of rechargeable batteries. They typically move about on wheels, although the number and positioning of the wheels vary. Personal robots can be programmed to perform several tasks simultaneously or in sequence. They usually have an on-board microprocessor and keyboard, although some may be programmed by an external computer. Senses that are available on most personal robots include the ability to respond to sounds, light, motion, objects, touch, and heat. Some have an arm that extends and has a gripper at its end. The arms are currently limited in their strength and can lift no more than several ounces. Many have a built-in voice synthesizer that enables them to "speak" to their owners.

At this early point in their development, most service robots are not intended to be of significant use, but were created to demonstrate the capabilities of robots. Their actual use as personal robots is limited to some of the preprogrammed functions that are available from their manufacturers, or to the creative applications of technically talented individuals. The latter group, which consists primarily of robot hobbyists, is probably developing the robot programs that will make these devices usable over the next decade. Even now, these personal robots can be programmed to move about a room, bring a wagon to a person, wake someone in the morning, and even sing songs. With an attachment, some service robots can even vacuum a room.

Applications

Applications within a special education classroom are still limited and dependent upon the capabilities of both the service robot and its programmer (Figure 4–2). Given the many capabilities of service robots, however, it is not difficult to think about potential uses. Unfortunately, there is little, if any, evidence to demonstrate applications such as those listed below. Nevertheless, in an area that will see future technological development, the following activities can be hypothesized:

- Reminding the student of scheduled activities and responsibilities
- Demonstrating correct social behaviors

Figure 4–2. *Inexpensive toy robots that illustrate robotic functions in the classroom.*

- Reminding the student of a correct response
- Modeling language for language-impaired students
- Performing motor tasks for physically limited students
- Monitoring the environment for sounds, noises, or words for the hearing impaired
- Visually scanning the environment for objects or movement
- Monitoring stereotypical behavior and reminding the student to stop
- Planning a sequence of steps to accomplish a goal

In addition to these possible activities, there is a group of applications that promises to meet some of the social needs of exceptional children. One of the characteristics of some students with special needs is their relative lack of control over their environment, whether due to physical, cognitive, or emotional limitations. The ability to control a powerful robot can give the student feelings of power and control. Another possible application is the use of the robot as a substitute companion, an ever-present friend who reliably can listen to its owner, respond, remember things, follow obediently, and perform a myriad of tasks. For some individuals with handicapping conditions, such a companion may dramatically alter their lives (see Vignette 4–2). Again, there is little evidence at this time that such applications will actually develop or prove beneficial. However, during this developmental phase, such ideas should be encouraged to provide goals for the technical wizards.

Evolution of Service Robots

As the field of service robots has evolved over the past five years, several promising robots have been designed and marketed, only to find that the educational community is not yet ready to include such sophisticated hardware in its technology curricula. Thus, the early optimism of the use of service robots has diminished as many of the early service robots are no longer produced. In the field of special education, a recent study by the Cosmos Corporation, a research organization based in Washington, D.C., commented that there were too many barriers to the rapid and imminent application of robots into special education (Moore, Yin, & Lahm, 1985).

One of the service robots that has been produced continuously for several years is RB5X, manufactured by General Robots of Golden Colorado. RB5X is 23 inches high, weighs about 24 pounds, and resembles a canister. Among its specific characteristics are a built-in microprocessor, sonar and tactile sensors, built-in software that allows it to learn about its environment, the ability to be programmed in several computer languages, and an optional arm that can carry objects weighing up to 16 ounces. Using

VIGNETTE 4-2
A Service Robot for the Future

It's 1999. Marge is a 22-year old paraplegic who has just moved into her own apartment. She lives there by herself except for her robot, Robbie, the newest version of the personal robots designed for use for persons with disabilities. Robbie has all the latest applications of technology. He can move about the house, even up steps. He has an arm that can pick up and manipulate items up to 25 pounds and uses just the right amount of pressure. He can "speak" to Marge and understand much of what she says. He learns everything that Marge teaches him and even learns things that he senses in the environment. He, like his ancestors, still runs on batteries, but they only need to be charged once a week and he can take care of that need himself.

It's morning and Robbie gently rocks Marge awake while singing her favorite song. Robbie brings her robe and helps her to dress and then get into her wheelchair. While doing this, Marge is asking Robbie the time, and asks him to put on the morning news on his built-in radio. Robbie helps Marge wash and brush her teeth. He can even comb her hair for her. After dressing with Robbie's help (she's not embarrassed in front of him), Marge and Robbie go to the kitchen for her breakfast. Robbie is the chef, with Marge's directions, of course. Although he cannot make everything, he uses the microwave to heat foods that have been previously delivered. Also, Robbie is a very patient feeder. He will either talk to Marge during breakfast, sing to her, play music tapes, or the radio. Today, Marge asks him about her appointments for the day, which Robbie has kept in his calendar. Of course, Marge had to learn just how to talk to Robbie, but with the newer technological developments in language recognition, that wasn't really too hard.

After breakfast, Robbie cleans up, and puts the dishes in the dishwasher. He'll turn it on after lunch and then empty it when it's finished. Robbie and Marge go to her desk, where Marge does most of her work for the public relations firm that recently hired her, allowing her to work from home. Each day, she has several calls to make. Not only does Robbie bring her the phone, but his great memory remembers telephone numbers and dials for her. While at the desk, Robbie hooks himself to the computer and printer so Marge can dictate a message that needs to be filed and edited later in the day, or perhaps telecommunicated to the firm's main office. Marge, with Robbie's help, checks her telecommunications mailbox for her messages and answers some while filing others. She can't stand all the junk mail that she receives, and is thinking of asking Robbie to screen her mail during the night to get rid of it. While working at the desk, the doorbell rings and Robbie goes to open it. It's the local Fire Marshall, who is concerned about Marge's ability to get out of her apartment in case of a fire. He is cautiously satisfied when Marge has Robbie demonstrate how well he knows his way around the place and how he can call the police or fire department in case of a problem. Robbie can tolerate much greater heat and smoke than Marge and doesn't need any light to see where he's going. Later, when Marge takes a brief nap after lunch, Robbie cleans up the house, vacuuming the rugs, and even washing the windows.

(continued)

VIGNETTE 4-2 *(continued)*

Marge is thrilled with Robbie. She doesn't at all feel isolated, the way she used to before he arrived. She doesn't feel she has to be so thankful and nice as she was to the day worker who used to come and help her. She doesn't even have to talk to Robbie if she is not in the mood. Further, he is reliable and helpful. She knows that he is always there to help her. Her parents are also relieved to know he is there. It wasn't easy for them to get used to her living by herself. Marge just loves it, though. For the first time in her life, she really feels independent.

RB5X and an extremely user friendly programming language called *SAAVY*, youngsters involved in a remedial program in language, reading, and mathematics were soon able to devise simple programs to move RB5X around the room or use the sensing devices (Delgado, 1984). Thus, while the use of service robots in special education has not fulfilled early predictions of universal adoption, activities with both handicapped and nonhandicapped children are occurring at the grassroots level. In a recent survey of a small sample of educators involved with technology in New York state, 76 percent reported that they were giving their students some exposure to robotics (Zurhellen, 1986). Despite such growing interest, there may not be a robot revolution in the schools as had been predicted, but there may be slow and steady increase in the area.

Robotic Arms as Prosthetics

It is quite possible that much of the excitement that robots have generated in the field of special education is based on some very real and impressive research that has taken place at two locations in the country. Working with severely handicapped individuals and using the technology of robotic arms, these two projects have demonstrated a functional application that suggests that some of the science fiction thinking may be plausible. In both of these projects, robotic arms, controlled by the individual, are used to perform routine, daily tasks such as feeding, magazine reading, telephoning, and more.

At The Johns Hopkins University Applied Physics Laboratory, Seamone and his team have been working since 1974 on a robotic arm and worktable system for use with spinal cord injured persons. Designed to permit such individuals to perform table-top tasks with little or no assistance, the robotic arm is controlled by chin movements and permits activities such as picking up a telephone and placing it in position for use, picking up a tissue, placing paper in a typewriter, placing diskettes into a disk drive, putting a magazine on a reading stand, brushing teeth, eating a sandwich, or eating with a spoon. Significant field testing and modifications of the system have already occurred (Seamone & Schmeisser, 1985). At the present time, the robot arm and worktable system is still one to two years away from availability to consumers, at which time the proposed cost reportedly will be approximately $10,000 (Seamone, 1986).

A similar robotic arm system has been under development through the Veterans Administration/Stanford University Robotic Aid Project. This project also employs a robotic arm but establishes control through voice recognition, allowing the user to manipulate the arm through verbal commands. This project has studied the use of such a robotic arm in several areas: personal care such as cooking, serving, stirring, salt shaking; recreational tasks such as board games or painting; vocational tasks such as opening file drawers and removing files; and therapeutic tasks such as range-of-motion therapy. At the present time, evaluation of this system continues with individuals with severe disabilities as well as with the elderly (Englehardt, Awad, Perkash, & Leifer, 1984). The primary purpose of this research is to determine the problems in developing and implementing such a device, rather than making it available to the consumer (Seamone, 1986). Other activities are also under way at Carnegie Mellon University, where K. G. Englehardt heads a robotics laboratory focusing on the health care industry, and within the industry through the use of robotic work stations for disabled employees such as the one at Boeing Industries.

Many of the persons interested in service robot applications have ganded together in the National Service Robot Association, which is part of the Robotics Industries of America (RIA) association in Ann Arbor, Michigan. They represent such diverse fields as special education, rehabilitation, health services, security, aerospace manufacturers, robot manufacturers, and even toy manufacturers. Persons such as these, and their associations, will make the potential of robots meet early expectations.

The Future of Robotics

There is little doubt that robots are making an impact on our society in factories, offices, classrooms, and homes. Toy robots, small educational robots, and small robotic kits will continue to develop as long as consumer interest remains high. Based primarily on microprocessor technology, it is probable that they will continue to be available for use by special education teachers. Further, as increased attention is given to the vocational preparation of students with special needs, the vocational applications of robotics through the use of kits or educational arms should increase.

SUMMARY

Electronic toys and robots represent an application of technology of potentially great significance to the lives of children and adults who are disabled. Current uses, such as affording increased environmental control, providing motivation through the excitement and power of electronics, and demonstrating some of the simpler notions of programming illustrate some of the beneficial uses of these new technologies. It is the potential for the future, however, that is even more intriguing. Service robots, capable of performing many of the chores of daily living, hold great promise for individuals with disabilities. Although current roadblocks may delay such innovative uses, it is believed that we may someday see these potential applications come to fruition.

REFERENCES AND SUGGESTED READINGS

Burkhart, L. J. (1980). *Homemade battery powered toys and educational devices for severely handicapped children.* Millville, PA: Author.

Burkhart, L. J. (1982). *More homemade battery devices for severely handicapped children with suggested activities.* Millville, PA: Author.

Coker, W. B. Jr. (1984). Homemade switches and toy adaptation for early training with nonspeaking persons. *Language, Speech, and Hearing Services in the Schools, 15,* 32–36.

Decker, R., & Krajewski, R. J. (1986). For robotics, slow-scan video, satellite beams, and more — the future is now. *The American School Board Journal, 173,* 32–34.

Delgado, N. (1984). Robots in the classroom. *Robotics Age, 6,* 18–20.

Englehardt, K. G., Award, R. E., Perkash, I., & Leifer, L. J. (1984). Interactive evaluation of a robotic aid: A new approach to assessment. *Proceedings of the Second Annual International Robot Conference,* 145–152.

Friedman, M. (1986). Attention all humans: Robotics literacy captivates elementary students. *Tech Trends, 31,* 12–14.

Haring, T. G. (1985). Teaching between-class generalization of toy play behavior to handicapped children. *Journal of Applied Behavior Analysis, 18,* 127–139.

Heckard, M. (1986). Career-minded high school students are commanding robots. *Tech Trends, 31,* 15–17.

Howe, S. F. (1984). It's 1984 and robots are in the classroom. *Media and Methods, 29,* 9–14.

Hughes, K. (1981). Adapting audio/video games for handicapped learners: Part 2. *Teaching Exceptional Children, 14,* 127–129.

Jeffcoate, R. (1977). Electronic technology for disabled people. *Rehabilitation Literature, 38,* 110–115.

Keller, J., & Shanahan, D. (1983). Robots in the kindergarten. *The Computing Teacher, 10,* 66–67.

Kimbler, D. L. (1984). Robots and special education: The robot as extension of self. *Peabody Journal of Education, 62,* 67–76.

Lahm, E. A. (1984). *Robots and special education.* Unpublished manuscript.

Lange, M. (1985). Using the turtle tot robot to enhance *Logo* for the hearing impaired. *American Annals of the Deaf, 130,* 377–382.

Marsh, G., & Spain, T. (1984). Robots in the classroom. *Electronic Learning, 3,* 48–53.

Mittler, J. (1984, September). *Robotics and the handicapped.* Paper presented at the Computer Technology for the Handicapped Conference, Minneapolis, MN.

Moore, G. B., Yin, R. K., & Lahm, E. A. (1985). *Robotics, artificial intelligence, computer simulation: Future applications in special education.* Washington, DC: Cosmos Corporation.

Murphy, G., Carr, J., & Callias, M. (1986). Increasing simple toy play in profoundly mentally handicapped children: II. Designing special toys. *Journal of Autism and Developmental Disorders, 16,* 45–57.

Nietupski, J., Hamre-Nietupski, S., & Ayres, B. (1984). Review of task analytic leisure skill training efforts: Practitioner implications and future research needs. *The Journal of the Association for Persons with Severe Handicaps, 9,* 88–97.

Piers, M. W. (1972). Epilogue. In M. W. Piers (Ed.), *Play and development.* New York: W. W. Norton.

Seamone, W. (1986, November). Personal communication.

Seamone, W., & Schmeisser, G. (1985). Early clinical evaluation of a robot arm/worktable system for spinal-cord-injured persons. *Journal of Rehabilitation Research and Development, 22,* 38–57.

Sheets, E. (1984). Making an easy, inexpensive robot in the industrial arts/technology lab. *Technology Teacher, 44,* 28–30.

Smith, P. (1981). The impact of computerization on children's toys and games. *Children in Contemporary Society, 14,* 73–82.

Whittaker, A. (1985). Robots bring commerce to the classroom. *New Science, 107,* 29–32.

Wright, C., & Nomura, M. (1985). *From toys to computers: Access for the physically disabled child.* San Jose, CA: Author.

Zurhellen, K. (Ed.). (1986). *Robotics — the NYSAEDS database.* Unpublished manuscript.

APPENDIX 4-1. ADDITIONAL SOURCES OF INFORMATION ON ROBOTS

Books and Journals

Aleksander, I., & Burnett, P. (1983). *Reinventing man: The robot becomes reality.* New York: Holt, Rinehart and Winston.

Asimov, I. (1950). *I, robot.* New York: Fawcett.

Asimov, I., & Frenkel, K. A. (1985). *Robots: Machines in man's image.* New York: Harmony Books.

Berger, M. (1980). *Robots in fact and fiction.* New York: Franklin Watts.

Burkhart, L. J. (1982). *Homemade battery powered toys and educational devices for severely handicapped children.* Millville, PA: Author.

Burkhart, L. J. (1982). *More homemade battery devices for severely handicapped children with suggested activities.* Millville, PA: Author.

Chester, M. (1983). *Robots: Facts behind the fiction.* New York: Macmillan.

D'Ignazio, F. (1982). *Working robots.* New York: E. P. Dutton.

Hawkes, N. (1984). *Robots and computers.* New York: Franklin Watts.

Henson, H. (1981). *Robots.* New York: Warwick Press.

Knight, D. C. (1983). *Robotics — Past, present, and future.* New York: William Morrow.

Krasnoff, B. (1982). *Robots: Reel to reel.* New York: Arco.

Marrs, T. (1985). *The personal robot book.* Blue Ridge Summitt, PA: Tab Books.

Marsh, P. (1983). *Robots.* New York: Warwick Press.

Minsky, M. (Ed.). (1985). *Robotics.* New York: Anchor Press/Doubleday.

Paltrowitz, S., & Paltrowitz, D. (1983). *Robotics.* New York: Julian Messner.

Reichardt, J. (1978). *Robots: Fact, fiction, and prediction.* New York: The Viking Press.

Robot experimenter. P.O. Box 458, Petersborough, NH 03458-0458.

Robot reader: The magazine for the personal robotics community. P.O. Box 3243, El Paso, TX 79923-3243.

Silverstein, A., & Silverstein, V. B. (1983). *The robots are here.* Englewood Cliffs, NJ: Prentice-Hall.

Warring, R. H. (1984). *Robots & robotology.* Blue Ridge Summit, PA: Tab Books.

Winkless, N. III. (1984). *If I had a robot . . . what to expect from the personal robot.* Beaverton, OR: Dilithium Press.

Wright, C., & Nomura, M. (1985). *From toys to computers: Access for the physically disabled child.* San Jose, CA: Author.

Electronic Toys

Steven Kanor, Ph.D.
Medical Engineer
8 Main St.
Hastings-on-Hudson, NY 19706
914-478-0960

Handicapped Childrens Technological Services
Box 7
Foster, RI 02825
401-861-3444

R & H Pharmaceuticals–Northside Surgical Supply
1165 Portland Ave.
Rochester, NY 14621
1-800-828-4242

National Lekotek Center
Civic Center
21 Ridge Ave.
Evanston, IL 60204
312-328-0001

Personal Robots

RB5X
General Robotics,
Golden, CO

Hubot
Hubotics Inc.
Carlsbad, CA

Hero 2000
Heath Corporation
Benton Harbor, MI

Hero I
Heath Corporation
Benton Harbor, MI

Hero, Jr.
Heath Corporation
Benton Harbor, MI

Educational Robots and Kits

Compurobot
Manufacturer unknown
Available through distributors

Fishertechnik
Fisher America, Inc.
Fairfield, NJ

Hobbybot
Branch and Associates
Available through distributors

Avoider
OWI, Inc.
Compton, CA

Turn Backer
Owi, Inc.
Compton, CA

Line Tracer
Owi, Inc.
Compton, CA

Piper-Mouse
Owi, Inc.
Compton, CA

Peppy
Owi, Inc.
Compton, CA

Mr. Bootsman
Owi, Inc.
Compton, CA

Circular
Owi, Inc.
Compton, CA

Navius
Owi, Inc.
Compton, CA

Medusa
Owi, Inc.
Compton, CA

Memocon-Crawler
Owi, Inc.
Compton, CA

S-Cargo
Owi, Inc.
Compton, CA

Wao
Owi, Inc.
Compton, CA

Multibotics
Multibotics, Inc.
Available through distributors

TSI Educational Robot Systems
TSI Inc.
Available through distributors

Toy Robots

Omnibot 2000
Tomy Corporation
Carson, CA

Omnibot
Tomy Corporation
Carson, CA

Chatbot
Tomy Corporation
Carson, CA

Verbot
Tomy Corporation
Carson, CA

Dustbot
Tomy Corporation
Carson, CA

Crackbot
Tomy Corporation
Carson, CA

Dingbot
Tomy Corporation
Carson, CA

Hootbot
Tomy Corporation
Carson, CA

Spotbot
Tomy Corporation
Carson, CA

Flipbot
Tomy Corporation
Carson, CA

Heroid
TTC Corporation
Carson, CA

Programmable Robie, Sr.
Radio Shack
Fort Worth, TX

Remote control Robie Jr.
Radio Shack
Fort Worth, TX

Petster
Axlon, Inc.
Sunnyvale, CA

Robopup
Axlon, Inc.
Sunnyvale, CA

Talkabot
Axlon, Inc.
Sunnyvale, CA

Spybot
Axlon, Inc.
Sunnyvale, CA

Armatron Robot Arm
Radio Shack
Fort Worth, TX

Remote Control Robot Arm
Radio Shack
Ft. Worth, TX

Educational Robot Arms

Rhino Robots Inc.
Champaign, IL

Microbot, Inc.
Mountain View, CA

Robot Vendors

Northeast Robotics
55 Earle Street
Milford, CT 06460
203-877-4400

Rio Grande Robotics
1220-A N. Third St.
Las Cruces, NM 88005
505-524-9480

Robot Vendors *(continued)*

Rainbow Adventure
14 N. Penn St.
Shippensburg, PA 17257
717-532-9149

Midwestern Robotics
P.O. Box 7483
Powderhorn Station
Minneapolis, MN 55407
612-722-6008

The Robot Store
1001 North Swope
Colorado Springs, CO 80909
303-635-1157

Marilyn Henry Childs
15408 111 Ave. N.E.
Bothell, WA 98011
206-488-3805

Universal Valex Inc.
1313 King Arthur Blvd.
Alexandria, LA 71303
381-487-2079

CHAPTER 5

Using Authoring to Individualize Instruction

MARION V. PANYAN

E ducational progress is dependent on the extent of individualization and the intensity of instruction. As Cosky (1980) and Eisele (1980) have noted, microcomputer based instruction has the potential to create individualized learning opportunities by presenting different content in different ways to different students. Microcomputers can also provide the repeated exposure to a problem required by many students to master a concept. Furthermore, computer programs provide examples and feedback in a way which could be characterized as nonjudgmental, predictable, and "patient."

Despite the promise of computer based instruction there are many barriers to its successful integration in the curriculum. One barrier is the lack of relationship between the student's goals and the instructional programs. A common scenario finds that a catalog featuring educational software is reviewed and programs previewed on the basis of their availability and attractiveness. A better approach would be to first identify the student's needs and then decide whether computers could be used to teach that skill. If the decision is to use computers then a search could begin for the most suitable program.

In searching for a match between the student's needs and the appropriate software the teacher basically has three choices. One is to locate professionally programmed software. Despite the proliferation of educational software, few professionally programmed and commerically produced programs incorporate sound instructional design principles. Furthermore, many programs present training on a limited spectrum of skills suited only to a small number of students or to a small portion of a student's curricular needs. More importantly, the lesson content and presentation features usually cannot be changed (Zawalkow, 1982). Thus, although software with established features ranks high in terms of ease of use, it lacks the flexibility to meet specific student needs.

A second choice, and perhaps one solution to the software adaptability problem, is to provide programming expertise to the teacher. If teachers programmed in a general purpose language such as *BASIC* or worked with programmers, lessons could be created that are more responsive to student needs. The time required to program with any sophistication makes this an unlikely alternative for many teachers. Time is also a factor in securing the services of a programmer and submitting exact design specifications, but more to the point, it is simply not economically feasible for most school systems to hire programmers.

A third alternative, and one that is being increasingly adopted, is for teachers to create computer lessons via an authoring language or system, which enables nonprogrammers to make existing products more meaningful or to create entirely new educational programs. Authoring tools come in a variety of forms but serve the common function of enabling teachers, aides, parents, and others to change and create software so that it is suitable for their students' needs.

AUTHORING SOFTWARE: COMPARING THE SYSTEMS

Four types of authoring tools or programs can be identified for organizational purposes: authoring languages, authoring systems, mini-authoring systems, and authoring utilities.

An authoring language is a special purpose programming language designed for creating instructional programs. *PILOT* and *Tutor* are examples of two such languages. An authoring system, on the other hand, is a software program that allows an author (e.g., teacher, parent, or other individual) to generate an instructional program without any explicit programming, simply by specifying the instructional content and teaching logic. The authoring system automatically generates the debugged code that corresponds to these specifications (Kearsley, 1982, 1984). Lessons generated by an authoring system typically are stored on individual student disks that are separate from the master disk used to create the lesson.

Both authoring languages and authoring systems make it possible to create courseware faster and more easily than using a general purpose programming language (such as *BASIC* or *Pascal*). Indeed it was the inadequacies of these general programming languages for teachers that led to the development of authoring systems or specialized languages for educational use (Pogue, 1980).

The two major advantages of authoring systems over authoring languages are that programming skills are not required, and considerable time is saved because no debugging is needed (Kearsley, 1984). Despite these advantages, authoring systems are used more by curriculum developers and instructional specialists than by the adults who are in direct contact with the needs of their students. Authoring systems have not been universally adopted by the teachers for whom they were designed. This may be due to the still extensive time requirements related to structuring the design of the program as well as developing content. Thus another authoring tool has evolved — mini-authoring systems.

Mini-authoring systems provide flexibility in the creation of instructional programs and sufficient structure to minimize the time and effort required in the authoring process. Mini-systems permit teachers to enter their own content (graphics and text). Additionally, there may be provision for specifying the lesson pace, student input mode, instructions, and consequences for correct and incorrect answers. The lessons that are generated generally reside on the master disk. In most instances mini-systems generally include a preset format for the lesson that is not alterable (i.e., game, matching, fill-in-the-blank). Examples of mini-systems (see Appendix 5-1) include *Game Frame* (Houghton–Mifflin), *TIC TAC SHOW* (Advanced Ideas), and *Word Attack!* (Davidson & Associates, Inc.). While these programs do not offer as much flexibility in lesson design, they require less time to prepare a lesson. Typically, sample lessons are included in the software package of mini-systems.

A fourth type of authoring tool is software that permits teachers to generate quizzes, tests, or worksheets. Such authoring utilities provide a fixed structure for the teacher to enter the information in response to a series of prompts. The materials generated through the utilities can be responsive to individual needs while saving teacher time. The programs provide automatic student performance data, and in some instances, error analysis.

Just as there are times to use computer aided instruction (CAI) and times not to, there are also situations in which professionally programmed software is sufficient, and in which authored lessons are appropriate. Authoring can be beneficial when: a program for a particular instructional objective is not available; currently available programs for a particular instructional objective are not producing gains; the level of personalization needs to be heightened for motivational purposes; and programs need to be adapted to a particular learner's style and background.

The lessons generated through authoring tools should be evaluated according to the same criteria that have been established for educational software. One should not sacrifice instructional integrity or value when authoring progams. Instructional integrity should actually be maximized because the lesson design and sequence are in the hands of the teacher.

Limitations of Using Preprogrammed Software

VIGNETTE 5-1
Software Limitations

A group of teachers has gathered in the teacher's lounge for a user's group on technology applications. The topic for this meeting is the value of educational software. John, the language arts coordinator, opens the discussion by commenting: "The vocabulary program I'm using with Mark is very motivating for him, however, he's mastered all the words in the lesson and I can't find a new program that picks up where that one left off."

Alice, a third grade teacher says, "I had just the opposite problem: the program I was using had a 2,000-word bank, however, the feedback it provided was not meaningful for the student using the program."

Margie, the social studies teacher, has a similar complaint. She relates: "I was so glad to find a program to support my teaching of the unit on continents. Yet the program asked the student to type in long sequences of information, which was prohibitive for the students with physical impairments with whom I work. I wish the program could be customized to accept a single input answer."

Finally, George, a resource room teacher, made the following observation: "Every time Maria gets an answer correct an animated clown dances across the screen. That little routine takes more time than the time devoted to presenting new information. I wish that I could control the timing and length of the reinforcer."

The comments in the vignette reflect some of the current frustrations experienced by teachers who are finding that existing commercial instructional software programs, though certainly improved over the past several years, fall short when it comes to meeting specific needs of specific students. Existing software is deficient on several counts, as evidenced by these teachers' first-hand observations.

First, there is frequently no opportunity to enter new content or add to existing content. There may be some discretion used over the level of difficulty, but these levels are equivalent to grade levels, not task-analyzed performance levels.

Second, there is rarely an opportunity in existing programs to specify the instructional cues. Yet the type of cue may determine the student's attentiveness to relevant stimuli and subsequently, the student's accuracy. Therefore, the capability to generate instructional stimuli through different sensory modalities is an essential ingredient in customizing software. At the same time, it provides a means for evaluating the student's learning style in an empirical way. Thus, authoring programs that enable their creators to specify whether the instructions will be written, voiced, or through picture cues are preferable to those without these features.

A third limitation of preprogrammed software relates to the way in which students interact with the computer. Whereas many students can use common keyboard entry, very young students or those with different physical impairments are penalized for not having a means to indicate their answers or knowledge. Alternate keyboard entry devices are necessary to accommodate these students. Authoring programs that do not address these needs fall short of being fully responsive to special education teachers and their students.

Teacher as Lesson Designer and Author

An important feature of authoring programs is the ability to specify relevant feedback and corrective consequences. The effects of reinforcing and corrective consequences must be continually assessed during instruction. Violations of this principle are evident when identical consequences are routinely evoked for students of differing needs and preferences. The sooner the teacher has information relative to the impact of the various consequences and adjusts the consequences for each student, the greater the probability that instructional decisions will result in skill acquisition. It is the classroom teacher who is singularly positioned to make these decisions for each student, not a programmer who makes a decision that is then binding for all students.

Another consideration in the use of appropriate consequences is a determination as to when they are to occur. As suggested by George's comments (Vignette 5–1), the reinforcers need to be presented on an appropriate schedule. Continuous reinforcement schedules are critical for acquisition of new skills, but intermittent schedules are the optimal ones for maintaining a skill (Ferster & Skinner, 1957).

Finally, teachers need to have before them a record of just how well the student performed in order to make decisions that will further the student's progress. Computers can easily provide such records, although many software programs that are not authorable do not include this feature. Computer users should require that a record keeping function be part of their educational programs as it is these data (analyzed and interpreted) that form the basis for program modifications. As Haring, Liberty, & White (1980) have noted, valuable time is lost if student results fail to direct the course of instruction.

The major purpose of educational software is to complement the curriculum so that students may achieve their objectives. Authoring software permits teachers to generate lessons tailored expressly to the needs of individual learners within their classrooms. Theoretically this will help to insure progress toward objectives. If students are not progressing, authoring system features can again be used to redesign software that may better promote learning. Several years ago most of the programs for microcomputers were designed to be used in one way. Today an ever increasing number of programs offers the teacher options to use the program in many different ways. This important step helps teachers to insure that the content of CAI is in sync with the curriculum.

Individualizing Programs

One method of enabling teachers to individually tailor courseware is through the use of "selectable options," which vary according to the program and collectively enable the teacher to individualize the program. There are many programs with selectable options and each program typically has a set of options suitable for the content area addressed in the software. For example, *Special Skill Builders I* (Compu-Tations, Inc., 1981), designed to teach color and shape recognition, counting, and a number drill, offers teachers options of adjusting the presentation speed, number of problems, type of student input (keyboard, game paddle or joystick), and whether to present musical feedback for the correct answer.

In the reading and language arts area, *The Contained Reading Series* (A/V Concepts Corp., 1983) is a program designed to improve the student's comprehension and vocabulary skills. The only authorable component is that the reading rate can be set from 40 to 250 words per minute. On the other hand, Laureate Learning System's *First Words, First Categories,* and *Micro-LADS* (1984) permit teachers to choose the categories of instruction (individual words within categories cannot be changed or deleted), the student input method (single switch or keyboard entry), response time, scan speed, criteria for advancement, remediation, or to end the lesson. Also the author can decide whether to use text or voice during the lesson.

The *Math Power Program* (Instructional/Communications Technology, Inc., 1985) allows teachers to make group or individual assignments, set pass/fail parameters, set number and sequence of steps to be completed, eliminate graphic reinforcers, and choose between tutorial or drill modes in teaching basic math computational skills. The *Math Competency Series* (Zeitgeist, 1982) is another math program that allows the teacher some discretion over the games' parameters. This program allows the teacher to modify the student's required response time, problem type and difficulty, and duration of game and help messages.

Many of the programs listed in this text include selectable skill levels and lesson parameters. Generally these programs define a range of levels so that the teacher cannot create a new level or new items within a level. Similarly, the teacher is given choices among two or three alternatives regarding the feedback options, and rarely has the opportunity to enter new consequences. These programs and others like them are valuable and can serve an important function. However, because they do not permit the teacher to enter new content, they will not be considered authoring programs.

Ease of use, although critical for the successful implementation of computers in special education, is a relative concept. Many companies claim that their products are easy for teachers to use, yet have not obtained direct reports from teachers on this dimension. Ease of use is clearly in the eye of the beholder or in the hands of the user. Selectable options provide this ease for new and experienced users.

MINI-AUTHORING SYSTEMS

One type of program teachers have consistently and clearly supported and used is the mini-authoring system. Unlike a full-fledged authoring system, a mini-system requires that the teacher enter content within a structured framework. The mini-system then incorporates the teacher's information in the resulting lesson. Many of the mini-systems are constructed around a game show or game-like format. Thus, it is sometimes difficult to determine how much the widespread use of these systems is due to their motivational appeal and how much is due to the individualized nature of the lessons.

All mini-systems include authoring capabilities and almost all contain sample lessons. These lessons demonstrate the flow of the program and how a to-be-authored lesson would be presented. These demonstration or sample lessons are helpful to review before constructing a lesson and in some instances are appropriate for students in their original form. For example, *Game Frame* (Houghton–Mifflin, 1986) includes 120 lessons for Grades 1 through 6. If one of these games is not suitable, then teachers can use one of the six game frames (Smileage, Tug-a-Grug, Shafts and Stairs, Bowling for Scholars, Factman, and Satellite Rescue) to insert content more relevant to their needs.

Generally, mini-systems allow for the creation of drill and practice or basic tutorial programs without branching capabilities. These systems are useful in situations in which the student has acquired a skill and requires review and repetition before mastery or automaticity are achieved. These systems are rarely useful without accompanying off-line instructional procedures. At their best, programs generated by mini-systems provide individualized lessons in terms of age-appropriate content and relevant feedback, while at the same time affording the student the other benefits associated with any form of CAI (immediate feedback, self-pacing, etc.).

Mini-authoring systems are available for many content areas including reading, language arts, and mathematics, as well as programs that are content-independent and can apply to various subject areas. Currently available mini-authoring systems and some of their features are listed in Appendix 5-1 along with their publishers.

Game Formats

An example of how a mini-system works can be seen in the program *The Game Show* (Advanced Ideas, Inc., 1982, 1986). This software is based on the popular game of Password, in which partners give clues to one another in order to identify a secret word or concept. The program comes equipped with items in 15 subject categories ranging from nursery rhymes to algebra. The authoring part comes into play when the teacher wants to add a new category or items within a category. Without any prior programming experience, the teacher can create new target words and clues tailored to the level and interest of particular students. The program can also be used by students to author games. In addition to the educational benefits derived from the game itself, the authoring feature teaches students dictionary and research skills as well as planning and organization skills. According to the program's author, Geoff Zawalkow, "*The Game Show* was meant to give people the ability to create their own material. That was a flexibility we wanted to build in, rather than stay tied to what the programmer felt was important." (Moylan, 1984, p. 51).

Companies claim that software programs in a game format are an effective and educational way to give students practice in the respective skill areas, and in many instances, teachers applaud the program. Results of controlled research, however, do not totally support this optimism, particularly with under-achieving students. Semmell (1986) found that learning handicapped students performed better on a straight drill-and-practice software program (*Plain Vanilla*) than they did on a program addressing the same content but presented in a game situation (*Alien Addition,* Developmental Learning Materials). Thus, while a game format is intrinsically appealing and sustains the learner's attention, it may not be sufficient for promoting skill acquisition and retention. More research needs to be conducted on the results of programs generated through these game-like mini-authoring systems. In the meantime teachers need to collect data (generated by the lessons themselves over time) to evaluate the usefulness of specific programs for individual learners.

Other Formats

There are a number of mini-authoring systems that don't rely on the game format. These include but are not limited to *E-Z Learner* (Silicon Valley Systems), *Reading Tutor* (Harding & Harris, Inc.), *Scanning with Language Arts* and *Scanning with Math* (Computability), *Spell and Define*

(Electronic Courseware Systems, Inc.), *Spelling Machine* and *Vocabulary Machine* (SouthWest EdPsych), and *Watchwords* and *Wordisk Maker* (Micromedia Software).

E-Z Learner is a program designed to provide drill and review in any content area. It is ideal as a self-teaching tool because the student can enter the items to be learned and then indicate the accuracy of the response during the program. It has no graphics capability and was originally designed for grades six and up.

Reading Tutor allows the teacher to write special stories and prepare exercises based on the student's ability level, special interests, and the skills that need to be strengthened. Students can help create these stories, which enable them to practice and improve skills in a dynamic reading context.

Vocabulary Machine contains more than 1,000 words and sentences for grades 1 through 12 and displays a high resolution graphic to accompany each word. It presents each word in a sentence to improve contextual analysis. Teachers can customize the lessons by inserting their own words and pictures. The record keeping system enables teachers to review progress on a lesson by lesson basis.

Watchwords is a drill-and-practice program that is designed to teach spelling, spelling recognition, and familiarity with the keyboard. The accompanying *Wordisk Maker* enables teachers to enter any list of words. The student can either select the correct spelling among two options or type the word when it is displayed.

Spell and Define is designed to increase the student's familiarity and knowledge of any set of terms provided by the teacher. The student matches one of 10 words to its definition. Records are kept of the student's progress, words missed, and percentage correct.

Scanning with Language Arts and *Scanning with Math* are similar programs in that they permit the student to use one or two switches to complete the work on the video screen and to reproduce printed work. The language arts program includes Word Attack, Crossword, and Phonics Machine. The math programs include addition with carrying, subtraction with borrowing, multiple digit multiplication, long division, constructive geometry, fractions, and story problems. In each case the teacher types in the lesson material to meet the student's current academic objectives.

VIGNETTE 5-2
Application of a Mini-Authoring System to Individual Needs

Nancy Coleman, a teacher in the Boston Public Schools, reports on the results of *TIC TAC SHOW* in her class.

(continued)

VIGNETTE 5-2 *(continued)*

Walter is a 10-year-old 4th grader who was identified as needing remedial help in the areas of math and language arts. Two years ago he was placed in the special needs program. Walter is a healthy but unhappy child who is profiled as being intellectually average but who has serious emotional problems and lacks motivation. He has difficulty concentrating, does not follow directions, and tends to complete work too fast, resulting in careless mistakes and illegible handwriting.

Walter participates in competitive games with other children and free time is given to him as reinforcement if seatwork is finished accurately.

Walter reads at grade level and his receptive vocabulary and understanding are good. He has difficulty expressing his ideas in writing, as evidenced by his poor sentence structure and organization. One of the specific objectives in Walter's Individualized Education Program was to teach him to identify the parts of speech and thereby facilitate correct language usage.

Walter found the worksheet exercise of identifying parts of speech within a sentence boring and the traditional practice routines failed to improve his accuracy. Therefore, I decided to use the mini-authoring system, *TIC TAC SHOW,* as one way of enabling him to identify verbs in sentences. I selected this program because I could put in words he was working on and because I felt the game format might be motivating to him. I chose 11 sentences from Walter's reader that included action verbs. Walter was required to read the sentence and choose the correct verb. He was able to control the length of time needed to respond to a question. If his response was correct an "X" was entered in his square. if his answer was incorrect, an "O" was entered in his opponent's square.

Walter loved the game! During the first three sets of questions he identified the verb correctly 70 percent of the time. If he missed a question, he would work harder the next time to respond correctly. He did not want to lose a space on the board to his opponent.

The mini-authoring systems can be used to create programs for groups of individuals. Following is an illustration of how the game designed for Walter can be adapted to the needs of a group.

VIGNETTE 5-3
Application of a Mini-Authoring System to Group Needs

Pam Davis, a Boston public school teacher of ten learning-adaptive behavior students ranging in age from 8 to 12, reports on the use of *TIC TAC SHOW.* Pam used this program to review science concepts. According to Pam:

> I decided to use *TIC TAC SHOW* to review the science material already covered through our class readings and discussions. We are currently working on the human body, and specifically the skeleton and muscles.
>
> Ten questions were put into the format with one wild card. All the questions required a one-word answer. Before playing the game, I went over how to play the game with the group using a sample game. I divided the group into two teams and told them that the team would have time to think of an answer but that they must all agree on the answer to be given.
>
> Before the game, I had difficulty obtaining the students' interest in science. They would look around the classroom and were not attentive. Once the game started, they became interested as the excitement in the class grew. Some students took out their science notebooks. One student turned to his vocabulary words to help him find the answers for his team. This game has made science interesting to all my students now. It demonstrated that they knew where to look for information and that they could work together for a common goal. Students are eager to continue with the game and have asked that the brain (which we are studying) questions be put into the *TIC TAC SHOW* game.

AUTHORING SYSTEMS

Sometimes mini-authoring systems are not flexible or powerful enough to create the type of lessons required for special learners. In these cases the use of an authoring system may be indicated. The use of an authoring system puts lesson development in the hands of the teacher and is much faster and easier than programming. As with mini-systems, there is a great range of authoring systems.

Blocks

One of the earliest systems developed specifically for special educators was *BLOCKS* (Slovick, 1982). This system was developed at The California School for the Deaf in response to the needs of hearing impaired students. The name of the program was derived from the fact that the author places images or information in blocks (graphics areas) on the screen and generates one or more questions associated with that graphics area. One or more blocks make up a lesson. Consequences for correct, anticipated incorrect, and unanticipated incorrect answers can also be specified in advance.

BLOCKS consists of three components. The first component is the Teacher Authoring Program, which allows the teacher to create and edit lessons. The second component is the Student Presentation Program, which displays the pace of the lesson except for the actual typing of the answer, which is teacher controlled. The final component is the Lesson Planning and Management System, which provides teachers with the means to plan which lessons the student will do, specify criterion levels, and print student performance summaries.

The advantage of *BLOCKS* is that it offers great flexibility in screen arrangement, question format, the use of graphics, and content area and difficulty. The major disadvantage is the time required to block out areas of the screen and to write lessons with the program.

The designers of *BLOCKS* characterize their system as explicit authoring. "An explicit author is one in which the teacher authoring program displays all options available to the teacher so that no 'command vocabulary' need be mastered. By using the 'explicit' format and care in design and programming of the authoring system, the curriculum designing teacher is sheltered from the increase in complexity that often accompanies increase in flexibility." (Slovick, 1982).

According to the developers, *BLOCKS* is used in schools in Canada, Scotland, Australia, and the United States. However, creating lessons with *BLOCKS* is a time-consuming task, a factor that argues against widespread adoption of the program by teachers.

In recognition of the need for flexible authoring systems for the microcomputer, the Technology and Marketing Branch, Division of Educational Services, Special Education Programs, U.S. Department of Education, funded three projects to design and develop authoring systems that would be more responsive to teacher needs. The resulting products were a Multisensory Authoring Computer System (MACS), developed at The Johns Hopkins University, SPE.ED, developed at Kent State University, and the HELPmate Authoring and Instructional Delivery System, developed at the University of Denver (Hummel & Farr, 1985).

Multisensory Authoring Computer System (MACS)

MACS was developed by an interdisciplinary team of computer technologists and special educators at The Johns Hopkins University (Kossiakoff, Hazan, & Panyan, 1984). This system consists of an authoring disk, lesson programs, two graphics and speech disks, and an instructional manual. The software requires a dual disk drive to author the program and a single drive to run the lesson. Other optional but recommended system requirements include an Echo II speech synthesizer, a printer, and a color monitor if graphics are included in the lesson. MACS enables teachers and curriculum developers with no knowledge of computer programming to prepare instructional lessons for the Apple II family of personal computers.

Creating Lessons with MACS

MACS is most suitable for teaching visual discrimination, identity matching, relational concepts (e.g., opposites, size), receptive vocabulary, elementary reading and mathematical skills, and paired associates (e.g., states and their capitals, a foreign word and its equivalent).

The basic structure of a MACS lesson is a matching/discrimination paradigm whereby the student selects the correct answer among a group of items. An application of the word-to-picture association is illustrated in Figure 5-1. In this case, a picture called a "target" is displayed above a set of words, one of which is directly related, or a "match" to the target picture. The nonmatching members of the word set are called "distractors." In this example, the match selection is made by the student pressing the space bar at the appropriate time to stop a scanning box that successively frames each candidate word. Feedback and reinforcement are given according to the teacher's specifications. A series of target pictures is displayed during the entire lesson, with the matching word and distractors appearing in random positions so that the match cannot be identified with the position it occupies.

There are 12 lesson types and two screen formats to choose from in preparing a lesson, as shown in Figure 5-2. It is important to note that more than one instruction can be used with each lesson type, accounting for the system's flexibility.

Figure 5-3 illustrates how the objective of a lesson can be changed by altering the instruction. Three different instructions for the picture-to-picture lesson type, "Which one is the same?" "Which one goes with it?" and "Which one is like it?" represent progressively more difficult skills ranging from identity matching to classification.

Similarly, a different skill would be tapped by one question for the picture-to-word lesson type (i.e., "Which picture goes with the word?") than by another question (i.e., "Which picture is an example of the word?"). In the

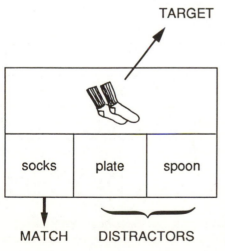

FIGURE 5-1. *Example of word-to-picture matching lesson.*

Picture to Picture	Picture to Letter	Picture to Word

Picture to Number	Letter to Picture	Letter to Letter

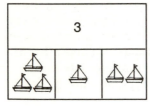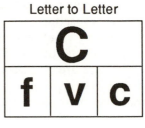

Number to Picture

	4	
🛥	2	
	6	

Number to Word

	2
ten	10
	1

Number to Number

	1
10	10
	100

Word to Picture

	socks
🧦	plate
	spoon

Word to Number

	one
10	ten
	two

Word to Word

	telephone
fork	chair
	fork

FIGURE 5-2. *Examples of twelve lesson types and two screen formats.*

1. Which one is the same?

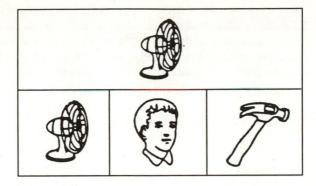

2. Which one goes with it ?

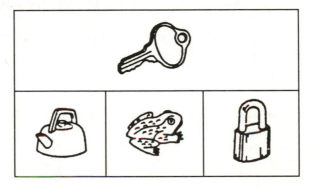

3. Which one is like it? (same category)

FIGURE 5-3. *Three objectives for picture-to-picture lesson type.*

first case, a simple picture-word association is the expected outcome; in the latter case, demonstration of a general concept is the desired learning outcome. In both instances, all lesson parameters such as scanning time, feedback and reinforcement options could be the same as previous lessons for the same individual. This organization facilitates editing and enables a teacher to quickly construct different lessons.

The complete path that can be used in learning or using the system's full capacity consists of a series of menus through which the teacher can make instructional decisions. These decisions concern lesson type, format, medium (instructions, content, feedback, and reinforcement), schedule for presentation (instructions, content, and reinforcement), lesson content (targets, matches, and distractors), input device, scan control time, feedback (correct, no answer, and incorrect answer), reinforcers, remedial prompts, and difficulty level. The menus that relate to feedback, reinforcement, scan control, response time, and screen format are constant across the different lesson types, facilitating ease, and hopefully frequency of use. The menus related to the instructions and lesson content vary slightly in accord with the requirements for composing lessons.

Features

An important feature of the lessons created with MACS is that through the use of an ECHO speech synthesizer the instructions, corrective feedback, and reinforcement can be voiced. Earphones can be plugged directly into the jack of the ECHO card for use in a group situation.

Another valuable feature is that students can use the program with a single switch or joystick. This feature enables students with physical disabilities to benefit from the program.

A third and final distinctive feature is the ease of graphics selection and entry into memory. The program comes with 96 stored high-resolution graphics grouped into 12 categories on each graphics disk. Items from these categories are selected by pressing the number associated with their name.

The MACS system has been extensively field tested and reports of its successful use with every disability group have been submitted. Teachers who had more than six months' experience with computers initially authored lessons more quickly than teachers without previous computer experience. However, after several lessons, some of the new users authored as quickly as the experienced users. These initial field tests demonstrated that after a one-hour orientation, teachers learned to author, preview, and save complete lessons in 10 to 30 minutes requiring minimal assistance from the manual.

MACS has a record-keeping feature that can be presented in summary, graphic, or replay of trials form. It automatically stores and later presents the results of student performance at any level of analysis that may be needed for decision-making purposes. Because of these capabilities it provides a framework for applied research. The student data summaries provide session-by-session accounts of the student's responsiveness to particular instructional stimuli. If the student is not progressing, new choices can be made and the program quickly edited and examined in its revised version.

Teaching and Applied Research Applications

The following vignette represents how MACS can serve both as a teaching and applied research tool.

VIGNETTE 5-4
How Effective is the Feedback Provided by CAI?

There are many unanswered questions with respect to the effectiveness of CAI or ways in which CAI lessons are constructed. One feature common to all lessons is the provision of feedback for incorrect answers. In some cases, it may be a blank screen, in other instances corrective information may be supplied. The exact form of feedback that best facilitates learning in CAI has not yet been determined for different types of students. Therefore, the purpose of the present study conducted by Sr. Christine Manlove, during her doctoral studies at The Johns Hopkins University, was to evaluate the effects of descriptive and nondescriptive feedback on the acquisition of three basic reading skills.

The subject of this study, Monique, was a 14-year-old female with Downs Syndrome and moderate intellectual limitation. She attended a nonpublic special secondary school in Baltimore. At the beginning of the study she was about to begin the second of three first grade readers in the Merrill Linguistic Reading Program.

Three software programs using MACS were developed on the basis of teacher reports and Monique's responses to a paper and pencil pretest. The programs contained five items each and were of three types: association (e.g., lock: key, bed, look), word completion (e.g., nu: t, d, p), and sentence completion (e.g., the cup is: big, bag, bug). The software programs were presented daily in the order just mentioned. Sessions lasted approximately 15 to 25 minutes.

A multiple baseline design across the three aforementioned programs was used to evaluate the effectiveness of corrective feedback. During baseline the computer reading programs were presented with non-descriptive feedback. In this phase correct answers merely prompted the computer to present the next item and incorrect answers produced the textual response of "No, try again." The treatment phase consisted of descriptive feedback for both incorrect and correct re-

(continued)

VIGNETTE 5-4 *(continued)*

sponses. In this phase correct answers flashed and the message "Good" or "Right" appeared on the screen. When incorrect answers were selected, the distractors were erased so that only the correct answer with the message "Look at the right answer" appeared on the screen. The percent of items answered correctly was the major dependent measure.

Figure A shows a complete account of Monique's performance across the three programs. Monique demonstrated a stable baseline for each program prior to treatment. A slight increase in her baseline score was noted on the word com-

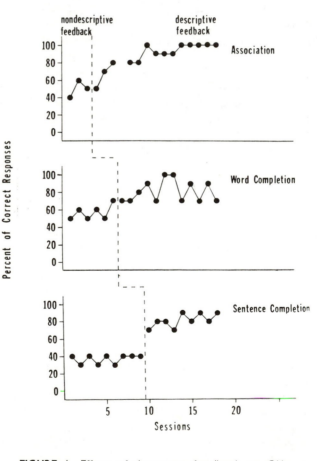

FIGURE A. *Effects of descriptive feedback on CAI.*

pletion program just prior to the treatment phase of that program. Monique performed more accurately once the treatment of descriptive feedback was instituted, especially for the first and third programs. She reached and maintained the criterion of 80 percent or higher for four consecutive sessions on the first and third programs under treatment conditions. Although her performance on the last four sessions of the second program averaged 80 percent, she did not consistently achieve the 80 percent criterion level. A paper and pencil post-test yielded an improvement of 80 percent, 80 percent, and 40 percent for the association, word completion, and sentence completetion items respectively.

This case study exemplifies several important points. The major finding was, of course, that descriptive feedback that provides additional information may be necessary for efficient learning to occur. However, this finding must be interpreted cautiously, since only one subject and one curriculum area were studied.

In this study, Monique transferred two reading skills learned on the computer to the paper after the test. However, even though she maintained an 80 percent average on the sentence completion program, Monique did not transfer these skills well to a post-test of the same items. A planned proactive integration of CAI software and regular curricular activities is strongly recommended.

This study also points out how MACS can be used to determine the effects of different consequences on student performance. Similarly, the impact of different cues (simple versus complex or text versus voiced) on performance could be evaluated. Intuitions, even of master teachers, sometimes are at variance with what a particular student may need at a particular time. MACS and programs like it enable teachers to discover first hand from their students exactly what variables aid or impede learning.

SPE.ED Authoring System

The SPE.ED authoring system was developed at Kent State University, also under contract to the U.S. Department of Education. The SPE.ED system is a frame oriented system in which the author creates fields of information or questions. These frames can be introductory, text frames, test frames, practice frames, criterion frames or end lesson frames which permit the orderly completion of the program. There is no provision for graphics to be incorporated in the lesson. However, SPE.ED does support a varied response format. Questions can be generated in multiple choice fashion, true-false, yes-no, matching, and fill-in-the-blank. There is also provision for using up to 80 columns of text in presenting information.

Two helpful utilities for teachers include the grade readability file command, which permits the author to check a file for the reading grade level, and the help command, which provides the user with brief on-line text information about each of the utilities.

SPE.ED allows teachers to select how students will interact with the courseware program. Switches, joysticks, keyboard, trackball, or a mouse can be used as the interface. The author can also select the type of output desired: video display, speech synthesizer, or both, or a printed display.

SPE.ED is public domain software that can be obtained for a registration fee of $50. The system consists of several diskettes and a 50 page user's manual. The system can be run under a CP/M 80 environment (Barton, 1985).

The HELPmate Authoring and Instructional Delivery System

The HELPmate system was developed at the Denver Research Institute of the University of Denver (Lamos, Amundson, & Winterbauer, 1984). It was the third authoring program developed under funding from the U.S. Department of Education. This system is based on a different conceptual approach than either MACS or SPE.ED.

In recognition of the diverse learning needs of special students as well as the different roles that special education teachers, curriculum specialists, and administrators have in meeting those needs, the HELPmate system was designed to be modular. This modularity allows for professionals to use the system in different ways and at different levels. For example, HELPmate provides a means for instructional designers and curriculum specialists to create new courseware that later can be integrated into the curriculum by special education teachers.

HELPmate provides two levels of authoring capability, micro and macro. The micro level allows authors to produce CAI modules, called microunits, that provide direct instruction in a single concept, skill, or strategy. These micro-units may consist of text, graphics, or both. The text can be accompanied by audio messages; the pictures can be animated; and questions can be presented in multiple formats (e.g., short answers, multiple choice). HELPmate provides four different text fonts and sizes along with color highlighting and line drawing (freehand and geometric) capabilities.

Teachers can organize, integrate, and sequence micro-units into lesson units through a macro level editor. Using this editor, the teacher can control which micro-units the student will see and when and under what conditions the units will be viewed. Furthermore, the teacher can construct a daily or a weekly schedule designating the micro-units a student will use during different hours of the day and different days of the week. The macro level editor also allows the teacher to monitor student progress and have the results displayed or printed. The micro level was designed for curriculum specialists and instructional designers, whereas the macro level was designed for classroom teachers. The macro level enables teachers to selectively combine the instructional modules created at the micro level into a variety of lessons best suited to the needs of a particular student as well as to the ongoing activities in a particular classroom.

Figure 5–4 shows the complete structure of the HELPmate Systems and the relationship between the Micro-editor and the Macro-editor (Lamos, 1986). The major advantage and distinction of HELPmate is its flexibility, which appeals both to novice teacher-authors who are arranging simple supplemental courseware, and to more experienced authors who wish to develop more sophisticated tutorial instruction. The system was designed for use in an MS DOS environment.

Authoring Systems Designed for Regular Education

In addition to these authoring systems designed for special educators, several commercially available systems offer teachers in regular education a means to create their own courseware. These authoring systems may of course be used in special education, but were not specifically designed for that purpose. The following brief synopsis of several such systems illustrates their salient features and applicability to special educators.

Voice-Based Learning System (VBLS)

The *VBLS* authoring system allows creation of computer courseware that accepts the student's response either through the keyboard or verbally. Six study session modes are available with author-determined question formats. Branching, alternate character sets, and verbal feedback through a cassette option make this system suitable for special education instruction. The distinctive feature of this authoring system is that the programs it generates can accept voice input, differentiating different verbal commands, as an alternative to keyboard input.

MicroTutor II EZ Authoring System

The *MicroTutor II EZ Authoring System* provides interactive individualized courseware ranging from simple drill and practice to sophisticated tutorials to complex simulations. The system includes high-resolution graphics, automatic maintenance of student records, animation, shape creation, branching between items and modules, sound, diagnostics pretesting, and retention post-testing.

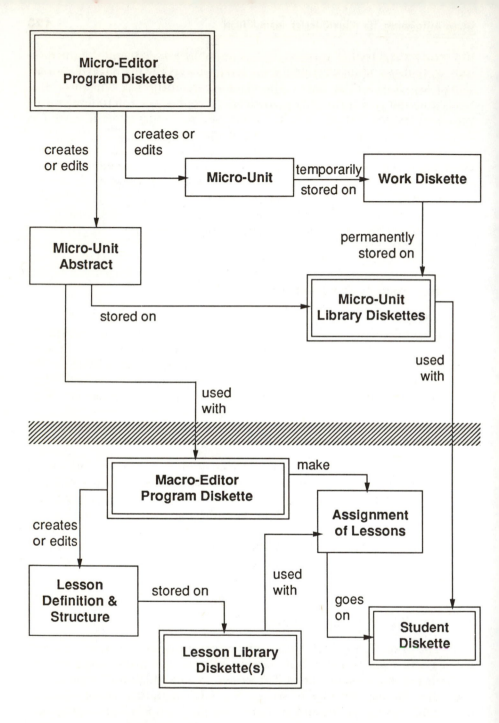

FIGURE 5–4. *Structure of the HELPmate system.*

The *EZ Authoring System* consists of an author disk and a tutor disk. The author disk provides a means for teachers to enter the desired content and presentation modes and to store them on the tutor disk. The tutor disk is used by the student during instruction on the content determined during authoring.

Ghostwriter Authoring System

Ghostwriter (Closing the Gap, 1984) is an authoring system that includes interactive video lessons. The lessons consist of a series of presentations of teaching material interspersed with interactions that require an active response of the student. The presentations may consist of text, graphics or video segments. Unlike some authoring systems, this system offers extensive branching capabilities. A student record keeping function is also an integral part of the lesson.

Authoring System Supplementing Instruction Selected by Teachers (ASSIST)

ASSIST was designed to enable teachers to create and assign CAI lessons in any curriculum area for any student population (Chiang, Stauffer, & Cannara, 1979). *ASSIST* specifies 10 different models of lesson presentation formats. A format may, for example, be a multiple choice type question. After selecting the lesson format the teacher enters the lesson content, which is textual only. This system has been enthusiastically received as measured by the responses of 20 teachers who have written over 1,000 lessons in an eight-month time frame.

EAZYLEARN

EASYLEARN is an authoring system developed for the IBM PC that enables users to create professional quality training materials. It was not originally designed for use in special education, but it can generate tutorials, demonstrations, and interactive instructional material using sound, graphics, and video displays.

McGraw-Hill Courseware Authoring System

This system consist of five disks: two authoring disks (master and back-up), one delivery system disk, one practice disk, and one demonstration disk (Closing the Gap, 1984–1985). Teachers can design lessons including five different question formats: multiple choice, yes-no, true-false, fill-in-the-blank, and word selection. Many options are available in the construction of the lesson. The lessons can include animation, scrolling, windows, six colors, five text sizes, four type fonts, and time delays. Graphics can be included with any standard graphics package. A record keeping function is also included for evaluation of student performance.

Super Sofcrates

This system is an expanded version of *Sofcrates–The Courseware Creator*. *Super Sofcrates* permits the author to use several learning formats, hi-resolution color text, graphics, and animation in lesson construction. It contains record keeping functions and easy-to-use interfacing capabilities. It is a menu-driven system and novices learn to create lessons in 4 to 6 hours.

AUTHORING LANGUAGES

If teachers cannot generate the programs they need through the use of mini-systems or authoring systems or cannot find a suitable program, then consideration should be given to the use of an authoring language. Authoring languages employ a special purpose programming language to create and design instructional programs. Authoring languages offer more power and capability especially in terms of creating screen displays and tutorial sequences, but at the same time are more complex than either mini or full-fledged authoring systems.

The function of authoring languages is aptly described by Grabinger (1985, p. 20) when he says: "Authoring language software is designed to interpret or translate a simple, English-like computer command into several lines of complex code understood by the computer. An authoring language keeps the power inherent in programming languages, such as *BASIC* or *Pascal*, but makes your job of writing lessons simpler. It enables you to concentrate on the message you want to convey and on the instructional sequencing rather than on arcane, complex codes." The major advantage of authoring languages is that they afford the teacher-author the flexibility to utilize the full capabilities of the computer (Johnson, 1984).

According to Johnson (1984), an authoring language should contain four characteristics in order to achieve interactive courseware that is superior to that produced by mini-systems or authoring systems. First, the language should be able to provide the major modes of presentation and accompanying answer-judging capabilities (i.e., drill and practice, tutorial, and simulations). Second, the language should provide a way to guide the learner through the material based on mastery of previous frames or presentation of remedial frames for items requiring more practice. Third, the language should permit the author to present lesson material in text, graphics, animation, alternate character sets, color, and sound. Finally, the language should allow the student to enter or indicate a response by a variety of inputs.

Languages Designed for Educators

Grabinger (1985) evaluated and compared three authoring languages particularly designed for use by teachers using Apple computers. These languages were *SuperPILOT, E-Z PILOT,* and *Super Sofcrates. SuperPILOT* and *E-Z PILOT* are variations of *PILOT* (Programmed Inquiry Learning or Teaching) (Smith, 1982). *Super Sofcrates* is based on design systems and the task is similar to creating a storybook. The three languages were judged on the following criteria: cost, copy protection, ease of learning (*Super Sofcrates* was rated the easiest), ease of use (*Super Sofcrates* was rated the easiest in this dimension as well), graphics/sound, peripherals, documentation, performance (*SuperPILOT* and *Super Sofcrates* were judged the best in overall performance), tutorials, screen design, instructional design features, and management features. Grabinger felt that *E-Z PILOT* was rather limited and that *SuperPILOT* was the most powerful of the three systems. However, the reviewer recommended *Super Sofcrates* because of the manner in which it helps teachers and instructional designers concentrate on the task of instruction rather than on programming.

Pattison (1985) recommended *E-Z PILOT* as the language for novice authors and *SuperPILOT* as a valuable language for more experienced authors because of its structure of menus leading to lesson composition. *PC/PILOT* (Washington Computer Services) is now available for the IBM PC. It conforms to the *COMMON PILOT* standard, thus allowing teachers to run programs developed on a variety of other computers.

Other Languages Available

In addition to these languages for educators there are a number of additional authoring languages available for computer based instruction that are more difficult to learn and may be good tools for computer programmers. For example, the *TenCORE Authoring System* for the IBM PC has an English-like authoring language, integrated source, graphics, and character editors, complete calculational capability, automatic built-in computer based instructional (CBI) functions including student input processing, and instantaneous switching between authoring and student modes (Klass, 1984).

Another recently released authoring language for the IBM computers is the *Multipurpose Authoring Language (MPAL)* (Nix, Gaudreau & Lathrop, 1986). In addition to the standard capabilities of text, graphics, animation, and sound of sophisticated systems, *MPAL* allows the use of optional equipment such as a component monitor and a video disk player to freeze frames of movies and superimpose text over the frame.

AUTHORING UTILITIES

Authoring utilities refer to software programs that permit teachers to generate quizzes, tests, worksheets or gamesheets. Such tools not only can save time but also provide an analysis of learning patterns and errors not easily retrieved through traditional testing methods. Authoring utilities differ from other authoring programs in that they do not provide instruction or interactive lessons. Typically there is no differential feedback for correct and incorrect answers.

There is a frequent need for testing to determine the student's progress and mastery level. Test results give the teacher directions for instruction. By comparing the results of successive tests the teacher has objective consistent evidence of skill progression or regression.

The tests generated through authoring utilities may take many forms (e.g., constructed answer, matching, multiple choice, fill-in-the-blank). Examples of authoring utilities are *Multiple Choice Files, Study Quiz Files,* and *Test Made Easy* (Computations), which enable teachers to create tests in any subject area. *Fastrack Quizzer* (Creative Publications) provides tests in a racetrack game format and *Quizmaster, Teacher's Helper* (Sunshine Software) enables teachers to author, edit, and assign quizzes. This latter program has a character modification that allows the teacher to use high resolution graphics for special characters needed for math, science, or foreign languages. *Questions* is a quiz development program for the Tandy Color Computer that enables teachers to enter up to 25 questions in a variety of formats.

Generating Other Types of Materials

In addition to generating test or quizzes, teachers can use computers to generate printed copies of instructional materials. Such programs are capable of generating work and review sheets for previously introduced materials such as new vocabulary words or math problems from a recent lesson. These computer-generated exercises can be in the form of mazes, spelling exercises, word games, or worksheets. Examples of such utilities are: *Wordfind/Crossword Magic* from L & S Computerware; *Elementary Vocabulary/*

Spelling from Hartley; *Mastering Math Series* and *Puzzles and Posters* from the Minnesota Educational Computer Consortium; and *K-8 Math Worksheet Generator* from Radio Shack. The value of these materials depends on the way they are presented to the student and the manner in which they are related to the curriculum. In isolation the materials generated through authoring utilities are meaningless and a waste of time. However, if they are preceded by personal teaching and followed by relevant feedback they can complement the curriculum. They also provide a permanent record of the student's performance that can be shared with parents.

In addition to providing copies of the student's actual work, other utilities permit the construction of personalized messages to parents. For example, *Parent Reporting* (Hartley) enables teachers to combine standard messages about events at school with specific messages related to an individual student's performance or requests to parents. This program and others like it increase communication with parents without a heavy time investment.

EVALUATION, SELECTION, AND USE OF AUTHORING PROGRAMS

After teachers analyze the instructional needs of their students and state their instructional objectives, the next step is to assist the students in accomplishing these objectives. Teachers need to secure the proper materials and use appropriate methods that will help the students acquire, retain, and use academic skills. CAI is one form of instruction that is being increasingly integrated in the curriculum. One type of CAI that permits teachers to prepare materials that reflect the skill level and needs of their students is authored programs.

Once a decision has been made to use an authoring program, the teacher must determine what type will most effectively and efficiently generate appropriate instructional lessons. There are two aspects of evaluating an authoring program: the lessons that are authored, and the procedures used to create and edit these lessons.

Evaluating the Products of Authoring Programs

The lessons generated through authoring programs should be judged on the same criteria applied to educational software (Council for Exceptional Children, 1983; Hannaford & Sloane, 1981; Microsift, 1982; Taber, 1983). Although the actual items on each of these software evaluation forms differ slightly, the major considerations are consistent and relate to the degree to which the software meets the learner's and teacher's needs, is instructionally sound, and is technically adequate and useful.

Lessons generated through authoring programs have an edge over other programs because of their level of individualization. For example, the first six items on Hannaford and Sloane's evaluation system relate to meeting the student's needs and are as follows:

- Does the program reach the target population for which it was designed?
- Will the program motivate the students to learn?
- Is the content relevant to the instructional needs of the student?
- Will the material be effective with individual learning styles?
- Does the format appeal to the students?
- Is the material relevant to daily living experiences?

An affirmative answer to these questions is much more likely if an authoring program has been used to generate the lessons. Thus, the very features that are critical to good software, are those which are made possible through authoring tools.

Evaluating the Authoring Process

With respect to the evaluation of authoring programs themselves and the authoring process inherent in these programs, Milone (1982) has constructed a checklist (Table 5–1) that lists ten major considerations in evalua-

TABLE 5-1. *Authoring System Checklist*

	Yes	No
Is the program easy to use?	☐	☐
Is the user's manual understandable?	☐	☐
Is the publisher dependable?	☐	☐
Will the publisher or dealer support the authoring system?	☐	☐
Does a curriculum exist that is compatible with the authoring system?	☐	☐
Do utility programs exist to support the authoring system?	☐	☐
Will I be able to create lessons in all the subject areas I want?	☐	☐
Will I be able to create lessons that meet the needs of all my students?	☐	☐
Will I be able to use the lessons on other computers in my school or district?	☐	☐
Does the cost of the authoring system seem justified, given the number of features it possesses?	☐	☐

Adapted from Milone (1982).

ting these tools. Table 5–2 illustrates 19 additional evaluation features Milone has identified that relate to the type and range of programs that can be generated through authoring systems. Collectively, these two tables include factors relating to ease and speed of operations, ease of lesson creation and editing, versatility, flexibility, portability, support, interface with other devices, report generation, compatible curriculum, and answer judging.

Pattison (1985) has also identified particular requirements to consider in choosing an authoring tool. She makes the logical but sometimes forgotten recommendation to think of the type of lesson desired, the authoring capabilities needed, and then locate an authoring program that has these

TABLE 5–2. *Authoring System Checklist*

	Yes	No
Does the authoring system allow		
tutorial screens	☐	☐
multiple choice questions	☐	☐
fill-in-the-blank questions	☐	☐
true-false questions	☐	☐
short answer questions	☐	☐
matching questions	☐	☐
answer judging	☐	☐
graphics	☐	☐
alternate character sets	☐	☐
sound effects	☐	☐
hints	☐	☐
several correct answers and responses	☐	☐
several wrong answers and responses	☐	☐
unexpected answers and responses	☐	☐
response when the student fails to answer a question within a specified period of time	☐	☐
response when the student fails to answer a question within a specified number of attempts	☐	☐
easy editing	☐	☐
easy record keeping	☐	☐
interface with other devices such as cassette, video tape, or video disk players	☐	☐

Adapted from Milone (1982).

capabilities. Pattison suggests that teachers consider the manner in which the program performs the following required functions: answer matching, feedback, flexible branching, record keeping, screen display features, and timing. Finally, the ease with which the author can revise a lesson is critical. Editing lesson content or features without reconstructing all the parameters of the original lesson is mandatory for teachers to author on a regular basis.

Selecting and Using Mini-systems

Mini-systems are a good choice for teachers who have never before used an authoring program. These systems include sample programs that can be used in their original form. If the student is not acquiring the target skill with the sample program the teacher can change the content, pacing, reinforcers, or other options. The teacher can evaluate the student's performance using this newly altered program. If the student's performance is satisfactory, the lesson can be continued. If the student is not progressing, there may be provision for an alteration that will address the areas of difficulty. With many systems it is easy enough to make changes that the teacher is likely to be willing to make the necessary accommodations.

Teachers who recognize the need for supporting practice in vocabulary and want to use CAI should first consult Appendix 5–1 or a recent authoring text (Davis & Budoff, 1986) to determine what authoring programs was available in this content area. Two other general resources for software in special education are the annual Closing the Gap Resource Directory (Closing the Gap, 1986) and The SpecialWare Directory (LINC Associates, Inc.). Let us suppose that the teacher knew from prior experience that the student was highly motivated by software that used a game format. The teacher also knew that record keeping was essential because it was important to compare the student's performance session by session. There are nine vocabulary programs with a game format and record keeping function are listed in Appendix 5–1. All nine programs were able to be used on an Apple IIe, which was the system in her classroom. The teacher chose *Race the Clock* (Mindplay) since it gave the option to enter original graphics, which might be useful and motivating to the student.

Selecting and Using Authoring Systems and Languages

Teachers have more control over the lesson design in an authoring system than in a mini-system. Because of this, it is helpful to prepare a written design document before proceeding with the authoring process. This document or blueprint should specify the series of frames or the screen that will be used to teach, as well as the order in which the author wishes to present the information. Many systems provide worksheets for this purpose. Once these plans have been specified, the teacher can enter the material in response to computer prompts. These prompts generally ask for instructional and tutorial information, questions, acceptable answers, hints, and consequences. The prompts provide a great deal of structure and support for the author, but at the same time may reduce the number of teacher options. Because of the capacity of authoring systems to provide detailed, sequential lessons it is helpful to preview a portion of the already constructed lesson before completion of the entire lesson. Therefore, authoring programs that enable the teacher to move back and forth between the authoring control commands and the lesson screen displays provide timely indications of the appropriateness of the lesson.

Authoring systems do not afford teachers as much free rein over the lesson progression as do authoring languages. However, one must seriously consider how much the added time in learning the language and preparing lessons contributes to a particular product that is superior to that generated through an authoring system. A major criterion for the evaluation of authoring systems and languages is the ratio between the time to author a lesson and the time a student will spend on that lesson. There is no correct ratio, but at a certain point constraints argue against the more sophisticated authoring languages in favor of mini- or full-authoring systems. Without sacrificing individualization, the extent to which authored lessons are suitable for more than one student determines the level of investment in time a teacher may be willing to consider.

Riedesel and Clements (1985, p. 252) suggest that potential authors ask themselves the following questions:

- Would I benefit from learning a more powerful computer language?
- Are the commands available in the system I am considering adequate for the type of courseware I want to write?
- What are the teaching strategies that are built into or encouraged by the program? Are these too limiting? Do they match what teaching strategies I would want to employ?

These questions illustrate the dual competencies required of teachers who would be successful authors. These teachers must know the specific curriculum needs and also the capabilities of a given authoring system in order to select the most appropriate authoring system or language. It is becoming increasingly evident that teachers do not have the time to use authoring systems and languages. Therefore, new mechanisms must be developed to permit teachers to contribute to lesson development through release-time, summer workshops, or other means.

Selecting and Using Authoring Utilities

Authoring utilities have a special purpose, and if used appropriately can save valuable teacher time. Two major considerations in selecting utilities are: does the utility provide an easy, more efficient way to compose and print materials than traditional methods?, and can the material generated by the utility be tailored to individual student needs? The value of utilities is in their ability to generate reviews, quizzes, and practice sheets whose content relates directly to the academic skills. There may be temptation to use the same program for all students rather than altering certain items based on the student's needs and performance levels. Therefore, utilities that enable teachers to generate multiple editions of a quiz or review are to be selected over those with a single option.

SUMMARY

This chapter has reviewed four types of authoring tools: mini-authoring systems, authoring systems, authoring languages, and authoring utilities. The most powerful and flexible programs (i.e., authoring languages) require the most time and are deemed very complex for the average teacher to use in the context of other teaching responsibilities. Mini- and full-fledged authoring systems were recommended for teachers to modify the content and lesson parameters. Authoring utilities were suggested as a means to generate review, practice, and test materials. Collectively, these authoring programs represent a means to give the teacher added control over CAI so that it can be responsive to identified student needs. As Eiser (1986, p. 28) has noted: "Determining what adjustments are appropriate for each student will become an important task for tomorrow's special ed teacher."

Authoring programs are tools, and as such, can be used to create responsive programs, or they can be unused or even misused. In the end, teachers as authors will determine the degree to which such tools will help them help their students. Given that there is an increasing number of authoring programs available, teachers are likely to find one or more that meet their needs. By examining the options, teachers may become more fluent authors and, in the authoring process, more discriminating users of technology.

REFERENCES AND SUGGESTED READINGS

Barton, L. E. (1985). SPE.ED Authoring system. *Analysis and Intervention in Developmental Disabilities, 5*(1–2), ix–xii.

Chiang, A., Stauffer, C., & Cannara, A. (1979, February–March). *A teacher-controlled, computer-assisted instructional system for special education.* Paper presented at the annual convention of the Association for the Development of Computer-Based Instructional Systems, San Diego CA. (ERIC Document Reproduction Service No. E 175 448)

Cosky, M. J. (1980, October). *Computer-based instruction and cognitive styles: Do they make a difference?* Paper presented at the National Conference on Computer-Based Education, Bloomington, MN. (ERIC Document Reproduction Service No. ED 201 299).

Council for Exceptional Children. (1983). *Software search evaluation form.* Unpublished manuscript.

Davis, K. Y., & Budoff, M. (1986). *Using authoring in education.* Cambridge, MA: Brookline Books.

Eisele, J. (1980). A case for computers in instruction. *Journal of Research and Development in Education, 14*(1), 1–8.

Eiser, L. (1986, October). "Regular" software for special ed kids? *Classroom Computer Learning,* pp. 26–35.

Ferster, C. B., & Skinner, B. F. (1957). *Schedules of reinforcement.* New York: Appleton-Century-Crofts.

Grabinger, R. S. (1985, May–June). An evaluation of three authoring-language software packages. *Tech Trends,* pp. 20–23.

Hannaford, A., & Sloane, E. (1981). Microcomputers: Powerful learning tools with proper programming. *Teaching Exceptional Children, 14*(2), 54–57.

Haring, N. G., Liberty, K. A., & White, D. R. (1980). Rules for data-based strategy decisions in instructional programs: Current research and instructional implication. In W. Sailor, B. Wilcox, & L. Brown (Eds.), *Methods of instruction with severely handicapped students.* Baltimore, MD: Paul H. Brookes.

Hummel, J. W., & Farr, S. D. (1985). Options for creating and modifying CAI software for the handicapped. *Journal of Learning Disabilities, 18*(3), 166–168.

Johnson, C. G. (1984). TenCORE and PC PILOT: A comparison of two authoring languages. *Interactive Learning International, 1*(2), 27–30.

Kearsley, G. (1982). Authoring systems in computer based education. *Communications of the ACM, 25*(7), 429–437.

Kearsley, G. (1984). Instructional design and authoring software. *Journal of Instructional Development, 7*(3), 11–16.

Klass, R. (1984). The TenCORE language and authoring system for the IBM personal computer. *Journal of Computer-Based Instruction, 11*(3), 70–71.

Kossiakoff, A., Hazen, P. A., & Panyan, M. V. (1984). Microcomputer-based individually managed instruction for the handicapped. *Johns Hopkins APL Technical Digest, 5*(3), 245–260.

Lamos, J. P. (1986, May). *The design of the HELPmate authoring and instructional delivery system as a tool for providing special education courseware.* Paper presented at the World Congress on Education and Technology, Vancouver, British Columbia, Canada.

Lamos, J. P., Amundson, J., & Winterbauer, A. (1984). *The HELP authoring system for special education.* Denver Research Institute Paper.

MicroSIFT. (1982). *Evaluator's guide for microcomputer-based instructional packages.* Eugene, OR: International Council for Computers in Education.

Milone, M. N. (1982). *Authoring system checklist.* Unpublished manuscript.

Moylan, M. (1984, June). The game show: Winning software. *Software Merchandising,* pp. 50–51.

Nix, D., Gaudreau, M., & Lathrop, F. (1986). Multipurpose authoring language. *The*

Directory, 2(3), 10–11.

Pattison, L. (1985, March). Software writing made easy. *Electronic Learning,* pp. 30–36.

Pogue, R. E. (1980). The authoring system: Interface between author and computer. *Journal of Research and Development in Education, 14*(1), 57–67.

Riedesel, C. A., & Clements, D. H. (1985). *Coping with computers in the elementary and middle schools.* Englewood Cliffs, NJ: Prentice-Hall.

Semmel, M. (1986). "Plain vanilla" software teaches more than far-out games. *Educational Computer News, 3*(13), 3.

Slovick, L. (1982, September). CAI at CFSD: Microcomputer-based authoring systems. *American Annals of the Deaf, 127*(5), 537–545.

Smith, M. (1982, July). Pilot for the Apple. *Creative Computing,* pp. 62–68.

Taber, F. M. (1983). *Microcomputers in special education selection and decision making process.* Reston, VA: Council for Exceptional Children.

Zawalkow, G. (1982). Education software formats. In G. Van Diver & R. Love (Eds.), *The educator's handbook and software directory for microcomputers* (pp. 22–25). Overland Park, KS: Vital Information.

Title: Alge-Blaster
Publisher: Davidson & Associates, Inc.
Components: User's manual, disk
Cost: $49.95
Hardware: Apple II series, IBM, C-64/128
Peripherals: None
Question format: Constructed answer
Content area: Algebra
Features: Instructions, input, record keeping

Title: Alien Action
Publisher: DLM Teaching Resources
Components: Disk, 8 blackline masters, teacher's manual
Cost: $44.00
Hardware: Apple II+, IIe, IIc
Peripherals: None
Question format: Game
Content area: Various subject areas
Features: Input, consequences, pace, record keeping

Title: Alligator Alley
Publisher: DLM Teaching Resources
Components: Disk, 8 blackline masters, teacher's manual
Cost: $44.00
Hardware: Apple II+, IIe, IIc
Peripherals: None
Question format: Game
Content area: Various subject areas
Features: Input consequences, pace, record keeping

Title: Bainum Dunbar Brainz
Publisher: Bainum Dunbar, Inc.
Components: Two disks, user's manual
Cost: $230.00
Hardware: Apple IIe, IIc
Peripherals: None
Question format: Multiple choice, true-false, fill-in-the-blank
Content area: Various subject areas
Features: Graphics, instructions, screen format, consequences, pace

Title: Brainz Builder One
Publisher: Bainum Dunbar, Inc.
Components: Two disks, user's manual
Cost: $95.00
Hardware: Apple IIe, IIc
Peripherals: Echo speech synthesizer (optional)
Question format: Constructed answer
Content area: Various subject areas
Features: Voice, screen format, input, pace

Title: Campaign Math
Publisher: Mindplay
Components: Disk, user's guide, teacher's guide
Cost: $39.99
Hardware: Apple II series, IBM PC/PC jr
Peripherals: Joystick or mouse controls
Question format: Constructed answer
Content area: Social studies, math
Features: Screen format, input, consequences, pace, record keeping

Title: Cat'N Mouse
Publisher: Mindplay
Components: Disk, user's guide, teacher's guide
Cost: $39.99
Hardware: Apple II series, IBM PC/PC jr
Peripherals: Joystick and mouse controls
Question format: Game
Content area: Language arts
Features: Graphics, screen format, input, consequences, pace, record keeping

Title: Create-CCD Lessons
Publisher: Hartley Courseware, Inc.
Components: 1 Disk, teacher's guide
Cost: $29.95
Hardware: Apple II+, IIe, IIc
Peripherals: Cassette control device
Question format: Varied
Content area: Various subject areas
Features: Voice, instructions, record keeping

Title: Create-Fill in the Blanks
Publisher: Hartley Courseware, Inc.
Components: 1 Disk, teacher's guide
Cost: $29.95
Hardware: Apple II+, IIe, IIc
Peripherals: Cassette control device
Question format: Constructed answer
Content area: Language arts
Features: Voice, instructions, record
  keeping

Title: Create-Lessons
Publisher: Hartley Courseware, Inc.
Components: 1 Disk, teacher's guide
Cost: $29.95 Apple; $49.95 IBM;
  $69.95 Lab Pack
Hardware: Apple II+, IIe, IIc, IBM
Peripherals: None
Question format: Varied
Content area: Various subject areas
Features: Instructions, screen format
  pace, record keeping

Title: Create-Medalists
Publisher: Hartley Courseware, Inc.
Components: 1 Disk, teacher's guide
Cost: $29.95 Apple; $49.95 IBM;
  $69.95 Lab Pack
Hardware: Apple II+, IIe, IIc, IBM
Peripherals: None
Question format: Varied
Content area: Various subject areas
Features: Instructions, record keeping

Title: Create-Vocabulary
Publisher: Hartley Courseware, Inc.
Components: 1 Disk, teacher's guide
Cost: $22.95; Lab Pack $69.95
Hardware: Apple II+, IIe, IIc
Peripherals: Cassette control device
Question format: Constructed answer
Content area: Language arts
Features: Voice, instructions, record
  keeping

Title: Create-Vocabulary French
Publisher: Hartley Courseware, Inc.
Components: 1 Disk, teacher's guide
Cost: $22.95; Lab Pack $69.95
Hardware: Apple II+, IIe, IIc
Peripherals: Cassette control device
Question format: Constructed answer
Content area: Beginning French
Features: Voice, instructions, record
  keeping

Title: Create-Vocabulary Spanish
Publisher: Hartley Courseware, Inc.
Components: 1 Disk, teacher's guide
Cost: $29.95; Lab Pack $69.95
Hardware: Apple II+, IIe, IIc
Peripherals: Cassette control device
Question format: Constructed answer
Content area: Beginning Spanish
Features: Voice, instructions, record
  keeping

Title: Create-Spell It
Publisher: Hartley Courseware, Inc.
Components: 1 Disk, teacher's guide
Cost: $22.95; Lab Pack $69.95
Hardware: Apple II+, IIe, IIc
Peripherals: Cassette control device
Question format: Constructed answer
Content area: Spelling
Features: Voice, instructions, record
  keeping

Title: Early Skills
Publisher: Hartley Courseware, Inc.
Components: 2 Disks, teacher's guide
Cost: $39.95
Hardware: Apple II+, IIe, IIc
Peripherals: None
Question format: Matching
Content area: Beginning reading skills
Features: Instructions, record keeping

Title: Game Frame-One; Game
Frame-Two
Publisher: Houghton–Mifflin Company
Components: 3 Game disks, 1
content disk, 1 user's guide per
package
Cost: $126.00
Hardware: Apple II+, IIe, IIc
Peripherals: Printer (optional)
Question format: Game
Content area: Various subject areas
Features: Screen format, pace

Title: The Game Show
Publisher: Advanced Ideas
Components: User's guide, disk
Cost: $39.95 Apple & IBM; $34.95
Commodore
Hardware: Apple II, II+, IIe, IIc, IBM
PC/PC jr, PCXT, PCAT, C-64/128
Peripherals: C-disk drive; IBM-color
graphics card
Question format: Game
Content area: Various subject areas
Features: Instructions, input

Title: Game Power for Phonics
Publisher: Spin-a-test Publishing Co.
Components: User's guide, diagnostic
tests, disk
Cost: $75.00
Hardware: Apple II series, IBM PC/PC
jr, TRS-80 III/IV
Peripherals: C-disk drive
Question format: Game
Content area: Reading, word
structure, phonics
Features: Graphics, voice, instructions,
input, consequences, screen format,
pace

Title: Hinky Pinky
Publisher: Learning Well
Components: Teacher's manual, disk,
Hinky Pinky handbook
Cost: $39.95
Hardware: Apple series
Peripherals: None
Question format: Constructed answer
Content area: Creative expression,
vocabulary building
Features: Record keeping

Title: Idea Invasion
Publisher: DLM Teaching Resources
Components: Disk, 8 blackline
masters, teacher's manual
Cost: $44.00
Hardware: Apple II+, IIe, IIc
Peripherals: None
Question format: Game
Content area: Various subject areas
Features: Input, consequences, pace,
record keeping

Title: Jungle Rescue
Publisher: Learning Well
Components: Teacher's manual, disk
Cost: $49.95
Hardware: Apple series
Peripherals: None
Question format: Constructed answer,
game
Content area: Spelling, language arts
Features: Screen format, record keeping

Title: Lucky's Magic Hat
Publisher: Advanced Ideas
Components: User's guide, disk
Cost: $39.95
Hardware: Apple II, II+, IIe, IIc, III
Peripherals: None
Question format: Game
Content area: Various subject areas
Features: Graphics, instructions, input,
consequences, screen format, pace

Title: Magic Castle
Publisher: Learning Well
Components: Teacher's manual, disk
Cost: $49.95
Hardware: Apple series
Peripherals: None
Question format: Game
Content area: Vocabulary
Features: Record keeping

Title: Make-A-Match
Publisher: DLM Teaching Resources
Components: Disk, 8 blackline
   masters, teacher's manual
Cost: $29.95
Hardware: Apple II+, IIe, IIc
Peripherals: None
Question format: Matching
Content area: Various subject areas
Features: Input, consequences, pace,
   record keeping

Title: Master Match
Publisher: Advanced Ideas
Components: User's guide, disk
Cost: $39.95 Apple & IBM; $34.95
   Commodore
Hardware: Apple II, II+, IIe, IIc, IBM
   PC/PC jr, PCXT, PCAT, C-64/128
Peripherals: C-disk drive; IBM-color
   graphics card
Question format: Matching, game
Content area: Various subject areas
Features: Graphics, instructions, input

Title: Math Blaster
Publisher: Davidson & Associates, Inc.
Components: Teacher's manual, disk
Cost: $49.95
Hardware: Apple II series, IBM, C-64/
   128, Atari, Mac
Peripherals: None
Question format: Game
Content area: Math
Features: Instructions, input, record
   keeping

Title: Math Magic
Publisher: Mindplay
Components: Disk, user's guide,
   teacher's guide
Cost: $39.99
Hardware: Apple II series, IBM PC/PC jr
Peripherals: Joystick and mouse
   controls
Question format: Game
Content area: Counting, addition,
   subtraction
Features: Graphics, screen format,
   input, consequences, pace, record
   keeping

Title: Meteor Mission
Publisher: DLM Teaching Resources
Components: Disk, 8 blackline
   masters, teacher's manual
Cost: $44.00
Hardware: Apple II+, IIe, IIc
Peripherals: None
Question format: Game
Content area: Various subject areas
Features: Input, consequences, pace,
   record keeping

Title: M-SS-NG L-NKS
Publisher: Sunburst Communications
Components: 1 Disk, backup,
   teacher's guide
Cost: $59.00
Hardware: Apple II+, IIe, IIc (48K),
   Atari 400, 800 (48K), IBM PC
   (64K), IBM PC jr (128K)
Peripherals: None
Question format: Fill in the blank
Content area: Language arts
Features: Input, consequences, screen
   format, pace

Title: Race the Clock
Publisher: Mindplay
Components: Disk, user's guide,
   teacher's guide
Cost: $39.99
Hardware: Apple II series, IBM PC/PC jr
Peripherals: Joystick and mouse
   controls
Question format: Matching, game
Content area: Language, verb
   recognition
Features: Graphics, screen format,
   input, consequences, pace, record
   keeping

Title: Reading Tutor
Publisher: Harding & Harris, Inc.
Components: Manual, master program
   disk, reading text disk, student disk
Cost: $79.95
Hardware: Apple II+, IIe, IIc
Peripherals: Printer (optional)
Question format: N/A
Content area: Reading, word structure
Features: Pace, record keeping

Title: Robomath
Publisher: Mindplay
Components: Disk, user's guide,
   teacher's guide
Cost: $39.99
Hardware: Apple II series, IBM PC/PC jr
Peripherals: Joystick and mouse
   controls
Question format: Game
Content area: Multiplication and
   division
Features: Graphics, screen format,
   pace, input, consequences, record
   keeping

Title: Speed Reader II
Publisher: Davidson & Associates, Inc.
Components: Teacher's manual, disk
Cost: $69.95
Hardware: Apple II series, IBM, C-64/
   128, Mac
Peripherals: None
Question format: Multiple Choice
Content area: Reading
Features: Instructions, input, record
   keeping

Title: Spell It
Publisher: Davidson & Associates, Inc.
Components: Teacher's manual
Cost: $49.95
Hardware: Apple II series, IBM, C-64/
   128, Atari
Peripherals: None
Question format: Game
Content area: Spelling
Features: Instructions, input, record
   keeping

Title: Spelling Machine
Publisher: Southwest EdPsych Services
Components: 1 Teacher's manual, 2 disks
   (main & backup) student record forms
Cost: $49.95
Hardware: Apple II, IIe, II+
Peripherals: Printer (optional)
Question format: Multiple choice
Content area: Spelling
Features: Graphics, consequences,
   record keeping

Title: Spelling Sorcery
Publisher: Southwest EdPsych Services
Components: 1 Teacher's manual, 2 disks
   (main & backup) student record forms
Cost: $34.95
Hardware: Apple II, IIe, II+
Peripherals: Printer (optional)
Question format: Multiple choice
Content area: Spelling
Features: Graphics, consequences,
   record keeping

Title: Tic Tac Show
Publisher: Advanced Ideas
Components: User's guide, disk
Cost: $39.95 Apple & IBM; $34.95
  Commodore
Hardware: Apple II, II+, IIe, IIc, IBM
  PC/PC jr, PCXT, PCAT
Peripherals: C-disk drive, IBM-color
  graphics card
Question format: Game
Content area: Various subject areas
Features: Voice, input

Title: Vocabulary Challenge
Publisher: Learning Well
Components: Disk, teacher's manual
Cost: $39.95
Hardware: Apple series, Commodore
Peripherals: None
Question format: Multiple choice
Content area: Vocabulary, analogies
Features: Screen format, record keeping

Title: Vocabulary Machine
Publisher: Southwest EdPsych Services
Components: 1 Teacher's manual, 2 disks
  (main & backup) student record forms
Cost: $59.95
Hardware: Apple II, IIe, II+
Peripherals: Printer (optional)
Question format: Multiple choice
Content area: Vocabulary, reading
  comprehension
Features: Graphics, consequences,
  record keeping

Title: Watchwords and Wordisk Maker
Publisher: Oakland Group
Components: User's guide, 2 disks,
  utility on 3rd disk, separate manual
Cost: $19.95
Hardware: Apple II series
Peripherals: Printer (optional)
Question format: Constructed answer
Content area: Spelling and language arts
Features: Instructions, input,
  consequences, pace, record keeping

Title: Wizard of Words
Publisher: Advanced Ideas
Components: User's guide, disk
Cost: $39.95 Apple II & IBM; $34.95
  Commodore
Hardware: Apple II, II+, IIe, IIc, IBM
  PC/PC jr, PCXT, PCAT, C-64
Peripherals: C-disk drive, IBM-color
  graphics card
Question format: Game
Content area: Vocabulary, spelling,
  dictionary skills
Features: Input

Title: Wiz Works
Publisher: DLM Teaching Resources
Components: Disk, 8 blackline
  masters, teacher's manual
Cost: $44.00
Hardware: Apple II+, IIe, IIc
Peripherals: None
Question format: Game, multiple
  choice
Content area: Various subject areas
Features: Input, consequences, pace,
  record keeping

Title: Word Attack
Publisher: Davidson & Associates, Inc.
Components: Teacher's manual, disk
Cost: $49.95
Hardware: Apple II series, IBM, C-64/
  128, Atari, Mac
Peripherals: None
Question format: Multiple choice, fill-
  in-the-blank, game
Content area: Vocabulary, reading
  comprehension
Features: Voice (Mac only),
  instructions, input, record keeping

Title: Word Bank
Publisher: Learning Well
Components: Disk, teacher's manual
Cost: $49.95
Hardware: Apple series
Peripherals: None
Question format: Classify items, game
Content area: Vocabulary, vowel
   sounds
Features: Screen format

Title: Word Spell
Publisher: Learning Well
Components: Disk, teacher's manual
Cost: $49.95
Hardware: Commodore
Peripherals: None
Question format: Constructed answer
Content area: Spelling
Features: Record keeping

Title: Word Magic
Publisher: Learning Well
Components: Disk, teacher's manual
Cost: $49.95
Hardware: Apple series
Peripherals: None
Question format: Game
Content area: Word structure,
   vocabulary, reading
Features: Screen format, record
   keeping

PUBLISHERS OF MINI-AUTHORING SYSTEMS

Advanced Ideas
2902 San Pablo Avenue
Berkeley, CA   94702
(415) 526-9100

Bainum Dunbar, Inc.
6427 Hillcroft, Suite 133
Houston, TX   77081
(713) 988-0887

Davidson & Associates, Inc.
3135 Kashiwa Street
Torrance, CA   90505
(800) 556-6141

DLM Teaching Resources
One DLM Park
Allen, TX   75002
(800) 527-5030 or (800) 442-4711 (TX)

Harding & Harris, Inc.
P.O. Box 1599
Orem, UT   84057
(801) 224-2014

Hartley Courseware, Inc.
133 Bridge Street
Dimondale, MI   48821
(517) 646-6458

Houghton-Mifflin Company
Educational Software Division
P.O. Box 683
Hanover, NH   03755
(603) 448-3838

Learning Well
200 South Service Road
Roslyn Heights, NY   11577
(516) 621-1540

MECC
3490 Lexington Avenue North
St. Paul, MN   55126
(617) 296-6400

Mindplay
Division of Methods & Solutions
100 Conifer Hill Drive, Suite 301
Danvers, MA   01923
(617) 774-1760

Oakland Group
675 Massachusetts Avenue
Cambridge, MA   02139

Southwest EdPsych Services
P.O. Box 1870
Phoenix, AZ   85001
(602) 253-6528

Spin-a-test Publishing Co.
3177 Hogarth Drive
Sacramento, CA   95827
(916) 369-2032

Sunburst Communications
39 Washington Avenue
Pleasantville, NY   10570
(914) 769-5030

CHAPTER 6

Computer Assisted Instruction in Special Education

DIANNE TOBIN

You have to feel sorry for computers. They are having a hard time living up to peoples' expectations.

— Behr, 1986

T he educational community has been no different from the rest of the world in that it has embraced computers as a panacea for the future. "As sure as a blizzard can be forecast, the educational forecast for the future is that the microcomputer will be an essential part of every classroom," wrote Flo Taber (1983).

The special education community has been caught up in the excitement of using computers in the schools as well. In many ways, computers offer even more to special education students than their regular education counterparts. Although special education usually refers to children with a multitude of handicapping conditions, physical as well as mental, this chapter will focus primarily on the learning handicapped. Learning handicapped students (learning disabled, emotionally disturbed, behaviorally disordered, mildly mentally retarded, and communicative disordered) make up more than 80 percent of the identified special education students in the United States.

OVERVIEW OF COMPUTER ASSISTED INSTRUCTION

Computer assisted instruction (CAI) and programmed learning were used even before the development of microcomputers. Early research generally agreed that students using CAI showed improved achievement or no difference in learning compared to students who did not use CAI (Tabor & Hannaford, 1984; Torgesen, 1984; Atkinson, 1984). Achievement was independent of the specific program, computer system, age, or instrument used for data collection. CAI helped students review material and retention rates may be greater than for regular instruction. Even where there was no difference in achievement per se, learning time tended to decrease. Of special interest is that CAI may be more useful for lower ability and special education children than higher ability children (Taber & Hannaford, 1984; Torgesen, 1984; Atkinson, 1984). In addition, CAI was found to promote cooperative learning (Fitzgerald, 1986; McGregor, 1986). Not unexpectedly, it was found that learning was most effective when the teacher was actively involved. In fact, the computer has done nothing to destroy the teacher's job. Computer instruction is no more or less effective than other methods unless it is used properly by the teacher.

The educational community bought more equipment. Henry Becker (1987) reported that, while few schools had computers seven years ago, currently 90 percent of U.S. school children attend school with at least one computer. Because the number of computers quadrupled between 1983 and 1985, a typical student in 1985 had twice as much computer time as a student did in 1983 (Becker, 1987). Becker suggests that 10 percent of the teachers using computers are special education teachers, so by extrapolation, 50,000 special education teachers were using computers in 1985 (reported in Blackhurst & MacArthur, 1986).

Transforming the Nature of Special Education

With the increase in hardware, CAI could lead the way to a transformation of education, particularly special education. At last, the opportunity was available to truly individualize instruction; each student could be given material based on instructional needs (Taber, 1983; Hagen, 1984). In most states, children with learning problems must have an individual diagnosis and prescription which for both ethical and legal purposes the school and teacher is duty-bound to carry out. Learning handicapped children suffer from many different cognitive processing problems and must be diagnosed and instructed based on individual needs. Therefore, particularly in special education, the need for individualized instruction is critical.

In addition, CAI could supply the repetitive practice so necessary in working with learning handicapped students. Computer practice can help make essential skills become automatic, and students can proceed to higher level skills without needing to concentrate on basic facts. Computer instruction was thought to increase the self-esteem of learning handicapped children by allowing them to fail without fear of peer ridicule and because the computer is patient and nonthreatening. Feedback for wrong answers could be given to the students immediately and consistently so they would know their answer was incorrect and relearn material immediately, saving them the process of unlearning wrong material before they could learn the material correctly. Computer programs could be paced so that a student who needed extra time was not at a disadvantage. In addition, the computer could quickly record the student's work so that the teacher could know immediately how well the student was learning the material and could individualize and prescribe precisely what the next step in the child's learning should be. The computer, therefore, was expected to accomplish feats that had previously not been possible for learning handicapped children (Budoff, Thorman & Gras, 1985; Schiffman, Tobin, & Buchanan, 1982; Schiffman, Tobin, & Cassidy-Bronson, 1982).

Recent Trends

Hardware purchases have increased dramatically in schools; however, there is some concern that computers have not been effectively integrated into the school environment. Reasons that are cited relate to the quality and expense of software on the market, the difficulty of training teachers to use a machine with which they are unfamiliar, and the difficulty of integrating computers into an established school schedule and curriculum.

Bitter (1984) points out that most technological developments have taken a number of years from their inception to their integration in society and our awareness of the implications they have wrought. It is only the first decade since the birth of the Apple microcomputer, the first to be developed, and schools have only begun to test the potential of this machine in the last several years. It may be that the educational community has expected too much too soon. As late as 1984, the Secretary of the U.S. Department of Education was warning about the justified skepticism with which to view the entry of computers into the educational scene, suggesting that education has seen too many "new fangled" ideas (Bell, 1984).

In recent years, there has been a shift from the extremes of viewing microcomputers as education's savior or as a silly fad to a more sensible approach. Educators are beginning to be concerned about software more than hardware, and about using computers effectively in the classroom.

TYPES OF CAI PROGRAMS

There are two major types of CAI programs. One emphasizes building skills and concepts in a logical step-by-step approach, and includes practice situations. These are usually described as drill and practice or tutorial programs. The other type suggests a more holistic approach to learning, engaging the students in activities that enhance learning but are not easy to document on objective tests or define precisely what skills are being taught. Software in that category includes problem-solving, simulations, and writing programs. Computer games can take either learning approach depending on the design of the program.

Drill and Practice

Since learning disabled children are usually skill deficient in one or several areas, many teachers prefer to instruct them in the step-by-step approach. In fact, the behavioral objectives defined by students' Individualized Educational Plans (IEPs) almost require that this approach be taken. This explains, in part, the popularity of drill and practice software. Justification for using tutorial or drill and practice programs is usually based on the need to teach, reinforce, or create automaticity for certain skills or ideas. These programs rarely purport to teach beyond the knowledge level to the realm of higher level thinking skills.

This should require no apology. As Lesgold (1983) pointed out, there is more known about how to provide practice than good initial instruction. Hofmeister (1984) also pointed out that drill and practice programs are the flash cards of CAI and, to the extent that flash cards are necessary, drill and practice programs can be substituted. Torgesen (1984) agreed that increasing practice opportunities on component skills may be the most effective way to use computers with mildly handicapped children.

In an article entitled "Drill and Practice's Bad Rap," Grabe (1986) described the curious phenomenon of research evidence indicating that drill and practice software is effective, yet educators are complaining that many software programs are only drill and practice. He pointed out that teachers' worksheets and practice activities are commonplace in schools and computerized drill and practice offers advantages over more traditional activities — immediate feedback, potential for individualization, ease of repeated trials.

The key to using drill and practice programs in the classroom is to recognize that they are not intended to teach a skill. It is assumed that the skill has already been taught. These programs, therefore, should be seen as a way to help the student reinforce already-learned material. In mathematics, number facts are obvious choices for drill and practice programs, and because these programs are easy to write, there are many on the market. In reading, the teacher may want to develop sight vocabulary words, grammar usage, phonetic elements. Terminology in science and social studies can similarly be reviewed. The key to choosing good drill programs with students is that the program should relate directly to the content in which the student needs practice and that the content and format match the learner styles. A program that puts a premium on speed is not appropriate for a child whose reaction time is slow. A program with a lot on the screen is not appropriate for a child who is easily distracted, for example. It is important to remember that drill and practice programs serve only one purpose: to reinforce and provide practice in one skill. Hofmeister (1984) points out that drill and practice programs are best used immediately after a skill has been taught for reinforcement, as a review for teaching the next level skill, and to guarantee that mastery of a prerequisite skill exists before a teacher attempts to teach a new skill.

Ease of Use

Drill and practice programs are easy to use, and for the teacher unsophisticated in the use of the computer, they may be the best way to start using a computer with students. They rarely require curriculum revisions by the teacher and they fit neatly into the organization of the school day. In addition, because they usually require minimal keyboarding skills from the student, they are easy to use as well. These are not trivial considerations and, although it has become fashionable to speak of using drill and practice programs with derision, if they are used properly, they are very effective instructional aids to the teacher. Drill and practice programs are best used by individual students in a timed practice situation. They rarely are effective as demonstration lessons or small group lessons.

Tutorial Programs

Tutorial programs are another form of CAI. Theoretically, they are programs that teach students a skill or concept. They may or may not have testing procedures to check on students' progress, or branching procedures to reteach materials students have not learned. Tutorial programs are usually designed for individual student use, and their branching techniques are supposed to ensure individualization of instruction, but may be used for a group lesson as well. Tutorials can be designed to teach one concept, for example, a specific prefix, or they can teach a series of skills and concepts.

Courseware

Software that teaches whole units is usually called courseware to distinguish it from the single-subject tutorial. Tutorial courseware that relates to objectives and curriculum is available and has been used in some school systems. *Plato,* by Control Data Corporation, one of the best known and earliest versions of courseware, was developed for larger computers rather than microcomputers, although microcomputer modules are now available. Textbook publishers, such as Houghton Mifflin, Macmillan, Harcourt, Brace, Jovanovich, and Scott Foresman are now producing software that is related to their reading series in much the way they used to produce workbooks (Smith, 1986). Management packages are included as well, so students' work can be monitored as they progress. Networking has given rise to Integrated Learning Systems (ILS). A list of several such systems, appearing in an article entitiled "Courseware for the ILS" (1986), revealed prices ranging from $30,000 to $100,000 for hardware and from $300 per work station for software to $10,000 for site licenses. These systems have sophisticated management programs that move students along the lesson sequences. In most, teachers can designate content areas and lesson sequence.

Some companies are writing software that can be purchased with lessons related to various reading series. A semantic mapping program by Teacher Support Software can be bought for many Basals. Some smaller companies are using authorable programs and writing their own lessons. For example, one company, Computer Tutor, has a series of lessons using *Word Attack* (Davidson) coordinated with both the Ginn and MacMillan readers. Tutorial couseware is not usually available to the special education teacher unless the school district has decided to buy into a system, in which case teachers may be required to use the material that has been purchased. It rarely happens that a school chooses to buy one piece of software in a series.

Evaluating Student Peformance

Tutorial software (and drill and practice) should include record keeping functions so teachers can evaluate students' performance. *Aimstar* (ASIEP Education Co.) can be used with several software packages to graph individual student data in the classroom as well. Many packages include such record keeping, but it is the teacher's responsibility to use the computer-generated information to evaluate students' progress and prescribe the next step.

Tutorial programs are the most difficult to write since, at their best, they must take each skill and concept, present it to the student, make sure the student really understands, go back and reteach if the student does not, and then repeat the process. Reteaching should not mean repeating the same material again, but approaching the same topic somewhat differently. It is important, too, that the second explanation be easier for the child to understand, not harder. One mathematics program, for example, which teaches students how to add two numbers, goes into a complicated series of word problems to explain a process students had not learned when they were shown two sets of items to be merged and counted. If the students could handle the word problems, they wouldn't have needed the remediation, and probably didn't need the software to teach them to begin with.

Application of Various Levels of Instruction

Tutorial programs that teach new material to young children, especially those with learning problems, are increasing. One of the major problems has been the difficulty of teaching on the computer without providing text instruction on the screen. Early learners or students with reading problems often cannot read the text to be able to understand what it is the program is trying to teach. Graphic representations have provided one solution. Some tutorial programs have begun to include the use of voice synthesizers as another method. Voice is usually used to give instructions and for reinforcement, and recently software producers have introduced stories that talk. Students can read along with the entire story or select individual words to have read if the student does not know the words (e.g., software by Laureate, Hartley, Teacher Support Systems, Mindscape, Read Well Media, Inc., Voice Learning Systems-Chatterbox). Although these programs are superior to the ones that try to use text to explain ideas, they often require additional hardware and the placement of computers in a separate room so that the talking computers do not distract other children. In some cases, teachers have hooked the computer to earphones so that only the child working on the program can hear the sound, but this still requires additional hardware and management problems.

For older children, other techniques are possible. In its *Developing Reading Power* series, Mindscape uses modified cloze techniques and contextual clues to work on comprehension skills. Stories that are interactive (i.e., have different storylines depending on students' responses) also are proliferating. Technically, these programs do not teach reading at all, but they do provide strong motivation for students to read.

At the high school level of instruction, tutorials are somewhat easier to write because the reading level of the students has become high enough for them to read from the screen. Many programs have been written in mathematics, physics, and social studies. They are usually highly text-oriented, although graphics are sometimes used for illustrative purposes. Information is presented on the screen, and then questions about that information follow. If the questions are answered incorrectly, the student is referred to the original screen on which the information was first presented. Sometimes the correct answer is highlighted, sometimes not. Branching into different instructional modes is rare because of the difficulty of writing such programs and because the program designers usually feel they have used the best instructional explanations the first time, and are not sure how to improve upon them if the student did not understand. It is assumed that the student did not read carefully enough or just forgot, and should go back to the original with or without hints.

Teaching of Skills Versus Concepts

Programs that teach skills are easier to write than those that teach concepts. Good examples of tutorial software can be found among several of the typing tutorial packages. This skill lends itself well to computer instruction. A picture of the keyboard can be displayed on the screen; the students' finger positions for each key can be displayed; and after showing them where and how to place their fingers, they can be asked to type. Repeated trials and practice are necessary to gain typing speed, and the computer can keep track of students' attempts. In addition, these programs usually require a minimum of teacher intervention while the students are working at the computer.

For the most part, however, teachers cannot rely on computers to teach material. In fact, most tutorial packages are thinly disguised drill and practice programs. Even with the best of tutorial software, teachers need to plan to be actively involved in the teaching of an idea or concept even if a tutorial program is available. Two approaches are possible. Teachers may want to introduce a concept, introduce the software, and then let the students work through the tutorial as added practice and reinforcement. In this case, it may serve the same purpose as a drill and practice program, although it has some additional teaching components. The teacher may also choose to use tutorial software as the initiator of a unit, and an introduction and motivator for a topic the student will be studying. The teacher may choose to make the software program part of a large group demonstration, with the class working it through together, or have individual students try the program, and then discuss the ideas as part of a group lesson later on.

With the development of artificial intelligence techniques and interactive (videodisc, for example) technologies, the future may still hold great promise for tutorial software. All the techniques for effective teaching could be presented. Using video, the students could see real examples of the idea to be taught, simulate the experience directly, and the master teacher can model the lesson that would have been done in a regular classroom. Students could then work on a problem related to the lesson, and punch the answer into a computer, and the teacher, monitoring at a master screen, could know instantly how many students did not understand, and who they are. Those students could then be branched to an alternate teaching mode while the other students continued to slightly different versions of the problems. Because the computer could analyze the type of error the child was making, the branching would be specifically related to that error. At some point, the teacher might have to work with children individually and could do so without the other students losing instruction time.

Follow-up activities, related to higher level thinking skills, could be encouraged through problem-solving situations created by the computer as well, and of course, everything would be recorded as the child proceeded through the material.

It is tutorial software that is supposed to foreshadow the end of teachers, but with the current state of the art, this appears highly unlikely. Advances in technology may produce expert systems and artificial intelligence programs that will make true tutorial programs a reality, but the teacher must continue to play an active role in the instructional process for the programs to be meaningful to the children.

SOFTWARE FOR GENERALIZING LEARNING

Software that takes a more holistic approach to the learning process is usually categorized as problem-solving software and simulation software. One additional category that needs to be added under this approach is the new programs related to writing that are increasingly appearing on the market and becoming a category of their own.

Problem-solving Software

Elements of a problem-solving situation are discussed by Eiser (1986). Skills that are necessary for effective problem-solving such as recall, noting patterns, breaking a task into parts, trial and error experimentation, note-taking, and drawing conclusions from clues, can all be developed or reinforced through various software packages. Eiser includes a list of 21 problem-solving software packages and the problem-solving skills they reinforce. O'Brien (1986) also lists criteria for problem-solving software related to mathematics and suggests eight software packages that apply. When students use problem-solving software, however, they are not taught the skills in isolation (in fact, they are usually not taught the skills at all), but as part of a broader problem to be solved.

Problem-solving software is usually not curriculum-specific. It puts heavy emphasis on understanding a process rather than on content. This has both advantages and disadvantages for the teacher. In order to relate the software to the curriculum, the teacher must carefully select the software and plan for its proper use. This takes considerably more time and imagination than planning to use a drill and practice package. On the other hand, the same program may be used in several different instructional situations. Problem-solving programs, which use graphing techniques as part of the problem-solving situation, can be used in social studies, mathematics, and science. Programs that emphasize logical thinking can be used in most subject areas as well, but it is the teacher who must relate the program activities to classroom content.

Problem-solving software can involve no reading at all; for example, students need only to manipulate a frog in a lily pond working through a series of patterns (*The Pond*, Sunburst, see Appendix 6–1). Others involve knowledge of some words that may have to be taught by the teacher in preparation for the children using the software. One early problem-solving package (*Moptown*, The Learning Company) that has students manipulating four variables —color, height, thickness, and name identification — requires that students recognize words like red, blue, tall, and short in order to work with the program. Although this would seem a limitation, the vocabulary can be easily taught and then students can proceed through the program. If an IEP requires that a child be given help in sequencing or organizing thoughts, some of these software packages may be helpful.

As a guest lecturer on problem-solving software, the author demonstrated *The Factory* (Sunburst) to a group of special education teachers and discussed ways in which it might be integrated into the curriculum. Ideas related to geometry, mathematics, and economics were the most common until one teacher said "I think this program would be wonderful in language arts." She then explained that students could describe what they saw orally or in writing, and describe how they were solving the problem. In addition, students designing products could write how they designed the object for other students to copy. By having the students verbalize and write their actions, a problem-solving package with almost no verbal content could become a language arts activity.

Problem-solving software can be used by a child working alone, but it is also highly effective when used by several students working cooperatively and by a teacher doing demonstrations as well. One of its greatest strengths is that it can encourage a spirit of cooperation rather than competitiveness in a classroom, and children enjoy working with these programs, so they are strong motivators.

Simulations

CAI programs labeled as simulations present the learner with a real-life situation and expect decisions to be made that open up a chain of events related to that situation. Although research results related to simulations are mixed (Sherwood & Hasselbring, 1985–1986), this may be due in part to their holistic approach to learning and the difficulty of objectively measuring specific learning.

Advantages of Use

Advantages of simulation programs are numerous. They can offer children experiences that could not normally be given in a classroom (e.g. being an airline pilot or running for office). They are often more economical than trying to reproduce a real situation. They may be easier for the teacher to organize than their regular classroom equivalent, role playing activities, because the software manages many of the elements the teacher would have to do. In addition, they are usually fun, help integrate learning, and create cooperative, interactive learning environments (Foster, 1984). For learning handicapped students, they can make abstract concepts more concrete, encourage students to take active rather than passive roles, allow students to make low-risk decisions, encourage collaborative decisions, and increase socialization skills (Hasselbring & Cavanaugh, 1986). They should be used when learning objectives are too complex to be broken down into minute steps, when the time-scale of real life activities is too long to fit in the classroom setting, or when real-life situations are too costly or dangerous to be used in the classroom (Taber, 1983).

Simulations can be used for training and have been extremely successful when used to train adults in various skills such as flying a plane, fixing an engine, or diagnosing an illness. A good simulation program should simulate real events or phenomena, and the decisions students make should have reasonable consequences. For example, in one of the earliest programs, a simulation in which students make decisions related to operating a lemonade stand, students are given information on weather conditions and road traffic before they decide whether they need to advertise, cut costs, or produce large quantities. If the weather is hot and the street is clear, a lot of lemonade is sold. If the weather is cold and there is construction on the street, an oversupply of lemonade will result if the student anticipated the same sales as in the first condition. Real principles of economics are at work in the program.

In the classroom, a program that simulates the dissection of a frog (*Operation Frog,* Scholastic) could save the science department a lot of equipment time and laboratory space if it is used in place of the frog dissection lab. It allows students to identify organs and work through the frog's various internal systems, but it is no substitute for an actual dissection. It probably would be better to use this program in addition to a real dissection, rather than instead of one. One approach might be to have the students work with the program before they actually do the real dissection so they will be better prepared.

Social studies simulation programs in which students make decisions about budgets, campaigns, immigration, or resource allocation are probably best used in the opposite order. The students should learn about the variables that enter into the decisions and then try to work them through as they work with their classmates to solve the problem (*Decisions Software,* Tom Snyder Productions).

A software package on eco-systems allows students to simulate survival on an island. They must pick species of animals and plants, build shelter, and not only survive themselves, but plan so that the other species on the island live as well. Unfortunately, this program is not sold separately but is part of *The Voyage of the Mimi* series (Holt, Rinehart & Winston), which includes videotapes, workbooks, and other computer programs and is very expensive.

Elements of Effective Programs

A good simulation program should simulate real events or phenomena, and the decisions students make should not only have reasonable consequences, but they should be similar to the decisions made in real situations. Although unusual variables, such as luck, may play a role in real-life situations, too much emphasis on this in simulations defeats the learning purpose. The child is not sure why the expected did not happen. Some decisions that students make appear to have more random consequences than algorhythmic ones. This is because programmers sometimes try to instill a little random luck into the simulation so students find the situation more appealing, but one wonders what the students are really being taught.

Good simluation programs should be written so that the simulation of reality actually comes as close to reality as possible. A simulation game involving chemical properties mixes real and imaginary chemicals so, although the problem-solving activity may be valid, students, especially those with learning handicaps, may have difficulty separating the true content from the imaginary.

At their best, simulations can sharpen decision-making skills, teach cause and effect, and encourage cooperation and logical thinking as well as develop a sense of familiarity with the skill that is being simulated. For reluctant readers, simulations often supply a motivation for reading for understanding.

Although simulations, like problem-solving software, can be used by individual students, simulation software can be very effective when used by the teacher as a demonstration lesson with the entire class working through the simulation together, or with several students working at the computer at the same time.

WRITING PROGRAMS

A new breed of programs has recently emerged on the market that does not neatly fit into the familiar categories for organizing educational software. These programs emphasize writing skills, are usually limited word processors, and encourage activities that are open ended. Student learning based on these types of programs has not been systematically evaluated, partially because the programs are relatively new and partially because the open ended nature of the activity makes it more difficult to set up systematic research designs. Right and wrong answers are less important than taking notes or writing stories based on pictures. Programs in this category take several approaches. In one case, a picture can be drawn and then the students can write a story about the picture. Some programs have the student write the story first and then the computer draws a picture of their story. In other programs, students are asked to take notes about a picture they have seen, for example, noting particular details about shapes or colors. Some programs suggest outlining activities, or offering prompts to help students think of good opening or topic sentences, or supporting ideas. These programs serve several purposes for the learning handicapped student. They prepare students for using the word processor, a writing tool that can be of enormous benefit. They allow students to focus on the writing process rather than just the grammar skill components emphasized in drill and practice or tutorial programs. Writing programs are usually motivating and help create a feeling that writing can be fun, which is often not the case for learning disabled students.

Because of their open ended nature, writing programs may be used in a variety of ways in the classroom. For younger children, they are suitable for large group instruction, with the teacher using the computer and the students suggesting what to write. As students get older and are more familiar with the keyboard, they can be used in small group activities. In some cases, they may be useful for a single student working in the back of the room or in a laboratory situation. Writing programs are best used as part of an overall school system plan to encourage education related to the writing process to be computer based.

GAMES

Games have always presented somewhat of a problem for the educator. They are fun, and usually a great motivator for children, especially those with learning problems. There is some evidence that computer games promote cooperation and have a positive impact on learning (McClung, 1986; Bright & Harvey, 1984). However, the transfer of learning is unclear and there is a danger that students may come to expect excitement from learning and lose the sense of learning for its own sake. Bright and Harvey (1984) point out that computer games are preferable to regular games in that they do repetitive tasks like rolling dice or shuffling cards more efficiently than if the students have to do them. Small pieces that easily get lost are not a problem. This is especially convenient in the special education classroom. The computer can use missed problems several times so students get practice in what they need rather than rely on randomization patterns in real games, and can adjust difficulty levels to the skill of the players. Of course, for the physically handicapped learner, computer games may be the only way they can play.

Types of Games

There are three types of computer games. Some computer games are simulations of real games, such as chess, mastermind, or backgammon. These obviously should be used the way their real-life counterparts would be used.

Some computer games have question and answer formats in which students compete with themselves, the computer, or other students in order to win the games. They can be formatted like arcade games, quiz shows, and athletic competitions. These programs usually serve the same purpose as drill and practice programs, reinforcement of a specific skill. Many of them put a premium on speed and should be used with caution with learning handicapped youngsters. Game programs often do not explain wrong answers but merely subtract points from a score when the answer is wrong. In addition, some games have so much happening on the screen that easily distracted children may find it difficult to focus on the problem at hand. This type of game is best used at the end of a learning sequence when students have mastered the material and teachers want to encourage overlearning and retention.

The third type of computer game is usually labeled adventure games. Some of these overlap with simulations, but they are different in that they do not have to relate to specific real-life situations. Students usually have to travel to strange lands, solving problems and making choices as they go. Their payoff when they complete the game is usually untold wealth and power. Adventure games take a long time to play, so teachers need to plan several weeks for their use. They are excellent for small group activities rather than individual student use, and encourage cooperation and planning. They also help reinforce critical reading skills, because students usually cannot reach their destination without having understood pertinent clues along the way. Some games encourage the use of more traditional learning tools. For example, a game in which students travel all over the world in search of a thief is sold with an almanac to help students interpret clues.

As pointed out by Kuchinskas (1986), adventure games can be used in conjuction with literature units on mythology, science fiction, and fanstasy as well as characterization and plot development. She points out that reading skills can be taught or reinforced through adventure games, including getting the main idea, developing vocabulary, determining cause and effect, making predictions, determining sequence, and drawing conclusions. Writing skills that can be encouraged include note taking, outlining, spelling, and organizing. In addition, hypothesis testing and development, as well as other problem solving skills, can also be developed through adventure games. They can be played by individual students over several weeks because most of the programs automatically record where students interrupted their game. They are also excellent for small groups and promote cooperation among the participants. Under some circumstances, they can even be used in a demonstration lesson with the teacher and the class playing the adventure together. Many adventure games are available inexpensively or as public domain, and that becomes an additional advantage for the classroom.

SOFTWARE EVALUATION

Software evaluation is tricky. Good software in the hands of a teacher who doesn't plan carefully just serves as a time killer. Poor software in the hands of a skilled teacher can often help augment a lesson very well. Software may be good for one student and harmful for another. A spelling program that mixes up letters or misspells words may be confusing for one learning disabled child and a learning experience for another. Certain teaching and learning styles may lend themselves better to one student than another. The issue of software evaluation, therefore, may be less critical than knowledge of the software in the marketplace (or the school) and the teacher's ability to integrate the software into his or her children's learning needs.

Gaining Knowledge of the Marketplace

Magazines and journals often have software reviews of new products on the market and various organizations publish reviews of software for both regular and special education. Teachers are sometimes advised to look through these for sources of software. In addition, many school systems now have software review committees that provide lists of software available to the schools. In fact, all of this takes an enormous amount of time, time that teachers do not usually have, if they need to search through all these materials, review the software, and then individualize it for each child. Theoretically it sounds wonderful, but realistically, teachers not only do not have the time to do all that but, in some school systems, are not permitted to make those individual decisions. In many cases, teachers find out about software from each other, from seeing other people use it, or from recommendations from supervisors.

Although Carter (1984) suggests that software designed for normal students cannot meet the needs of cognitively slow students, as with other kinds of materials used for children with special learing needs, CAI does not always have to be labeled "for special education" to be useful in special education classrooms. In fact, because of limited markets, many publishers avoid implying that their material is good for students with special learning needs, for fear it won't be bought for use in the regular classroom. The number of software companies is proliferating. As Komoski (1984) pointed out, there are currently about 100 textbook publishers, with 20 or so dominating the market, while there are 700 educational software companies producing thousands of educational software packages. It may be time to lay to rest the complaint that "there is no software out there" and ask instead, "how do I decide what to use?"

Using Forms for Evaluation

Standard forms for reviewing software have begun to proliferate in the literature. Several textbooks, for example, *Computers in the Classroom* (Bitter & Camuse, 1984) and *Choosing Educational Software* (Truett & Gillespie, 1984) include many software evaluation forms. Organizations, such as the National Education Association (NEA) and the National Council of Teachers of Mathematics (NCTM), have devised review forms. Books, including comprehensive software lists and reviews, can be purchased. The Educational Software Selector (TESS) contains reviews of almost every educational software package in existence. Forms related to special education needs have been devised by CEC for its software search, by Test (1985) and Luetke-Stahlman (1986). States and districts have developed forms for reviewing software in their localities for general and special education. The state of Kansas established a Microcomputer Information Coordination Center (MICC) to coordinate statewide activities related to technology applications in special education. It publishes reviews that are available statewide. Many of these are very thorough, reviewing every aspect of the program, including technical considerations, curricular considerations, and general characteristics. Software reviews are beginning to appear on various computer networks as well. However, after all the reams of paper have been read, what the teacher really needs to know is which software to use with the children and how to use it.

At the risk of adding to the proliferation of software evaluation forms, a form developed from the teacher's perspective is included in this chapter (see Figure 6–1). If put on a data base, teachers can key into specific content and objectives and then look at other information about the program. Teachers need to be able to locate resources quickly and easily. Their primary concerns are the resources available to teach a particular unit to a particular child or group of children. If materials are coded as specifically as

Name of Program _____

Brief Description _____

_____

_____

Curricular Area(s) _____

Specific Objective(s) _____

Program Characteristics:

Language experience   Tutorial Review
Drill & Practice   Simulation
Problem Solving   Other _____

Special Devices/hardware needed (list) _____

_____

Teacher can change:

Input options   Content of program
Speed of responding   Other _____

Prerequisite student skills needed:

Computer skills _____
Academic skills _____

Materials provided by manufacturer:

_____ Testing
_____ Worksheet/Follow-up activities
_____ Correlation with text, reader
_____ Correlation with reader

Classroom use

_____ Multiple copies/lab packs
_____ Multiple loads permissable
_____ Networking possible
_____ Licensing arrangements

continued

FIGURE 6–1. *Software planning/preview form.*

Program Use
_____ Introduction   _____ Enrichment
_____ Instruction   _____ Motivation
_____ Review   _____ Evaluation of Student Work

Student Use
_____ Individual student at computer
_____ Two students working together
_____ Small student group
_____ Evaluation of student work

Optimal Length of Time
_____ Minute session one time only
_____ Minute session multiple session
_____ Minute session continued over several weeks

Post Use Comments
Teacher's name _____
Decription of way program used _____
_____
_____

Teacher develop additional materials? ————————————

Did students benefit? _____

Suggestions for next time
_____
_____
_____

FIGURE 6-1. (continued)

possible by content area, the teacher does not have to wade through many irrelevant programs before appropriate ones can be found.

The form assumes that the software has already been ordered and runs on the equipment available in the school. As teachers review software (which they must do before using it with students), they complete the form so that other teachers can use the ideas in the future. This form is by no means complete. Information related to technical considerations and other questions on most forms are deliberately not included in order to emphasize information important to classroom use.

A separate section for comments by teachers after they have used the software is included so that teachers can begin to share ideas with each other. Teachers may think of creative ways to use individual pieces of software. By including these ideas on the form, teachers not only reap the benefits of others' success and failure but may be stimulated to think of new approaches as well.

Some states are already moving in the direction of teacher-centered or curriculum-centered reviews and evaluation forms. The California State Department of Education, for example, recently published a series of five books and disks entitled *Technology in the Curriculum*. Separate books in language arts, mathematics, history, social science, and science are available. Content objectives, by grade level for the K–12 curriculum, are listed and software that meets those objectives is suggested. Since this series was not developed for special education, questions concerning adaptive devices screen formats are not included. However, the format is very readable, and it is an easy guide for a teacher to use. In addition, at the end of each book, specific lesson plans and worksheets are included as additional support for the teacher.

Evaluating the Reviews

Software descriptions may be more meaningful than a software evaluation. Often, one evaluator thinks a program is outstanding, but that program does not work for an individual teacher or classroom. Sometimes the reverse is true: software that received a negative evaluation is used successfully in a number of classrooms. One evaluator may consider software poor if it does not have a management component, yet another teacher may believe that is less important than good learner interaction with the program. One danger of depending on software reviews and evaluations is illustrated in Vignette 6–1.

VIGNETTE 6–1
Software Reviews

The Media Services Division for the state of Maryland recently inaugurated a software data base for use by Maryland schools. A committee of special education teachers had reviewed several pieces of software and sent their reviews to be entered into the data bank. The review for one particular piece of writing software, a program that allows students to place graphic representations on the screen to design a picture, and then allows them to write a story underneath, was

(continued)

VIGNETTE 6-1 *(continued)*

somewhat negative. The review described the complexity of use for young children and learning handicapped children and suggested it not be recommended for classroom use.

What is ironic is that, two days earlier, another Maryland teacher had come to the office for counseling and, in discussing her needs for courses in the Masters Degree in Technology for Educators at The Johns Hopkins University, had described one of the most rewarding writing lessons she had ever taught. Using the same writing program on one computer in the front of the room, second grade students drew a picture on the large monitor by telling the teacher what pictures to use and where to place them. After they had drawn the picture, the teacher asked them to write a brief story about the picture at their seats, using pencil and paper. The students then shared their stories and the teacher discussed opening sentences, interesting ideas, and other aspects of the stories. Then, as a class, the students developed a combined story using ideas from several individual stories. The students were eager to repeat the activity, and the teacher promised to do so at a later date. Unfortunately, the second teacher's review did not make it into the data base. Which review is correct? Probably both. The program might not work for the teacher thinking of using it as an independent activity or as part of a large laboratory situation. On the other hand, it may work well as part of a demonstration lesson.

USING CAI

In their research on how software is used in schools, Williams and Williams (1985) reported that most programs in mathematics were basic skills and drill and practice oriented. Programs in reading were concentrated heavily in early reading skills, with comprehension exercises and some speed reading introduced at intermediate levels. Similarly, language arts programs emphasized basic skills in areas such as grammar and spelling, using graphics, color, and sound at younger levels, and text and multiple choice formats at higher levels. Science and social studies software was related more to intermediate grades than earlier ones, and tended to introduce concepts or terminology. In general, most educational software is intended for elementary school with an emphasis on mathematics and the language arts curriculum.

The typical decision process involved in deciding to use a particular piece of software in the classroom is described by Johnson (1986). Teachers find a piece of software, consider it briefly, let students try it, and then pat themselves on the back for integrating computers into the curriculum. One of the reasons CAI applications, particularly drill and practice programs, are used more extensively than other types of programs is that they can be used easily and without much planning. It is precisely for that reason, however, that CAI is often misused in the classroom.

Contrast this with an ideal scenario for integrating computers into the special education classroom:

■ The special education teacher reviews all IEPs for the student in all the content areas.

■ Classroom teachers are consulted to determine how students' needs and curriculum objectives match in the regular classroom if students are mainstreamed for part of the day.

■ Determination is made of which content areas the special education teacher needs to emphasize and the best approach for teaching the appropriate skills and ideas.

■ The special education teacher reviews software from catalogs, electronic bulletin boards, and software reviews in magazines, goes to meetings to find the best software on the market, and matches it with learning needs and curriculum areas for each student. Obviously, if there is a state curriculum guide matched with appropriate software, or a software center that can be called, it should be done as well. The technology for better search and retrieval techniques through larger data bases, CD, ROM, and easier telecommunications will make this increasingly common.

■ The teacher purchases those packages that are currently not available in the school system and orders the others to be sent to the classroom.

■ The teacher reviews each piece of software thoroughly, noting its strengths and weaknesses, appropriateness for learning style, readability level, and anything else that is significant.

■ The teacher takes each piece of software, checks that another instructional vehicle cannot do the job better, matches it with students' learning needs and the curricular objectives of the IEP, and carefully integrates that software into the instructional day.

It is not realistic, however, to expect that this scenario will ever occur. Several factors contribute to preventing the ideal from becoming a reality. The first, and probably the most important, is teacher time. Steps 1 through 4 in the ideal scenario must be done by the special education teacher, independent of the computer. These are time consuming by themselves. Steps 4 through 7 are mind boggling. There are too many programs from too many companies and reviews from too many sources for the classroom teacher to deal with, when the reality may be that only limited resources are available.

In addition, few classroom teachers have the authority to order software or hardware or determine how those will be allocated within their school or system. Often, only a few people are responsible for software selection in a school or system, and the classroom teacher must work with the selections available. It is foolish to suggest that the teacher embark on a research study of software on the market. To suggest that special education teachers be responsible for keeping current on software through reviews is also unrealistic. The speed with which software is introduced by a large number of companies makes that job virtually impossible, and previewing and reviewing every piece is also far beyond the time contraints of most special education teachers.

Planning for Classroom Use

It is far easier to cite the difficulties of using CAI in the classroom than to suggest practical yet effective ways to approach the problem. From a practical point of view, there appears to be little the average special education teacher can do to deal with the following variables: the hardware and related peripherals available, the compatible software accessible for classroom use, and the organizational structures set up for the use of the hardware and software. Except in unusual cases, these variables are controlled by someone else — a media center representative, the principal, the mathematics department, or at best, the special education coordinator. Special education teachers rarely have total control over these variables, even if they have input into some of the decisions. The special education teacher, therefore, has to make plans using what is available.

It is important to remember that software is an instructional tool for teachers to use to help their students learn better. It should not be used when another medium or approach can teach a concept better. One of the problems that has surfaced is caused by teachers trying to force software into their instructional day or using software that is totally unrelated to the needs of the students.

The special education teacher must begin with the assumption that it will not be possible to solve all problems for all students through the application of CAI. In addition, it is necessary to realize that systematic, long-term planning is virtually impossible, given the speed at which hardware and software are becoming available. Manageable small steps in the right direction are preferable to a scatter shot, hit-or-miss approach.

The teacher must establish a management system suitable to the particular situation that exists. This system will be different if the teacher has access to a computer laboratory once or several times a week, or has access to only one computer in the classroom all the time, or only once in a while. Although this is a critical element, it is no different from what the teacher must do as part of the preparation for instructional planning in general. No one method will work all the time for all teachers or all students.

Too much software, as well as too little, can present a major problem in implementing CAI in the classroom. Teachers may not know where to begin. It is important for teachers to plan for the use of CAI in their classrooms where it is effective and where it can fill a gap. Schiffman (1986a) uses the term "software infusion" to refer to the use of computer software to enhance instruction rather than as a primary educational delivery system. A similar approach suggested by Gardner (1986) is that teachers review the curriculum they are planning to teach, and the needs of the students they are teaching, and establish "targets of difficulty," that is, look at those areas in which traditional methods are weak, and then see if CAI can help.

Complementing Curriculum Goals

A similar concept for integrating computers into the curriculum is being piloted by Educational Products Information Exchange (EPIE). The aim of resource materials should be to complement the curriculum, and a system is currently being devised so that curriculum goals, textbooks, and assessment measures can be entered into a computer to test the fit. When the text and other supplementary materials do not match the curriculum goals, supplementary materials, including software, are suggested (Komoski, 1986). Whether the term used is "curriculum alignment" (Komoski, 1986), "targets of difficulty" (Gardner, 1986), or "software infusion" (Schiffman, 1986a, 1986b), each suggests a more manageable approach to the use of CAI in the special education classroom. By whatever name, CAI must become part of a total package of tools available to the special education teacher to help children with special learning needs. CAI must be treated as any other learning mechanism by the teacher. It requires the same planning and attention as a filmstrip or a resource book. Using the concept that software should be included in the curriculum only to help students who will be better instructed through the computer than through traditional means, the teacher can begin to approach the introduction of computers into the classroom in more realistic ways.

There are two ways to approach the situation. One is to fit the available software and hardware configuration of the school into the curriculum, and the other is to determine the needs of the child first and to find the hardware and software to fit those needs.

The first approach, although less desirable, may have to be taken if limited software and hardware is available. In that case, the teacher may have to target only a few children, those whose learning needs can be enhanced by the software that is available. If a teacher's guide to software is available, the teacher should obviously consult it. If not, the teacher would need to preview each piece and make notes on the characteristics of the software and the content learning and behavioral characteristics addressed by each piece. If the library is limited, this job is less time consuming. The teacher must also check the students, their objectives and needs. As the teacher reviews the CAI, all aspects of the software must be studied in order to capitalize on its strengths and adapt for its weaknesses. For example, some teachers place colored circles or pictures on certain keys so that students can be told to press the red button or the butterfly instead of the space bar.

Determining an Overall Instructional Plan

When there is a match between software and a student's needs, that student should be targeted to receive CAI. For example, if a computer is available for an hour a week and the school has only drill and practice programs in mathematics, the teacher would look for those students whose IEPs require help in mathematics and the narrow the range to those whose skill deficiencies match the skills reinforced in the software. Where no CAI software is available to meet some students' needs, the teacher should check programs that use game formats or drill and practice programs that allow the teacher to enter content to see if one or more of them can be adapted. Or, the teacher can look at programs that may not be suitable for individual students but could work if the teacher controlled the keyboard in a demonstration situation. If the teacher must include all students in computer-related activities, programs that have some instructional relevance and provide motivation should be selected, even if they do not meet classroom needs directly. A worksheet or other related activity can be used to capitalize on computer activity.

The teacher, who has a large selection of software to choose from, would proceed in a similar manner but would alter the order of the steps in the process. Student IEPs should be reviewed first to determine student needs, and an overall instructional plan should be determined. When the teacher has some concern over methodology or the materials available, that area should be flagged for possible CAI instruction. At this point, the teacher should see whether software is available in those areas. Checking with the individual responsible for the software library is the first step. In addition, a quick check with other faculty in the building, or other special education teachers, should be made to see if anyone has had success in using a particular software or management system. If a school has a software review library, similar to the California, Kansas, and Maryland systems mentioned earlier, the reviews should be checked. This is different from a thorough search of the literature and can usually be accomplished through the day-to-day interactions normally associated with a teacher's work situation.

Next, a manageable goal should be established. This would be different for each teacher, depending on the situation. For example, a teacher who has access to a resource laboratory every week for 45 minutes might decide to use that time only to reinforce weak skills by giving students extra practice. Software would be selected each week to match the skills that needed reinforcing. These can be supplemented by authoring packages when needed. The teacher would then assign each student to a piece of software for the period. The teacher could also decide to use that 45-minute period to train students on keyboarding skills so that they will be prepared to use word processors later on. Still another possibility would be to use the time for extra practice in reading and problem-solving through adventure games that would continue for several weeks. The teacher who has access to a laboratory only, therefore, would not be concerned with software for large group instruction.

A teacher who must send a child to the media center might want to select a child who is independent enough to leave the classroom, whose schedule can be accommodated to the computer use schedule, and whose learning needs fit the software available. Given those constraints, only two or three students might be able to use the computer each year, but it is better to pursue manageable goals and do them well than to attempt too much and do it badly, or waste the student's time.

A teacher who has only one computer available in the classroom might want to plan one demonstration lesson a week using the computer and set up a schedule where single students, or groups of students with similar needs, use the computer on different days. Some teachers have worked out complicated management strategies for students doing independent or small group work on the computer, and this can work, too, but it is probably not a good idea to try it until both the teacher and the students are comfortable with the machine. One step in the process that can never be skipped is that the teacher must become thoroughly familiar with the software to be used and plan for its use with the same thoroughness that would be used with a filmstrip or a learning kit. The teacher should also be familiar with the prerequisite skills for using a program (e.g., keyboarding, knowledge of addition, minimum reading levels). These may turn out to be less critical than expected since some children seem to be able to handle computer instructions better than textbook reading. The teacher, however, must be aware of the prerequisite variables in order to understand problems that may emerge.

Assessing Suitable Instructional Use

Previewing software before using it (something teachers do with any piece of instructional material) is essential so the teacher can prepare for its optimum use. Does it need to be booted up by the teacher and made ready so that the child sits down with the program already on the screen? Is it important for the child's name and date to be entered so that management information is available? Preparing the program for use by students saves lengthy start-up periods and conveys to the student that computer time is part of school work time.

If the software works with the student, some notation of its success and the type of student it was successful with should be made, both for the teacher's future reference and to share with other teachers. The following year, additional software or students might be included, using procedures similar to the previous year unless the software or hardware situation has changed, in which case a re-evaluation may be necessary.

In some cases, for administrative reasons, only software suitable for group instruction may be usable. If that is the case, the teacher can look for software packages that can be used in group situations. Many of these are available, and can meet a variety of classroom and content needs. An early program in which children teach the computer about animals is excellent for teaching understanding of categories and groups within categories. Writing programs can be used to generate story ideas, which can then be written individually. Simulations, adventure games, and tutorials can be used as introductory lessons to stimulate interest in a unit, or as applications of skills towards the end of a unit.

CAI can indeed realize the expectations that many predicted for it in special education when it first burst upon education. Computers are not a passing fad that will fade from the educational scene. They have become too ingrained in our society to be eliminated from our schools. As our educational tools increase, including artificial intelligence and videodiscs, teachers will find themselves trying to use these technologies as well. Like the special education students they teach, teachers must enter this new world one step at a time, not being afraid to try something new, but making sure they have not guaranteed failure by tackling too much. Our special education students need the benefits that CAI can give them.

SUMMARY

CAI offers teachers of learning handicapped children tremendous opportunities for enriching the learning of their students in two ways. As an aid for practice of learned skills, CAI is more motivating than standard workbooks and, if management capabilities are included, it allows the teacher instant access to the students' strengths and weaknesses in those skills. CAI, which gives a more holistic approach to learning, gives students a better understanding of how to apply learned skills and encourages higher level thinking. The critical element in the successful use of CAI, however, is the teacher. To make CAI more effective in the classroom, the teacher must take an active role in the process. It is the teacher who must decide whether a program works better for individual instruction, small groups, or as a demonstration lesson for the whole class. It is the teacher who understands the learning needs of the children. It is the teacher who must match the programs to the content in the classroom for CAI to be meaningful.

Teachers must use CAI as they use all learning materials. They should proceed in small, manageable steps, not attempting too much too soon. Special education teachers have been individualizing instruction for years, and the computer should become just one more tool in the process.

REFERENCES AND SUGGESTED READINGS

Atkinson, M. (1984). Computer assisted instruction: Current state of the art. *Computers in the Schools, 1*(1), 91–99.

Atkinson, R. (1968). Computerized instruction and the learning process. *American Psychologist, 23,* 225–239.

Becker, H. J. (1987, February). Using computers for instruction. *BYTE,* pp. 149–160.

Behr, P. (1986, July 17). Pity the poor computer. *The Washington Post,* p. E1.

Bell, T. H. (1984). Effective use of computers in school requires coordinated development. *T.H.E. Journal, 1*(3), 80–83.

Bitter, G. (1984). The future of education in the microcomputer revolution. In M. Behrmann & L. Lahm (Eds.), *Proceedings of the National Conference on the Use of Computers in Special Education* (pp. 28–38). Reston, VA: Council of Exceptional Children.

Bitter, G., & Canuse, R. A. (1984). *Using a microcomputer in the classroom.* Reston, VA: Reston Publishing.

Blackhurst, A. E., & MacArthur, C. A. (1986). *Microcomputer use in special education personnel preparation programs. TESE, 9*(1), 27–35.

Bright, G. W., & Harvey, J. G. (1984). Computer games as instructional tools. *Computers in the Schools, 1*(3), 73–79.

Budoff, M., Thormann, J., & Gras, A. (1985). *Microcomputers in special education.* Cambridge, MA: Brookline Books.

Carnine, D., Moore, L., Stepnowski, M., & Woodward, J. (1985). *Teacher net: A networking system for improving classroom efficiency.*

Carter, J. (1984). Learning characteristics of retarded persons as criteria for evaluating special education software. *SIG Bulletin of the International Council for Computers in Education, 1*(2), 4–9.

Chrosniak, P. N., & McConkie, G. (1985). *Computer-aided reading with reading discouraged children.* Paper presented at annual meeting of AERA, Chicago, IL.

Courseware for the ILS. (1986). *Electronic Learning, 5*(5), 45.

Eiser, L. (1986). Problem solving software: What it really teaches. *Classroom Computer Learning, 6,* 42–45.

Fitzgerald, G. E. (1986, June). *Computer applications in the behavior change curriculum: Increasing cooperative learning skills.* Presented at an invitational research symposium on special education technology, Washington, DC.

Forman, D. (1982). Review of the literature. *The Computing Teacher, 9*(5), 37–50.

Foster, D. (1984). Computer simulation in tomorrow's schools. *Computers in the Schools, 1*(3), 81–89.

Gagne, R. M. (1977). *The conditions of learning.* New York: Holt, Rinehart and Winston.

Gagne, R. M., & Briggs, L. J. (19XX). Principles of instruction design. New York: Holt, Rinehart and Winston.

Gardner, M. (1986). Developing and implementing a computer curriculum: The problems, the contents and the future. *Electronic Learning, 5,* 5.

Grabe, M. (1986). Drill and practice's bad rep. *Electronic Learning, 5*(5), 22–23.

Grimes, L. (1983). Computers are for kids: Designing software programs to avoid problems of learning. *Teaching Exceptional Children, 14*(2), 49–53.

Hagen, D. (1984). *Microcomputer resource book for special education.* Reston, VA: Reston Publishing.

Hasselbring, T. S., & Cavanaugh, K. J. (1986). Applications for the mildly handicapped. In C. K. Kintzer, R. D. Sherwood, & J. D. Bransford (Eds.), *Computer strategies for education: Foundations and content area applications* (pp. 289–312). Columbus, OH: Charles E. Merrill.

Hofmeister, A. (1984). *Microcomputer applications in the classroom.* New York: Holt, Rinehart and Winston.

Hofmeister, A. M., & Thorkildsen, R. (1984). Microcomputers in special education: Implications for instructional design. *Exceptional Education Quarterly, 4*(4), 1–11.

Johnson, J. (1986). It's April, taxman time. *Computing Teacher, 13*(7), 20–23.

Kneif, X. (1979). Effects of computer based instruction and tutoring in an elementary school system. *AEDS Proceedings.*

Komoski, P. K. (1984, December). Educational computing: The burden of ensuring quality. *Phi Delta Kappan,* pp. 244–248.

Komoski, P. K. (1986, February). *Curriculum alignment demonstration.* Presentation at the American Association of School Administrators meeting, San Francisco, CA.

Kuchinskas, G. (1986). Introducing adventure games. *Computing Teacher, 13*(6), 44–46.

Kulik, J. A., Bangert-Downs, R. L., & Williams, G. W. (1983). Effects of computer based teaching on secondary school students. *Journal of Educational Psychology, 29,* 19–26.

Kulik, J. A., & Bangert-Downs, R. L. (1984). Effectiveness of technology in precollege mathematics and science teaching. *Journal of Educational Technology Systems, 12,* 137–158.

Lesgold, A. M. (1983). A rationale for computer-based reading instruction. In A. C. Wilkensen (Ed.), *Classroom computers and cognitive science.* New York: Academic Press.

Litman, G. (1977). Relation between computer assisted instruction and reading achievement among fourth, fifth and sixth grade students. *Dissertation Abstracts, 38,* 2003A.

Luetke-Stahlman, B. K. (1986). Evaluating sofware for special needs students. *SIG Bulletin of the International Council for Computers in Education, 2*(3), 43–46.

Lysakowski, R., & Walberg, H. (1982). Instructional effects of participation and corrective feedback: A quantitative synthesis. *American Educational Research Journal, 19*(4), 559–578.

Majer, K. (1973). Computer assisted instruction in reading: How, what, when and where? *Educational Technology, 13,* 23–27.

McClung, P. A. (1986). A study of the effects of playing selected microcomputer games on the spatial ability of fifth, seventh and ninth grade males and females. In B. Cassas, Resarch windows. *The Computing Teacher, 13*(8), 10.

McGregor, G. (1986, June). *The use of microcomputer based adaptations to increase the social interaction between students with handicaps and their nonhandicapped peers.* Paper presented at the Invitational Research Symposium on Special Education Technology, Washington, DC.

O'Brien, T. (1986). Turning mysteries into problems. *The Computing Teacher, 13*(6), 39–43

Reinking, D., & Schreiner, R. (1985). The effects of computer mediated text on measures of reading comprehension and reading behavior. *Reading Research Quarterly, 20*(5), 536–552.

Schiffman, G., Tobin, D., & Buchanan, W. (1982). Microcomputer instruction for the learning disabled. *Journal of Learning Disabilities, 15*(9), 134–136.

Schiffman, G., Tobin, D., & Cassidy-Bronson, S. (1982). Personal computers for the learning disabled. *Journal of Learning Disabilities, 15*(7), 422–425.

Schiffman, S. S. (1986a, January). Software infusion: Using computers to enhance instruction. Part one: What does software infusion look like? *Educational Technology,* pp. 7–11.

Schiffman, S. S. (1986b, February). Software infusion: Using computers to enhance instruction. Part two: What kind of training does software infusion require? *Educational Technology,* pp. 9–15.

Sherwood, X., & Hasslebring, X. (1985–1986). A comparison of student achievement across three methods of presentation of a computer based science simulation. *Computers in the Schools, 2*(4), 43–50.

Slattow, G. (1976). *Demonstration of the PLATO IV computer based education system: Final report.* (ERIC Document Reproduction Service No. ED 158 767)

Smith, J. D. (1986). Managing reading software for use with reading textbooks. *Electronic Learning, 7*(5), 24–28.

Snider, W. (1986). Pioneers are harnessing computers to unlock learning for handicapped. *Education Weekly, 5*(37), 1, 10–11.

Stowischek, J. J., & Stowischek, C. E. (1984). Once more with feeling: The absence of research on teacher use of microcomputers. *Exceptional Education Quarterly, 4*(4), 23–39.

Taber, F. M. (1983). *Microcomputers in special education.* Reston, VA: Council for Exceptional Children.

Taber, F. M., & Hannaford, A. E. (1984). Introduction to the uses of the microcomputer in special education. In M. Behrmann & L. Lahm (Eds.), *Proceedings of the National Conference on the Use of Microcomputers in Special Education* (pp. 28–38). Reston, VA: Council for Exceptional Children.

Test, D. W. (1985). Evaluating educational software for the microcomputer. *Journal of Special Education Technology, 7*(1), 37–46.

The 1986 educational software preview guide. (1986). Sacramento: California State Department of Education.

Thorman, J. (1984). Sharing curriculum and decreasing paperwork in special education: Problems and solutions. *SIG Bulletin of International Council for Computers in Education, 1*(4), 53–56.

Torgesen, J. K. (1984). Instructional uses of microcomputers with elementary and mildly handicapped children. In R. E. Bennett & C. A. Maher (Eds.), *Microcomputers and exceptional children* (pp. 37–48). New York: Haworth Press.

Truett, C., & Gillespie, L. (1984). *Choosing educational software: A buyer's guide.* Littleton, CO: Libraries Unlimited.

Williams, F., & Williams, V. (1985). *Success with educational software.* New York: Praeger.

Woodward, J., Carnine, D., Gersten, R., Gleason, M., Johnson, G., & Collins, M. (1985, November). Instructional design principles for CAI: A summary of four studies. (Available from authors).

Woodward, J., Carnine, D., Moore, L., Noell, J., & Hayden, M. (1986). Teacher Net: An affordable networking system for every classroom. Unpublished manuscript, University of Oregon.

APPENDIX 6-1: SOURCES OF FURTHER INFORMATION ON CAI

The following is a list of software publishers, vendors, and sources of information on CAI applications for special education and their addresses. Most of the major software publishers and some of the smaller ones are included. Some companies have toll free 800 numbers, and individuals who wish to call should check the 800 directory. Inclusion does not mean endorsement.

Software Publishers

Aquarius
Indian Rocks Beach, FL 33535

ASIEP
3216 N.E. 27th Avenue
Portland, OR 97213

Baudville
1001 Medical Park Drive S.E.
Grand Rapids, MI 49506

Borns Software
198941 Sea Canyon Circle
Huntington Beach, CA 92648

Broderbund
P.O. Box 12947
San Rafael, CA 94913-2947

Collamore/D.C. Heath
Collamore Publishing
125 Spring Street
Lexington, MA 02173

Continental Press
520 E. Bainbridge
Elizabethtown, PA 17022

Data Command
P.O. Box 548
Kankakee, IL 60901

Davidson & Associates
3135 Kasluwa Street
Torrance, CA 90505

DLM
One DLM Park
Allen, TX 75002

Focus
839 Stewart Avenue
P.O. Box 865
Garden City, NY 11530

Ginn & Company
191 Spring Street
Lexington, MA 02173

Grolier Electronic Publishing
Sherman Turnpike
Danbury, CT 06816

Harcourt Brace Jovanovich
Orlando, FL 32887

Hartley
133 Bridge Street
Dimondale, MI 48821

Holt, Rinehart & Winston
383 Madison Avenue
New York, NY 10017

Houghton Mifflin
Educational Software Division
Dept. 217
Hanover, NH 03755

HRM Software
17 Tomkins Avenue
Pleasantville, NY 10570

I/CT
10 Stepar Place
Huntington Station, NY 11746

IBM Educational Systems
Dept. WH, P.O. Box 2150
Atlanta, GA 30035

Justens Learning Systems, Inc.
800 E. Business Center Drive
Mt. Prospect, IL 60056

Krell
1320 Stoney Brook Road
Stoney Brook, NY 11790

Laureate
110 E. Spring Street
Winooski, VT 05404

Learning Company
545 Middlefield Road
Menlo Park, CA 94025

Macmillan
866 Third Avenue
New York, NY 10022

Marble Systems
P.O. Box 750
Exeter, NH 03833

MCE
157 S. Kalamazoo Mall
Suite 250, Dept. 7
Kalamazoo, MI 99007

McGraw-Hill
1221 Avenue of the Americas
New York, NY 10020

MECC
3490 Lexington Avenue North
St. Paul, MN 55126

Milliken
2225 Grant Road
Los Altos, CA 94022

Mindplay
82 Montvale Avenue
Stoneham, MA 02180

Mindscape
3444 Dundee Road
Northbrook, IL 60062

Morning Star
P.O. Box 5364
Madison, WI 53705

Peal
2210 Wilshire Blvd., Suite 806
Santa Monica, CA 90403

Plato/Wicat
8800 Queen Avenue South
Minneapolis, MN 55431

Prentice-Hall
Allyn & Bacon
Englewood Cliffs, NJ 07632

Read Well Media, Inc.
P.O. Box 441047
Aurora, CO 80044

Remedia
P.O. Box 1788-C
Scottsdale, AZ 85252

Scholastic
2931 E. McCarty Street
Jefferson City, MO 65102

Scott Foresman
1900 E. Lake Avenue
Glenview, IL 60025

SEI
2360J George Washington Highway
Yorktown, VA 23692

Spinnaker
215 First Street
Cambridge, MA 02142

Springboard Software, Inc.
7807 Creekridge Circle
Minneapolis, MN 55435

Sunburst
39 Washington Avenue
Pleasantville, NY 10570-9971

Teacher Support Software
P.O. Box 7130
Gainesville, FL 32605

Tom Snyder Productions
123 Mt. Auburn Street
Cambridge, MA 02138

Voice Learning Systems
2265 Westwood Blvd., Suite 9
Los Angeles, CA 90064

Walt Disney Educational Media
500 S. Buena Vista Street
Burbank, CA 91521

Software Distributors

The following companies are primarily distributors, and do not develop and market their own software. Some sell software at a discount.

Alpha Resource Centers
804 Third Street, S.W.
Washington, DC 20024

CC
P.O. Box 23699
Tigard, OR 97223-0108

CDL
P.O. Box 605
Newton Falls, MA 02162

CEO Associates
201 Route 516
Old Bridge, NJ 08857

Chaselle, Inc.
Dept. ES, P.O. Box 2097
Columbia, MD 21045

Conduit
University of Iowa–Oakdale Campus
Iowa City, IA 52240

Educational Activities, Inc.
P.O. Box 392
Freeport, NY 11520

Gamco Industries
P.O. Box 1862L3
Big Springs, TX 79721

K-12 Micromedia
6 Arrow Road
Ramsey, NJ 07446

NCP
P.O. Box 61
1380 S. Pennsylvania Avenue
Morrisville, PA 19067

Opportunities for Learning, Inc.
Career Aids, Inc.
20417 Nordhoff Street
Chatsworth, CA 91311

Queue
562 Boston Avenue
Bridgeport, CT 06610

Software for Kids
P.O. Box 10376
Rockville, MD 20850

Sources for Special Education Software Information

Closing the Gap
P.O. Box 68
Henderson, MN 56044

Council for Exceptional Children
Center for Special Education
  Technology Information Exchange
Technology and Media
  Division (TAM)
Project RETOOL
1920 Association Drive
Reston, VA 22091

Educational Products Information
  Exchange (EPIE)
P.O. Box 839
Water Mill, NY 11976

International Council for Computers
  in Education
1787 Agate Street
Eugene, OR 97403-1923

LINC Resources
1785 Morse Road, Suite 215
Columbus, OH 43229

Microcomputer Information
  Coordination Center (MICC)
University of Kansas Medical Center
Room 139
Children's Rehabilitation Center
39th & Rainbow Blvd.
Kansas City, KS 66103

Special Education Software Center
3333 Ravenswood Avenue
Menlo Park, CA 94025

Special Education Technology
  Resource Center
Madeleine Pugliese, Director
c/o Emmanual College Library
400 The Fenway
Boston, MA 02115

Special Net
1201 16th Street
Washington, DC 20036

The Educational Software Selector (TESS)
P.O. Box 839
Water Mill, NY 11976

CHAPTER 7

Word Processing and Related Tool Applications

JEFFREY W. HUMMEL

I nstruction in writing includes the teaching of mechanics, that is, spelling, grammar, punctuation, handwriting, and a variety of writing conventions. Writing instruction also involves the development of a set of concepts and strategies for generating ideas and getting them down on paper.

Children may be more motivated to learn to write if they understand that writing is a way to communicate and if they are afforded appropriate learning opportunities. Adequate allotment of time for writing, adequate access to hardware and software, and the preferred patterns of use of computer time are preliminary considerations to any effort to provide these opportunities for handicapped students.

Word processors are software application packages for microcomputers or dedicated systems designed primarily for the documentation and manipulation of the written word. The basic features of word processing programs permit text entry, text editing, and the saving of text on disk and paper, or "hard copy." Full-feature programs let the user work with text in a variety of ways. These include underlining and highlighting text, formatting documents with tabs, making bulletted paragraphs, creating electronic forms, merging lists of information and forms, moving text between two files, sending files to different word processing programs, and altering the formats for printing files.

Teachers must understand how word processing and related applications (e.g., spelling checkers, thesauruses) can be integrated into handicapped students' writing instruction. Word processing programs are *tools* that can be used in writing instruction, to aid the special education teacher in communications with parents and in the preparation of instructional materials. These computer programs also have application in the real world beyond our classrooms.

WORD PROCESSING WITH HANDICAPPED CHILDREN

When looking at word processing applications for handicapped children, it is helpful to become familiar with the variety of ways information can be entered into the computer. The most familiar method is single character entry via a keyboard. However, through hardware and software adaptations, it is possible to enter and manipulate single characters, words, or phrases. The recognition of these options increases the availabilty of word processing technology to disabled people who may not be able to master single character entry.

Mildly Handicapped Children

Rosegrant's six years of work (1985a, 1985b) have contributed substantially to the knowledge available about the use of microcomputers to facilitate progress in the reading and writing of children with learning disabilities. She describes four factors central to making the microcomputer a valuable tool for these children: using the microcomputer to provide visual, auditory, and motoric modes of assistance; using it to lower the risks associated with making errors; providing a high degree of child control over reading and writing tasks involving the microcomputer; and providing a meaningful learning context in which written language exploration and analysis can occur.

Rosegrant (1985b) describes the key elements for fostering progress in reading and writing. The adult provides forms of assistance in order to enable the child to experience success at literacy. This maintains the child's sense of competence as a learner by providing encouragement for the essential learning behaviors, which foster progress in the acquisition of literacy. She has developed software based on this model, including *Listen to Learn* from IBM, and the Apple version, *Talking Screen Test Writer* (Scholastic). This software provides assistance in the form of multiple modality supports, and offers ample opportunity for feedback and repetition. The auditory support provided by a speech synthesizer is an important feature that makes it possible for the child to choose to hear letter names or words as they write, and hear lines or whole pages of composed text. This auditory cue helps children master the relation between the written and spoken word. If students request that the speech synthesizer say "cts," they hear that "cts" is not a real word, as opposed to when they hear the speech synthesizer say "cats," which sounds like a real word. While it is true that synthesized speech does not provide a consistently accurate reproduction of spoken language, Rosegrant has found that the auditory cues it does provide are adequate to aid learning. Her programs, which are designed for early literacy development, can help handicapped students learn complex phoneme, grapheme, and morpheme codes as they express themselves in written language. Her programs are not intended to be full-feature word processing programs, having only limited editing capabilities.

Magic Slate, by Sunburst, in contrast to Rosegrant's programs, comes with 20-, 40-, and 80-column versions. *Magic Slate* allows the user who would benefit from a 20-column screen displaying larger printed characters the chance to progress toward the full-feature 80-column version. Williams and Blauser (1986) report that, with some help from an adult, trainable mentally retarded high school students can be successful in using *Magic Slate* in a variety of writing activities. *Magic Slate* relies partially on a system of icons (pictographs that symbolize software functions), which seem to work nicely.

Older and more able handicapped students with good literacy skills (i.e., the visual acuity to handle the complexity of an 80-column screen display) might be better off starting with a program such as *Appleworks*, which relies heavily on mnemonic cues. *Appleworks*, from Apple, is particularly attractive in that it is an integrated utility package. This means it has a word processing program, a data base program, and a spreadsheet program that can be used together.

Other word processing programs, such as *Homeword* by Sierra Design and *The Milliken Word Processor* by Milliken can be used by mildly handicapped children. *Homeword* has been touted because of its use of icons. However, the logic of these icons breaks down for adults as well as for handicapped students. *The Milliken Word Processor* has some nice features, including the use of a desktop analogy for its three basic functions and a readily available help menu. However, this program also has some limitations in its applications with handicapped children (Hummel, Senf, & Mather, 1985).

The third edition of the *Bank Street Writer* includes some improvements over the earlier versions. It can be used with a data base program designed for younger children, the *Bank Street School Filer*. Both are available from Scholastic. MacArthur and Schneiderman (1986) have criticized early versions of *Bank Street Writer*, and have identified some additional pertinent issues for the evaluation and selection of word processing programs for handicapped students. In particular they advised against the use of programs with a separate mode of moving the cursor, which include the older versions of *Bank Street Writer*. MacArthur and Schneiderman resist a generalization regarding best overall organization of word processing programs, offering these two recommendations: provide instruction in the concepts used in the organization of the program and provide direct instruction and directed practice on points of difficulty.

Physically Handicapped and Developmentally Disabled Children

Brandenburg (1986) of the University of Wisconsin's Trace Center provides an analysis of the computer needs of individuals with physical handicaps and states that there are two kinds of writing needs of the physically handicapped that cannot be overlooked. These are portable writing (i.e., a portable "pencil and paper) that moves with the individual to different environments, and work station writing, which involves the writing of large amounts of text not handled by a portable "pencil and paper." The ultimate goal is a work station that provides the physically handicapped user access to the same software available to his or her nonhandicapped counterpart (see Vignette 7–1).

In addition, some form of adaptive access is required for both kinds of writing. Two basic types of adaptive access to computers and word processing are physical accommodations external to the computer that facilitate the use of the standard keyboard and electronically based accomodations that circumvent the standard keyboard by emulating keyboard activity.

The Adaptive Firmware Card, marketed by Adaptive Periphersals, permits different ways of inputting signals that result in keyboard emulation (see Figure 7–1). The Firmware Card is particularly important because it can be used with commercially available off-the-shelf word processing programs.

The *Trine System*, based on the Epson HX-20 computer, is under development at the Trace Center. This system, with its input interface and a variety of output functions, was evaluated as appropriate for some writing activities but inadequate for a number of other (Brandenburg, 1986).

The *Morsewriter*, designed for Morse code entry, (Farr, Hummel, Jadd, & Stein, 1986) has been used successfully for a variety of writing tasks but does not have the editing capability to qualify as a word processing program. Success with current efforts to develop the storage and printing capabilities of the *Morsewriter* will make this system competitive as a writing tool.

Peet (1986) describes an Hawaiian program designed to teach developmentally disabled adults word processing for the workplace. This program provides training in keyboarding, basic word processing, and mailmerge, also known as merge printing for mass mailing. The Hawaiian Developmental Disabilities Council has secured funding to expand this project, with the goal of placing trained developmentally disabled adults in a secretarial pool for word and

VIGNETTE 7-1
Engaging the Disabled Learner

Michael has been disenfranchised for almost all of his school career. He is severely handicapped with cerebral palsy. For the past six months as a student in a neighborhood fourth grade class, he has been using a microelectronic augmentative communication system that affords three levels of communication. The first level is a message system of frequently used brief utterances, some words and phrases, and simple sentences. The second is a simple word processing program, sometimes referred to as a mini word processing program. The third level is a more complex message system that permits the combination of selected messages from a catalog of messages designed for Michael, and the unique text that Michael composes with his mini word processor.

Based largely on his receptive language ability and a gleam in his eye, Michael's parents and some of his teachers were convinced of his cognitive potential. Michael is a nine-year-old, wheelchair-bound quadriplegic with physiologically inadequate speech production mechanisms. Prior to receiving his microelectronic augmentative communication system with synthesized voice and printed output, he had not been able to talk, write, or read. Now he is doing all three.

Michael's expressive communication is bimodal, using synthesized speech and printed hard copy. Some of his "talk/write" communication is dialogue or conversation, some is what most of us would call a written exercise. Both modes can be produced as he composes, or can be saved on disk. He also spends time composing for his dialogue journal. He uses the electronic mail and bulletin board system in his school to deliver messages to other students and teachers in his own and other classrooms. Previously Michael had been disenfranchised and largely disengaged. Now, for the first time, Michael is fully engaged in communication, language, and literacy learning. For the past month Michael has enjoyed communicating with Linda, who, like Michael, recently moved from an east coast beach community on Cape Cod to the Great Plains. Michael and Linda, who is hearing impaired, love to reminisce, and both have learned how to write about sand dunes, surf at high tide, and lobster tails. They have co-authored an essay, "The Surf and Sand," for their school's desktop publication, *Essays about Our Country*.

data processing and other services. These adults are placed according to their skills and are paid for their work.

Visually Impaired Children

The special needs of persons who cannot read 40-column text require some extra attention. As a result, an array of software and hardware for the visually impaired is appearing. The City University of New York, Baruch

FIGURE 7-1. *An adapted keyboard that can be used for word processing: Unicorn Board used with the Adaptive Firmware Card.*

College, resource guide, *Computer Equipment & Aids for the Blind and Visually Impaired* (Gerber, 1985), provides a useful description of these materials. *Addons: The Ultimate Guide to Peripherals for Blind Computer Users* from National Braille Press is a second important source. In addition to the Computer Center for the Blind at Baruch College, there are numerous other centers for the visually impaired across the country. A listing of these centers can be secured from the American Foundation for the Blind (15 West 16th St., New York, NY 10011).

Young readers needing large print may find the 20-column option of *Magic Slate* with a high density printer helpful. The high density printer provides better contrast for easier reading. The large print screens marketed by Visualtek offer another option. This company's large print screens read information from several computers and display it in large type. If enlarged print does not provide the requisite accommodation, the low cost of computers with voice output offers further possibilities for adapting technology to meet individual needs. *Double Touch,* a sub-program of *Dr. Peet's Talk/ Writer* (Hartley), provides a voice synthesized keyboard to assist blind children learning to use word processing.

Word Talk (Computer Aids, Fort Wayne, IN) is a full-feature word processing program that can use a variety of speech synthesizers and computers. Information displayed on the screen and all key presses are simultaneously spoken, with a raised pitch indicating capital letters. The documentation for *Word Talk* is available both in print and on audio cassette and is organized so that it is easy to learn by listening. The publisher claims that the program has been learned by cognitively intact blind children as young as nine years old. One very important feature is that text files composed with *Word Talk* can be used by commercial word processors.

A blind person interested in using the same word processing program as a sighted person could use *Screen Talk*. Using a speech synthesizer, *Screen Talk* reads the screen for a number of commonly used commercial word processing programs that run on IBM PCs. Speech can be turned on and off and set at three rates. Four different speaking modes provide control over the voicing of punctuation and other special characters.

Grade one and two braille translation can be achieved with a variety of computers using Computer Aid's *Braille-Talk*. With a braille printer, a voice synthesizer, and standard text files from popular word processing programs, braille hard copies and voice output can be secured. TSI of Mountain View, California, AVOS of St. Paul, Minnesota, and UTER of Santa Monica, California, all offer interesting and competitive options.

Hearing Impaired Children

Children with hearing problems typically do not have physical limitations in their ability to use word processing systems. However, they often have difficulty learning grammatical syntax and structure. To teach deaf and hearing impaired students to communicate via correct English language forms, teachers at Gallaudet College are using the popular CB (Citizens Band) type telecommunications and a set of microcomputers linked together into what is called a local area network. Each student uses a keyboard to participate in classroom conversation, which is displayed on one large screen. Emphasis is placed on the use of correct grammatical English.

The Department of Communication Arts and Sciences of New York University has been conducting a project based on an appreciation of writing as a way to communicate to actual audiences. Hearing impaired and deaf students have been successful users of this project's systems, which are also available to students with other handicapping conditions. This prototype project, directed by Dr. Doris Niaman and supported by the U.S. Department of Education, uses electronic telecommunication systems provided by General Telephone and Electronics Corporation. These systems include a school bulletin board, which allows students the chance to publicly share the final drafts of their writing; student mailboxes, used by students to privately communicate with other students participating in the project; a research bulletin board, used by participating teachers and project staff to communicate publicly about related questions and comments; and research mailboxes, used by participating teachers and staff to communicate privately. Using these systems, handicapped students are able to use word processing to facilitate communication through writing.

Need for Training in Computer Skills

If special education fails to train handicapped students in real world computer skills, a special-needs student's lack of facility with word processing or with other technology applications may block access to the full complement of life's experiences and opportunities. While there is no evidence that handicapped students have less access overall than their non-handicapped peers, there is reason to believe that they spend relatively more time with drill and practice programs and less time with real world applications such as word processing (Mokros & Russell, 1986). In the NCEP report, *Uses of Computers in Education,* technology experts predict a convergence of telecommunications and the microcomputer, and the emergence of societal demands for "technological literacy," a broader concept than the current dominant notion of computer literacy. They also predict that tool applications software will be increasingly integrated into school programs unless teachers' lack of knowledge and experience blocks that integration into the curriculum.

WORD PROCESSORS TO FACILITATE WRITING

The Nature of Writing

McNutt (1980) describes a holistic, integrated, meaning-centered approach to language arts instruction for special needs students. The approach de-emphasizes the learning of discrete skills in isolation, while emphasizing the importance of deriving and extracting meanings when we listen, talk, read, and write. Graves (1986), whose approach to writing is compatible with the ideas outlined by McNutt, describes writing as a medium through which people communicate with themselves and others. The teaching of writing involves choreographing opportunities to learn, instruction embedded in meaning-centered writing activities, and teacher and student modeling of the process of writing.

The act of writing itself is a complex process of linking ideas to expressive language forms, which can be externalized, or put down on paper. The writing activities of some writers may be accurately characterized as involving linear, though not discrete, stages. For others, writing activities are more correctly described as involving recursive and idiosyncratic processes. Crowley (1977) argues that the work of inexperienced writers can be characterized as linear, with perhaps only two discernible stages, drafting and revision of mechanical errors. Others, following Emig's (1971) discredit of the product approach of writing, have differentiated the writing process into three stages: prewriting and planning, writing, and revision.

Flowers and Hayes (1981) view writing as a complex series of actively employed cognitive processes. They define writing as four basic processes uniquely applied by each writer. These are planning, which involves the organization and production of ideas as well as the setting of goals; translating, which is the changing of thoughts into written language forms; reviewing, which entails evaluation and revision of the written product; and monitoring, which involves keeping track of progress and the use of the three other processes. Each of these processes can be applied at any point, depending on the goals of the writer.

Research seems to indicate that, for some handicapped students, writing is basically linear with very little planning or prewriting. The production of drafts is followed by only limited efforts at revision. For other handicapped students, the Flowers and Hayes notion of unique and varying use of the four cognitive processes may capture the nature of writing. Whether successful writing is done in linear stages or involves the varying applications of four cognitive processes is a function of the student's opportunities to learn to write as well as any relevant emotional, cognitive, or physical limitations. Some handicapped students have difficulty organizing their ideas in a coherent fashion and have problems using the correct language forms. The application of word processing to the needs of handicapped children may help alleviate some of these problems.

Teaching Word Processing

Word processing programs are often used with handicapped students to avoid the difficulty of writing by hand and to take advantage of the easy editing (Degnan & Hummel, 1984). Existing research suggests that students with special needs may need close monitoring and explicit instruction in keyboarding (Neuman & Morocco, 1986). In addition, instruction must also be provided on the use of editing and on other features of word processing programs (MacArthur & Shneiderman, 1986).

Keyboarding

It is unfair to compare students' handwritten products to products composed at the keyboard for those students with decent handwriting skills but poor keyboard skills. Attention must be given to keyboarding so that students move beyond "hunt and peck." However, keyboarding should not be viewed as a prerequisite for the use of word processing, but rather developed along with other composition skills. Neither should teachers assume that keyboard skills are easier to acquire than good handwriting skills (Degan & Hummel, 1984). A small subset of students with fine motor coordination or visual-motor integration problems may have more trouble with keyboarding than with handwriting. Thus, word processing may not be a preferred option for them.

The teaching of keyboarding requires an awareness of the factors affecting the handicapped individual's performance. For example, instructors should be cautious about using typing tutors requiring timed responses. Racing to beat the clock can be very frustrating for anyone, and for the student with visual-motor problems, the pressure of a timed task makes it even more difficult.

A second factor in the teaching of keyboarding is the selection of effective instructional materials. The use of typewriters or simulated keyboards does not seem to be an effective teaching tool because the habit of pressing the return key at the end of a line can be difficult to unlearn. The wraparound function of a word processing program results in a rhythm different from that of a typewriter's required press of the return key.

Neuman and Morocco (1986) recommend avoiding the use of transcription as a tool in teaching keyboarding. This raises the related issue of choosing between transcription keyboarding (in which students are required to both read text and to type) and compostion keyboarding (in which the focus is placed on composing original text at the keyboard). Some students may benefit from the opportunity to become facile with composition keyboarding before they take on the different demands of transcription.

Writing and Editing

Investigation results at the University of Maryland (MacArthur & Shneiderman, 1986) suggests that particular features of word processing programs offer challenges to some students with special needs. Learning to move the cursor on the screen or to use simple commands to insert and delete text may require specific instruction. In addition, understanding the difference between the edit option that results in new text being inserted at a point in the existing text, and the edit option called "overwrite," which writes new text over the existing text, could be difficult for some students. Screen formatting, characters and key presses that are recorded on the screen, and the overall operation of the basic features of the program are other areas that may be difficult to learn.

This research also suggests a number of other word processing features that may present a particular challenge to some students with special needs.

The concepts associated with moving, storing or retrieving files, or moving and deleting blocks of text are difficult ideas to grasp. MacArthur and Shneiderman report observing students who loaded the original copy of the file into the computer, made corrections on the working area file, and again loaded the file from the disk. They thought they were saving the corrected copy when in fact they were erasing the corrected copy with the uncorrected version. Some students may require several explanations of these involved concepts and may need close monitoring as they learn the programs.

Formatting for Printed Text

Daiute's (1986) research with older handicapped writers suggests that reading and editing from the text on the screen may be more demanding than reading and editing from printed hard copies of the file. The physical demands of reading from the screen combined with the conceptual demands described above may be challenging for some handicapped students. A combination of revisions from printed copies and assistance from teachers to edit files may be necessary. In many settings the unfavorable ratio of computers to printers can create a problem for students who need printed copies to revise text.

Some word processing programs do not use a "what you see is what you get" system of displaying and printing text. Special markers and "empty spaces" may appear on the screen that do not show up on the hard copy. For special needs students to use programs in which the screen-displays text is formatted differently than the printed text, instruction in reformatting and "empty space" may be required (MacArthur & Shneiderman, 1986). Special instruction may also be necessary to help students understand that the insert mode enters new spaces and characters by moving the existing text, while an overwrite mode will replace any previously entered material.

As students become more proficient at editing and revising on the screen, the additional skill of reformatting the text for printing may be necessary to keep margins and indentations in the correct position. Although the complexity of this process depends on the software being used, special instruction will be necessary to familiarize students with the formatting capabilities of the programs in use.

Methods of Teaching Writing with Word Processors

Teaching students the mechanics of word processors is only one part of the process of the teaching of writing using word processors. Just as any instruction requires building blocks, facility with a word processor only provides the child with a tool with which to work on higher level skills.

Modeling

Modeling is typically an underutilized teaching technique. Examples of modeling techniques include providing students with a list of five topics of interest; discussing goals and means for monitoring achievement towards goals; allowing students to observe the creation of a composition via a large monitor with good resolution, while explaining the connection between thoughts and key words; and revising the draft text, with explanations. Depending on student reading levels, word processing programs can be used to compose the text and to include comments about drafting and revising in the margins. Classroom peers could, in the same fashion, illustrate progress through these stages (Sommers, 1985).

Assessment

In addition to modeling writing activities, it is important to assess the writing abilities of students. One method of assessment is an en vivo assessment, which includes observing students as they write and collecting samples of the students' writing under different conditions. These forms of writing include: expository, persuasive, expressive, narrative, poetry, and letter writing (Temple & Gillet, 1984).

Cartwright (1978) provides instructive guidelines for this kind of informal assessment. Informal assessment of features of students' writing samples, when complemented by information gathered from interviewing students as they write, provides useful direction for the development of a writing program. It is also useful to compare writing samples produced with a word processing program and teacher guidance to writing samples prepared with pencil and paper. With teacher guidance and a well-matched word processing program, most students do write better (Hummel & Rosegrant, 1986). This alone does not make a case for using a suitable word processing program, but suggests that handicapped students should be given this opportunity before conclusions are drawn about writing ability.

Prewriting

Many students, at first, have very little to write about. Expressive writing is often the easiest form of writing for these students. Drawing up lists of experiences and interest areas, coupled with a few phrases or key words, can be most helpful.

Lists of possible topics can be generated with the aid of prewrite computer programs or integrated packages that have compatible word processing and data base management files, such as *Appleworks*. Strickland (1985) points out that a good prewrite computer program is truly interactive, responding to the user and making the user feel in control. The prewrite program should help children identify what they already know, and not control their options. Computer-based prewrite programs can simulate some of the things that good teachers do in writing conferences. They can direct thinking, provide examples, suggest strategies, and be an imaginary audience. Computer-based prewrite programs can provide a catalogue of writing strategies and cues to particular prewrite strategies such as: "give it to me in a nutshell," wh-questions, brainstorming, or "picture the scene in your mind." Access to various strategies can encourage the user to try a number of options. Strickland (1985) describes a number of prewrite programs, most of which are designed for relatively able readers and writers.

Writing a Narrative (MECC) is appropriate for a secondary resource room (Hummel, 1985a). A particularly useful strategy included in this program is the presentation of open-ended questions designed to stimulate the student's own ideas and provide a framework for a narrative. The user writes a word or phrase about a few experiences, then chooses to describe one of these experiences by answering "who, what, and where" questions. *Quill* approaches writing in two ways. It encourages the teacher to work with the student to prepare writing planners, by first working with a group of students to establish lists of topics, and then generating questions for those topics (Hummel, 1985b). *Essaywriter* is a word processing program that provides guidance for prewriting, drafting, and revision. While prewrite programs may be able to simulate some of the facilitating strategies of writing conferences, they are no substitute for the conferences themselves.

Teacher–Student Conferences

An increasing number of authorities on writing suggest that individual teacher–student writing conferencing is the most effective approach to writing instruction (Carnicelli, 1980; Garrison, 1981). Sommers (1985) argues that teachers need to understand the individual's progress and provide feedback during writing activities. Newman and Morocco (1961), of the Educational Development Center in Newton, Massachusetts, highlight what they call the "accessibility" feature of word processing, discussing the importance of accessibility for writing conferences. They formulated this insight as a result of their two-year study of learning disabled students using word processing programs in writing instruction. Teachers and students taking turns at the keyboard, with the teacher entering prewrite kinds of questions, and teacher conferencing, are among these techniques.

Some important guidelines for teacher student conferences (Neuman & Morocco, 1985) include having the teacher:

- Reread, or have a student reread, the text to maintain or regain students' involvement
- Suggest ways to expand the child's text

- Engage the student in conversation about the topic
- Provide oral strategies for elaboration, such as "Pretend you are talking to somebody"
- Provide cognitive strategies for elaboration, such as, "Close your eyes and picture the scene," or "Draw a map of the scene or a picture of some part of it"
- Request that the student enter their own comments
- Help the student get focused
- Simulate audience response to the student's writing
- Foster the student's self-concept as a writer.

It is likely that such strategies will work with a broad set of handicapped students. They also express concern about teacher critiques of student writing. The teacher may be tempted to take too much control of content, or look for correct mechanics prematurely, being too concerned with the text looking nice. Additional areas of concern include the possibility that the more public nature of the text may inhibit writing that students want to keep private. A student may not want "faulty" writing, or the content of the text, accessible to others.

Feedback to Students

As teachers design environments for writing they should establish what Graves (1986) calls a community of learners. In addition to a priority on effective communication, the teacher should establish routines for writing and predictable patterns of feedback and direction. Purposeful, meaning-centered writing can include responsive teaching and incidental learning. As students are involved in their writing efforts to derive and relate meanings, the teacher provides instruction responsive to the students' needs as they emerge. Neuman and Morocco (1985) stress the point that the editing feature of word processing programs can result in a poorly timed emphasis on correcting mechanical errors.

Teacher-imposed emphasis on the correction of mechanical errors can interfere with the student's effort to develop ideas in writing. However, the teacher should be available to use minimal cueing when handicapped students get stuck attempting to develop their ideas or when trying to correct surface errors. With minimal cueing for surface errors, teachers ask students if they know how to change the surface problems and then provide some reminders of prior related instruction. The teacher then makes a decision whether to tell the student how to make the correction and then go back to developing the ideas, or to provide some incidental direct instruction on the spelling or grammar errors.

Spelling checkers can be used quite effectively in providing student feedback. These programs check the spellings of all the words in the text against their built-in electronic dictionaries. The spelling checker finds "suspected misspellings," which include typos, actual misspellings, and any word not in the electronic dictionary, such as proper nouns. They may also provide a list of correctly spelled alternatives. If students know the meaning of the word and can learn correct spellings by selecting them from a list of possibilities presented by the spelling checker, then the use of spelling checkers is instructive. The often-included feature of printed lists of misspellings and corrected spellings can provide the teacher with a useful record of student errors. A review of *Sensible Speller* (Hummel, 1985b) concluded that it is difficult to make any generalization as to whether using a print dictionary is more instructive than using a spelling checker.

Additional Applications of Word Processing

An appreciation of the importance of audience is reflected in enhanced software packages that include word processing capabilities and message delivery systems. This appreciation is also reflected in the entire desktop publishing movement. Once students have basic skills in writing and in use of word processing, there are a number of related computer activities to expand classroom applications of writing with computers. Integrated software combines word processing with other productivity tools and telecommunications. Desktop publishing provides students with combined graphics and text to express their ideas.

Integrated Packages

An integrated package may provide the incentive for students to use their word processing and writing skills for tasks other than those related to completing writing assignments. Through a combination of programs, computer applications may be expanded. Apple's *Appleworks* and IBM's *Assistant Series* combine productivity tools such as word processing, data base managers, spreadsheets, and graphics. Students can manipulate data and write reports using a single software package.

Quill is an example of an integrated word processing package with built-in features for publishing and telecommunications. The *Quill* package contains four programs: *Planner, Writer's Assistant, Library,* and *Mailbag.*

The *Planner* is a prewriting software package designed to assist users in developing written communication that can then be elaborated on by using *Writer's Assistant,* the word processing editor.

Mailbag allows for direct communication between individuals in the classroom, combining features of a post office, telephone, and bulletin board. Written messages can be exchanged between individuals, or posted for the group. *Mailbag* may enhance writing instruction by fostering written communication to real and varying audiences (i.e., friends, classmates, and teachers) and by providing additional incentive to write by personalizing the experience.

The *Library* creates an opportunity for students to share text. Writing is saved and stored with a simple data base program that records the author's name, title, and topic. At the election of the student authors, writing is entered and cataloged using the data base program, and can then be accessed by teachers and other students. In providing access to stored pieces of writing, *Quill* can create a communication environment that encourages students to write for others.

Desktop Publishing

Writing for others very often incorporates the publication of newsletters, journals, poetry, banners, and cards. *Printshop* and *Newsroom* are two very popular software packages that use a combination of menus and templates for the production of simple published materials incorporating both text and graphics. While viewed as limiting by some who have used far more elaborate systems, creative teachers have produced interesting projects, such as school newsletters and posters, with special needs students.

A growing number of schools are becoming equipped to do desktop publishing. Desktop publishing permits the production of text and graphics that approximate professional quality, using more powerful computers such as Apple Macintosh or IBM with laser printers. Digitized graphics, different sized and shaped fonts, as well as blocked, shadowed, italicized, and underlined text can be created with a reasonable amount of effort from teachers and talented students. It is likely that handicapped students will need some assistance in the selection of the various options; however, desktop publishing offers exciting possibilities for all students, and is a real world application of computers.

WORD PROCESSING SOFTWARE AS A TOOL TO AID THE SPECIAL EDUCATOR

Applications for Teachers

As teachers become more facile with word processing, they are likely to become more comfortable with other active, creative computer applications and may be more inclined to view the computer as an ally, rather than an adversary. At the same time, however, teachers may not have the time or may not want the challenge of learning more than one sophisticated word processing program. Therefore, the following simple six-step process to select appropriate software may be helpful:

- Define goals for using a word processor
- Determine whether existing hardware decisions will control selection of a word processing program, or whether there is flexibility to make software and hardware decisions at the same time
- Learn about capabilities of various software programs (e.g., costs, backup and licensing policies)
- Test a number of software packages before making a selection
- Begin with a pilot implementation of the selected program and reevaluate it before use is so extensive that it becomes almost impossible to change
- Stay abreast of new developments, remaining aware of the possibility of changing your selection decision.

Buyer's guides, such as the one offered by Heintz (1982), can also be very helpful. In addition, there can be reciprocal and cumulative benefits for teachers learning how to use word processing programs as a tool to prepare form letters and exercises for students. With their use of word processing programs as a tool, they are modeling the real world use of computers for their students. Teachers may also become better able to teach their students about the computer as an aid in the reduction of labor in various tasks. Finally, any increased practical knowledge of word processing programs may also complement their attempts to use these programs in their writing instruction.

Parent Communication

Word processing software can be used as a tool to help the special educator respond to all the information exchange requirements of their state regulations (Hummel & Archer, 1987). Existing regulations require a variety of formal communications that can be handled by form letters. Rather than the unpolished look resulting from a stencil or photocopy, sophisticated word processing programs produce a professional quality letter, letting the user enter information into a template that has been prepared by the word processor. A template is nothing more than an electronically stored form. With some word processing programs, this form is brought onto the screen, and the information is entered by keyboard. The results can then be printed. Figure 7–2 illustrates a template of a letter for parents.

Some word processing programs, such as *Wordstar* (Micropro), allow fast and efficient production of these letters. Others, such as *Displaywrite* (IBM) and *Appleworks* (Apple) require that user to first place markers in the form or template, and then enter the pertinent items for each student. With *Displaywrite* the template of the letter is on the screen. By entering a simple command that finds the markers in the letter as they appear, the user can

1987
1 Main Street
Office of Special Education
Your School
Your Town, USA

Re: The Committee on the Handicapped action on your child

Dear: []

At the 1987 meeting of the Committee on the Handicapped, the Committee recommended that your child be classified as [] and be placed in the [] program. Your child's teacher will be []. Your child's first day in this placement will be [].

We hope that the recommendations are satisfactory and the information in this letter is clear to you. You have the right to further discussions if you are dissatisfied with the recommendations, or confused about any of the information. It is your right to state any such dissatisfaction within 20 days of the date on this letter.

If you have any questions, please contact me at my office number.

Sincerely,

Chair of the Committee on the Handicapped

FIGURE 7-2. *A template of a letter for parents.*

then enter the items for each student. With simple commands the user saves a copy of the completed letter, sends one to the printer, and moves back to the template to begin the next letter. With *Appleworks*, portions of the letter are printed as they are completed. The disadvantage of *Appleworks* is that completed copies of each student's letters cannot be saved. Permanent hard copies could be made by using carbons.

Individual Education Plans (IEPs)

The development of Individual Education Plans (IEPs) is a key require-ment of state and federal regulations. Commercial computer programs pri-marily using a sophisticated data base management system have been designed to assist teachers in the development of IEPs. Some word process-ing programs, however, offer advantages over commercial IEP programs (Hummel & Degnan, 1986; Jenkins, 1986). Jenkins argues against the use of virtually all commercial computer programs that help the teacher write IEPs due to the high cost of most commercial IEP packages. Not only are some of these programs quite expensive, they can be difficult to learn and often can-not be adapted to local needs.

Jenkins describes an alternate approach that uses the word processor program *Word Handler* (Silicon Valley). In this approach, the word process-ing program has been used to prepare a special data disk, referred to as the "IEP Writer." Teachers use *Word Handler* and this special disk to write their own IEPs. Advantages of this approach include the ability to customize ob-jectives in response to individual needs and the ability to store those objec-tives. In addition, *Word Handler* has the ability to act as a simple data base program. The user must have files of IEP objectives on their special data disk. The teacher either enters original IEP objectives or uses a shared pool of objectives. With the *Word Handler*-based approach, the teacher can then "call up" objectives from these files, as lines or groups of lines, individu-ally, or in sets.

Hummel and Degnan's (1986) approach uses the word processing pro-gram and the data base management program of the integrated tool pro-gram, *Appleworks*. It is similar to the one based on *Word Handler*. *Apple-works* is used to prepare data disks of IEP objectives that can be customized. Developing IEPs with a sophisticated word processor should be viewed as a competitive and possibly more individualized alternative to commercially available IEP packages. Some computer-assisted approaches to IEPs may serve administrative purposes, but be of little help to teachers. It seems clear that one distinct advantage of using the word processor approach is the benefit of becoming familiar with a sophisticated program, as opposed to learning how to use a commercial package with IEP development as its only use (see Vignette 7–2). Teachers trained to use *Appleworks* for IEP develop-ment are pleased with their working knowledge of *Appleworks*, which en-ables them to use it for other purposes (Hummel & Degnan, 1986).

Creating Classroom Materials

Tamm (1985) has written (and desktop published) a 179-page book to illustrate how *Appleworks* can be used by teachers for a variety of purposes, including generating exercises, reading materials, study guides, tests and

---

VIGNETTE 7-2
Word Processing For Teachers

Standing in the hallway outside his resource room, Richard Johnson chats with Karen Peres, who has just completed a late August in-service course titled "Word Processing Can Lighten the Paper Burden." As he listens to her enthusiastic review of the highlights of that in-service course, he looks into his room and his eye catches the shelves of file folders in total disarray. He absorbs part of what she is saying, but thinks that Karen understands it all because she has a background in data processing. He thinks that learning to use a computer would be all new for him, and would simply take too much time. It is September 1 and all the students will be on the scene in four days, including five new students from out of state who have just been placed in his program, since the August meeting of the Committee on the Handicapped. These students do not yet have IEPs, and he has had no contact with their parents. He wonders what happened to his plans to be organized by now.

All of his mildly handicapped students, who are mainstreamed in third, fourth, or fifth grade social studies classes, will experience the changes in the social studies curriculum set for this year, including the new text. Plus, the fifth graders have to prepare for the writing competency test for the first time this year, and the spelling program for all third graders is different. He wonders again where his plans to be organized went to.

He hears Karen's enthusiasm, and asks her if she knows of any plans to repeat the course. She says that the course is scheduled for October, adding, "If I can learn it, you can learn it." She tells him that word processing software can help him with the preparation of IEPs, with parental communication, and with the development of instructional materials. She invites him to see some of the form letters and exercises she created in the in-service course.

---

worksheets. Other word processing programs could just as easily be used. The beauty of developing activities such as these on a word processor, instead of on a typewriter, is the ease of modification. Classroom exercises can be constructed with templates, which can be used and redesigned easily to fit content to the assignment. They can then be duplicated and passed out to students.

Hummel and Balcom (1984) illustrate how the "replace function" of many word processing programs can be used to generate vocabulary exercises. Portions of text can be substituted for other text, and students can determine the implications for the overall meaning of a passage after such changes are made. Alternate forms of reading materials can be prepared, making adjustments on readability and vocabulary level. Currently available readability software has some important shortfalls, but improvements in this type of software appear to be forthcoming. For persons interested in the ways that computers can be used in reading instruction, Geoffrion and Geoffrion (1983) provide useful ideas.

Appleworks and other word processing programs also afford some creative opportunities for teachers who are intrigued by computers and word processing programs to assist in the classroom organization and management. Tamm (1985) describes and illustrates a seating chart template, a sign-out sheet template, and one that serves as an assignment calendar.

Tamm also highlights the importance of formatting the text material when constructing any exercise or template. He recommends using all of the standard formatting parameters, including page width and length, and the four standard margins. However, when constructing an exercise as opposed to a template or form, it is often desirable to have more space than the standard margins permit, making the side margins less than one inch, or the bottom margin less than two inches, in order to increase the content or make the format more attractive. Similarly, the actual working space of the document may need to be smaller. It is crucial to remember to save the formatted document. Otherwise, the next time it is called up from the disk, the standard parameters will be applied, and the document will be re-arranged within them.

Testing

It is also possible to construct a standard format for a test or review by constructing a template that can be used over and over again. The typical exercise will have a standard heading and standard directions for different types of questions or tasks. Matching, fill-in-the-blank, true-false, multiple choice, and essay questions each have a specific format and standard directions. The headings and directions are entered into the template to look something like the test template in Figure 7–3. Components not needed can be deleted as the exam is constructed. Before saving this document, which will be printed and given to students, the new document must be renamed. If it is saved without renaming, this just-created exercise will replace the template. Retain the template with its original name, and give this exercise a meaningful title.

If budget permits, it is possible to purchase test making software such as *Quizmaster,* which has been used successfully in the field (Hummel, et al., 1985). Other test software is described in a recent article by Lodish (1986). Most of these test maker programs are templates that can be "filled in" by the teacher, and have nice features such as the randomizing of questions and items for matching exerciese.

Your Middle School Resource Room
American History — Review Exercise

Chapter

Matching Exercises

Your name_____

The date_____

Your American history teacher's name_____

At the right you see numbered descriptions.

At the left you see names, each with its own letter.

Pick the description at the right that most closely matches a name at the left.

Write the name that most closely matches the description in the space next to the description.

This is a required review exercise.

It must be handed in.

_____

_____

Your Middle School Resource Room
American History — Review Exercises

Chapter

Placing Events in the Correct Order

Your name_____

The date_____

Your American history teacher's name_____

Below you see pairs of events in American History

You are to decide which event in each pair happened first.

Put a "1" next to that event.

Remember there should be a "1" next to the first event in each pair.

The results of this exercise will count toward your grade.

_____

_____

FIGURE 7–3. *Template for matching and ordering exercises.*

SUMMARY

Word processing is a productivity tool that can assist students in computer assisted learning and teachers in computer assisted instruction and computer managed instruction. This chapter described only a few applications and approaches to using word processing to assist in a better education for handicapped children. Word processing can serve handicapped children by providing them with a tool that will enable them to be more fully integrated into today's society. The applications of word processing in educational environments are nearly endless and are limited only by the vision and creativity of the teachers and children who use this powerful tool.

REFERENCES AND SELECTED READINGS

Barenbaum, E. M. (1983). Writing in special classes. *Topics in Learning and Learning Disabilities, 3*(3), 12–20.

Brandenburg, S. A. (1986). Conversation, writing, computer access: Meeting the needs of individuals with physical disabilities. In M. Gergen (Ed.), *Computer Technology for the handicapped: Applications '85* (pp. 31–39). Henderson, MN: Closing the Gap.

Carnicelli, R. M. (1980). The writing conference: A one-to-one conversation. In T. Donovan & B. McClelland (Eds.), *Eight approaches to teaching composition* (pp. 101–131. Urbana, IL: National Council of Teachers of English.

Cartright, G. P. (1978). Written expression and spelling. In R. M. Smith (Ed.), *Teacher diagnosis of educational difficulties* (pp. 95–117). Columbus, OH: Charles E. Merrill.

Crowley, S. (1977). Components of the composing process. *College Composition and Communication, 28,* 166–169.

Daiute, C. (1986). Physical and cognitive factors in revising: Insights from studies with computers. *Research in the Teaching of English, 20*(2), 141–159.

Degnam, S. C., & Hummel, J. W. (1984). Word processing for special education students: Worth the effort. *The Journal: Technology Horizons in Education, 12*(6), 80–82.

Education Turnkey Systems. (1985). *Uses of computers in education* (Research rep. No. 7). Washington, DC: National Commission on Employment Policy.

Emig, J. (1971). *The composing process of twelfth graders.* Urbana, IL: National Council of Teachers of English.

Farr, S. D., Hummel, J. W., Jadd, E., & Stein, R. J. (1986). The development and educational application of a communications prosthesis for severely involved children. In M. Gergen (Ed.), *Computer technology for the handicapped: Applications '85.* Henderson, MN: Closing the Gap.

Flowers, L., & Hayes, J. R. (1981). A cognitive process theory of writing. *College Composition and Communication, 32,* 365–387.

Garrison, R. (1981). *How a writer writes.* New York: Harper and Row.

Gerber, J. (1985). *Computer equipment and aids for the blind and visually impaired: A resource guide 1985.* New York: CCVI Publishing.

Geoffrion, L. D., & Geoffrion, O. P. (1983). *Computers and reading instruction.* Reading, MA: Addison-Wesley.

Graves, D. H. (1986). All children can write. *Learning Disabilities Focus, 1*(1), 36–43.

Heintz, C. (1982, December). Buyer's guide to word processing software. *Interface Age,* pp. 19–25.

Hummel, J. (1985a). Courseware review: Writing a narrative. *Journal of Learning Disabilities, 18,* 119–120.

Hummel, J. (1985b). Word processing and word processing related software for the learning disabled. *Journal of Learning Disabilities, 18,* 559–562.

Hummel, J. W. (1986). The microcomputer: An opportunity to re-engage students with learning disabilites. Manuscript submitted for publication.

Hummel, J. W., & Archer, P. (1987). Implementing the computer concept. In J. Lindsley (Ed.), *Computers and exceptional individuals* (pp. 207–228). Columbus, OH: Charles E. Merrill.

Hummel, J. W., & Balcom, F. W. (1984). Computers: Not just a place for practice. *Journal of Learning Disabilities, 17,* 432–434.

Hummel, J. W., & Degnan, S. (1986). Options for technology-assisted IEPs. *Journal of Learning Disabilities, 19,* 529–536.

Hummel, J. W., Mather, N., & Senf, G. M. (Eds.). (1985). *Microcomputers in the classroom: Courseware reviews.* New York: Professional Press.

Hummel, J. W., & Rosegrant, T. (1986, March). *Using microcomputers to alter learning behaviors of children with learning disabilities in order to facilitate reading and writing.* Association for Children and Adults with Learning Disabilities International Conference, New York.

Jenkins, M. W. (1986). A new way of doing IEPs — Kill two birds with one stone. In M. Gergen (Ed.), *Computer technology for the handicapped: Applications '85* (pp. 286–288). Henderson, MN: Closing the Gap.

Lodish, E. (1986). Test writing made simple. *ELectronic Learning,* pp. 68.

MacArthur, C. A., & Shneiderman, B. (1986). Learning disabled students' difficulties in learning to use a word processor: Implications for instruction and software evaluation. *Journal of Learning Disabilities, 19,* 248–253.

McNutt, G. (1980). Perspectives on reading, language arts, and learning disabilities. *Learning Disabilities Quarterly, 3*(4), 3–9.

Morocco, C. C., & Neuman, S. B. (1986). Word processing and the acquisition of writing strategies. *Journal of Learning Disabilities, 19*(4), 243–247.

Mokros, J., & Russell, S. (1986). Survey of microcomputer application used with the handicapped. *Journal of Learning Disabilities, 19,* 150–159.

National Institute for Work and Learning. (1985). *Training for work in the computer age.* Washington, DC: National Commission for Employment Policy.

Neuman, S. B., & Morocco, C. C. (1985). *A model teaching environment for using word processors with LD children.* (Tech. rep. No. 2). Newton, MA: Education Development Center.

Neuman, S. B., & Morocco, C. C. (1986). *Two hands is hard for me: Keyboarding and learning disabled children.* Manuscript submitted for publication.

Palloway, E. A., Patton, J. R., & Cohen, S. B. (1981). Written language for mildly handicapped students. *Focus on Exceptional Students, 14,* 1–14.

Peet, W. (1986). Training the disabled young adult to word process competitively. In M. Gergen (Ed.), *Computer technology for the handicapped: Applications '85* (pp. 31–36). Henderson, MN: Closing the Gap.

Roit, M. L., & McKenzie, R. G. (1985). Disorders of written communication: An instructional priority for LD students. *Journal of Learning Disabilities, 18,* 258–260.

Rosegrant, T. (1985a). Using a microcomputer as a tool for learning to read and write. *Journal of Learning Disabilities, 18,* 113–115.

Rosegrant, T. (1985b, April). *Using a microcomputer to assist children in their efforts to acquire beginning literacy.* Paper presented at the American Educational Research Association Convention, Chicago, IL.

Sommers, E. A. (1985). Integrating composing and computing. In J. L. Collins & E. A. Sommers (Eds.), *Writing on-line: Using computers in the teaching of writing* (pp. 3–10). Upper Montclair, NJ: Boynton/Cook Publishers.

Strickland, J. (1985). Prewriting and computing. In J. L. Collins & E. A. Sommers (Eds.), *Writing on-line: Using computers in the teaching of writing* (pp. 67–74). Upper Montclair, NJ: Boyton/Cook Publishers.

Tamm, R. W. (1985). *Applying Appleworks.* New Hartford, NY: Bristen Press.

Temple, C., & Gillet, J. W. (1984). *Language arts: Learning processes and teaching practices.* Boston, MA: Little, Brown and Company.

Williams, S., & Blauser, D. (1986). Word processing using Magic Slate. In M. Gergen (Ed.), *Computer technology for the handicapped: Applications '85* (pp. 147–149). Henderson, MN: Closing the Gap.

CHAPTER 8

Electronic Spreadsheets and Data Base Management

CARL T. CAMERON
KATHY HURLEY
KATE WHOLEY

A s the availability of microcomputer hardware and software expands in the classroom, teachers appear to develop skills and interests in pursuing new hardware and software options, particularly for students who find it challenging to learn. One priority for teachers is the use of software that will allow individualization of instruction for a variety of student needs. Initially, the software that appeared to have the most promise for individualizing was authoring systems; however their relative complexity and the time required to learn them, have resulted in limited use by classroom teachers. In their place, software known as "productivity tools" has provided expanded options for developing customized instructional activities. Productivity tools are usually described as word processors, spreadsheets, data bases, graphic packages, printing and publishing, shells, authoring systems, and communication packages (Cameron, 1987). In this chapter, the focus will be on the use of data bases and spreadsheets, with specific information of how these tools can be used with disabled students.

PRODUCTIVITY TOOLS

Principals and teachers first introduced productivity tools to education for their own use in the planning and management of their schools, but classroom teachers have also discovered their usefulness in the instructional process. The use of these tools in the classroom is a relatively new focus for educators, even those who have been at the forefront of technological usage. There are a number of reasons why productivity tools are gaining popularity in classrooms.

First, the cost of conventional educational software, although not high in comparison to most other software, has been prohibitive for many states and school districts. Because of the cost, teachers are looking for software that can be easily adapted for a wide variety of uses and situations. Unless budgets for instructional software expand rapidly, productivity tool software will be found increasingly attractive. Rather than a single program that teaches students elements of the chemical chart or capitals of the 50 states, tool software, easily learned and customized for many purposes, allows instructors to provide a wide variety of instructional applications for acquisition and processing of both specific lesson content and cognitive skills.

Second, advancements in microchip technology that have boosted the capacity of the personal computer's memory have increased the usefulness and flexibility of the personal computer in virtually all areas. By allowing software, regardless of type, to contain more information, the computer becomes a more sophisticated and versatile tool. In a nutshell, it gives the use of computers a more exciting and realistic flavor.

Third, the recent trend in the "applied philosophy" of educators across the country of the purpose of teaching — to provide students with skills that allow direct application of knowledge to solve real world problems — has increased the use of microcomputers in the classroom.

Finally, educators realized that they have barely tapped the potential of the computer in the classroom, and have become fully aware of the challenge made to the profession to provide more appropriate instruction to a more diverse population of the disabled, limited-English-proficient and other students who find it difficult to learn. (See Figure 8–1 the terminology associated with productivity tools.)

The use of productivity tool software such as data bases and spreadsheets provides an opportunity for linking software use in school with the specific needs of our information age society. It may, however, serve another key role in the education of students who find it difficult to learn, our nation's more than four million students in special education. While much research needs to be done, it is apparent that the use of productivity tools to organize and retrieve information in an appropriate manner may very well make a major difference for handicapped students who need assistance in organizing, synthesizing, and using information in making personal and vocational decisions. In fact, the two most important uses of productivity tools will be the ability to transfer the computer literacy skills into appropriate employment and community living, and the ability to "break the code" for appropriate decision making.

Productivity Tools: Software designed to provide the structure for the completion of functional and specific communication tasks.

Spreadsheet: A productivity tool that provides a quick and diversified electronic ledger for accounting and record-keeping.

Data Base: A productivity tool that provides an electronic filing and retrieval system.

Integrated Packages: Software that combines and shares two or more types of productivity tools.

Template: A software file that is used to provide a format for use of a productivity tool for a specific application, such as a report that has standard categories.

FIGURE 8-1. *Productivity tool terminology.*

Living in the Information Age

The technology explosion during the last few years has revolutionized the way we live our lives, run our households, drive our cars, do our jobs, and even how we play. There is no doubt that we are in the process of moving our economy from providing goods and services to one that focuses on the developing, monitoring and retrieval of information. Currently there are few (if any) occupational areas that have not been drastically changed by the availability of low-cost and powerful microcomputer hardware and software. The building custodian, the auto mechanic, the teacher, and the accountant have all integrated productivity tools into their workplace. In fact, many occupational areas consider the use of productivity tools to be an entry requirement for employment.

Breaking the Code

In addition to providing skills that transfer from school to community, productivity tools have been used to assist students in examining the relationships among concepts, language, and mathematical symbols. Although research is still fragmented and scarce, it appears that using the microcomputer to model the process of sorting by relationships, calculating relatively large amounts of numbers and managing information easily, has provided significant support for students who cannot process this information effectively, if at all. Productivity tool software allows teachers to create lessons that create an environment for children to pose questions and quickly determine answers. It allows them to produce lists and organized reports in addition to singular answers, as it shifts a student's focus from the drudgery of locating, sorting, and calculating to the excitement of asking questions and obtaining and studying results.

Rationale for Use with Handicapped Students

When making the decision to invest the time and energy in using data bases and spreadsheets for instruction, it is important to determine what benefits will be derived from their use. Although there is a real lack of evaluation research related to the most effective use of productivity tools, the following benefits are often reported:

- Discovering commonalities and differences among groups of events and things
- Analyzing relationships
- Looking for trends
- Testing and refining hypotheses
- Organizing and sharing information
- Keeping information up to date
- Arranging information in more useful ways

DATA BASES

Basically, a data base is a storage system — very compact, very flexible — but a storage system nevertheless. They are most useful when one has a lot of information on one topic, hence they lend themselves well to scientific research, keeping recipes on a countertop computer, or storing attendance data in a school system.

Data bases have a wide range of applications, and as one might surmise, a wide range in levels of sophistication. Some of the most basic data bases allow a very limited number of fields (or data items), a limited number of fields in a record, and may also limit how the information can be sorted and retrieved. For example, some of the most basic data bases only allow sorting by one field, such as student number or last name. On the other hand, more sophisticated (and powerful) data bases like *dBaseIII* (Ashton–Tate) and *R:base System V* (Microrim) provide for creation of an almost unlimited number of fields and records and allow the user to create a large number of search routines, data entry screens, and report formats. In addition, these sophisticated programs also provide for user-friendly menus, ease of programming, and the ability to simultaneously search information that may be located in more than one file (called a relational data base).

The development of the data base concept originated in the government, businesses, and industry, which had critical needs to manage very large amounts of information like billing, making payments, locating clients, and examining personal histories. All data bases were originally designed to run on large mainframe machines, and were not considered practical for microcomputer use. With the advent of high-powered memory in microcomputers, a wide variety of data base applications opened up for home, business, and educational use. Not only were these traditional systems made more accessible, but new programs such as *PFS File* (Software Publishing Corporation) and *dBaseIII* (Ashton–Tate) became easier and easier to use. Data bases differ in their capacity, speed, and versatility, but their common features remain. A data base program is designed to provide both input and output control; typical options include the ability to modify the way information is entered, where the information comes from, and a wide variety of output options, like labels, reports and mailing programs. As a result, data bases are now one of the fastest selling software applications for personal, professional, and educational use.

To review the basic terminology used by data base management systems, we can choose an information base as an example and work backwards. For instance, suppose we decided to develop a data base of special education materials, encompassing a wide variety of instructional levels, content areas, media types, and publishers. In addition, there is a variety of ways that a teacher might want to locate materials: by name, by publisher, by media type, by activity, or by content area. In this example, the *file* will be the listing of all the instructional materials. Each specific material that is listed is a *record*. Each record contains a number of different types of information, each called a *field*. (See Figures 8–2 & 8–3.) For example, the fields may be designed to hold information on names of the materials, publishers name, type of media, cost, content area, relationship to assessment instruments, and many possible others.

When the actual information is entered, like Mindscape for the publisher's name (field), this is called a *data item*. If this data base is a relational one, then you could also select information from another file, like a name and address file for publishers that would allow Mindscape's address and phone to be retrieved whenever a Mindscape product is selected.

The organization of fields within the data base is called the *structure* of the data base. In some basic programs, organization of the fields may determine how you retrieve data. In the less flexible programs, the user is allowered to mark (sometimes referred to as the "index," or "key word") one or more fields for retrieval and to sort in a hierarchical manner the data contained in the fields. In still other data bases, all fields can be used for sorting and retrieving.

File: A collection of entries with the same categories of information such as student records, instructional materials or lessons.

Record: Information on one student, one piece of instructional material, or lesson.

Field: One space where information is to be stored in a record, such as a name, address or date of birth.

Data Item: Information that is to be entered for each field such as John Q. Public (for a student's name field), SRA Reading Series (for an instructional material field), or measuring to the closest inch (for a lesson field).

Relational Data Base: A data base that can locate information from more than one file at a time. For example, retrieving a name and address from one file, and that person's appointment record from another file, to merge into a summary statement.

FIGURE 8-2. *Data base terminology.*

Record No: 1

Instructional Material Name: Making Sense of Relationships

Publisher: Macro Press

Date: 1986

Instructional Content: Social Skills

Target Audience: Adolescent Mildly Handicapped

Cost: $49.95

Availability: Resource Room

FIGURE 8-3. *Data base record example.*

Using a Data Base

The use of a data base involves several steps that are relatively consistent, regardless of the data base software selected. The steps include creating a file, entering data, and displaying data.

Creating a File

Once you have made a decision on the type of information that you want to store, you need to create a file, which is a set of individual records. You are designing the record format at this point. Each item of information that you want to include in this file will become a field (See Figure 8–4). For instance, the student records file would have records each of which contained a field for the name of the student.

Entering Data

When you have designed your data base record format, you are then ready to load information into your file. Most data bases have a menu that provides a choice of activities, one of which is entering data. If you select this option, a blank format screen will appear that will allow you to enter each individual data item. When you have entered data for each field, the software will store your information and produce a new format with which to enter the next record. This sequence will continue until you decide to quit. In addition to entering new records, you will also have the option of updating existing records. Most programs allow you a variety of ways to search for the record you want to update, by a field name, or by record number.

Record No:

Name:

Address:

City:

State:

Zip Code:

Phone:

FIGURE 8–4. *Record format.*

Displaying Data

Once you have a series of records loaded into your file, you can retrieve your information in a variety of ways. You may want to look at a particular record, or print a copy of that record. More than likely, you will want to sort the records in order to obtain a list or other display of records with certain common characteristics. Most software includes some standard display formats, such as mailing labels, lists, or other standard options, and also allows you to develop a customized display of your data, such as a report, invoice, list of courses taken, or paychecks. Figure 8–5 depicts a typical listing of records.

Using Data Bases in Instruction

Many of the skills that come into play while working with data bases are useful for providing experiences for students (and in particular, handicapped students) to move from a concrete level of understanding to understanding symbolic and abstract representations of reality. Students may learn to classify appropriately, and develop skills in observation and discrimination. For example, with distinct data base categories before them, children must decide where the information belongs. In labelling things and grouping them into meaningful categories, the students find similarities among the isolated pieces of data. This similarity finding can lead to generalizing and inferring by students, making a leap beyond what is know by guessing, and to increasingly valid generalizations. This ability to analyze and synthesize data into comprehensible patterns is fundamental to more complex problem-solving. Some of the skills that are introduced and refined using data bases follow.

Instructional Material	Publisher	Date
[ ]	[ ]	[ ]
★★
Making Sense of Relationships	Macro Press	1986
Using the Bank	Motorcity Press	1983
Writing to Read	IBM	1985

FIGURE 8–5. *Listing of data base records.*

Discovering Commonalities (and Differences) Among Records in a File

This skill refers to comparing the contents of several records and noticing what they have in common. Examples of this skill include noticing that scales are attributes of both fish and reptiles, or that different chemical compounds are composed of the same elements, or that certain plants are indigenous to several countries. Such discoveries lead naturally to the question, "Why?"

Classifying

Generally, this refers to the ability to reason from specific facts to the broader category. Arranging, or seeking to retrieve information from, appropriate fields within a data base file requires an understanding of the purpose of the different fields, and placing data in them appropriately. One example is classifying petroleum as a source of energy, gasoline and kerosene as finished products, and transportation and heating as potential uses, in a study of natural energies.

Sequencing

Putting the steps within a process into order requires an understanding of the effects one step has on another. Sequencing involves thinking about what is needed to fill the black box between the question and the answer. Creating a search strategy, locating and isolating the data one wants to work with, and ordering data on a final printout according to a logical scheme are examples of sequencing skills.

Identifying Trends and Relationships

Identifying fluctuations and patterns in the results of a search allows students to stretch their thinking, to build relationships among the results, and extrapolate from what is known to what is unknown. Such a skill may be demonstrated in the classroom through examining import and export data, or numbers of immigrants over a period of time.

Hypothesis Testing

Hypothesis testing is another skill that can be acquired using data bases and direct instruction. Building on and practicing the above skills, hypothesis building and testing means stating that between the contents of two (or more) fields, a relationship exists. It involves identifying a cause and effect, guessing at which side of the equation influences the other, and attempting to judge whether or not that relationship is valid. Beginning with a series of questions asking students to look for similarities between factors of geography (climate, vegetation and elevation, for example) and population size, students can be directed to look for similarities and pose questions about their possible relationships. For instance, might elevation, or rainfall, influence a state's climate? Might climate influence population density? By testing for all records meeting one criteria (for instance, elevation), testing for all records that meet a second criteria (for instance, population density) and combining results from the two tests, students can see for themselves the results are similar.

In another example, a student might examine the sales of video cassette recordings, their prices, and the volume of rentals at the local video store. One might pose a hypothesis that as prices fall, sales and rentals increase. Or does sales influence the price? Additional data might be recognized as needed before any certain relationship can be established.

When students were comfortable with the initial data base, they enhanced it with additional fields (e.g., average income size, number of toxic waste sites) and further explored similarities and possible cause-and-effect relationships among the subject matter (Wheeler, 1987).

Decision Making

To determine what to include and what to leave out of a data base under construction, students must decide the amount of information each record needs. They will need to evaluate the available data and decide which of the many data items will be useful in future searches.

Problem-Solving

Problem-solving emerges as a useful skill and is used during many computer exercises. The first time through a search, it is often the case that the answer is not exactly right. Whether the student needs to redefine the search statement in a query, arrange the data so that it is more useful, or include additional fields in the report, some kind of refinement is generally called for. Programmers refer to this process as debugging.

Reports from field-based teachers describe how their students discover that the inconsistency in the data entered, typographical errors, and too narrow a search strategy, causes results to miss some records. Especially when working with computers, tiny errors make huge differences in the results people get. Often, there are many possible ways to get at the data; with data bases, students must find the most efficient mehtod of doing so. Error correction, or an evaluation of what caused the results displayed, is quite natural when working with computers (Hummel & Balcom, 1984).

These teachers also reported that their students independently discovered coding as a way of representing some defined terms, when the capacity of the data base would not allow all the information to be entered. Educators point to increases in the acquisition and practice for higher cognitive skill development that the use of data base software provides. Providing students with the opportunity to develop, explore, and refine the skills they are acquiring in the classroom is being used increasingly for basic as well as higher order skill processing.

Procedure for Teaching with a Data Base

Working with a prepared data base, students learn the terminology of data base management systems, the design of a particular piece of data base software, including commands for retrieving, arranging and displaying record contents, and procedures for printing out results of a search (e.g., APPEND, EDIT, DELETE, FIND, SORT, PRINT), and search strategies (the generalizable problem-solving skills needed to determine the sequence and format of their queries to the data base).

Generally, an introduction to data bases begins with asking students to find the answer to a factual question. The answer is retrieved using the correct query statement. For example, students might search for all countries (NAME) in Africa (CONTINENT) liberated in 1905 (DATE OF INDEPENDENCE), or the number of democracies (TYPE OF GOVERNMENT) in South America (CONTINENT).

Given the chance to explore and become familiar with the fields and command structures, students can begin creating their own data bases. Several teachers have found it helpful to supply a format for their students the first time through this process. Working in small groups, students research and enter the data they will use. Reference and synthesizing skills are inculcated and refined at this stage as students locate information. They can learn comprehension skills in order to avoid duplication of information they gather, and categorizing and synthesizing skills while identifying common traits for key word retrieval. And they can begin to use problem-solving skills while extracting information in the report formats they create.

As a culminating exercise in learning to use data bases, students often design their own. Given a topic, they build on their earlier experiences with the system, agreeing on the content and organization. They correct their own errors as they work with the data. Decision-making and consensus-building skills can be developed during these exercises. Evaluating and refining the usefulness of field content, key word choices, hierarchy (if any), and structure, can be encouraged.

Use of a data base includes the use of planning and researching skills for identifying and gathering data; problem-solving, analysis and decision-making skills for breaking down a given problem into manageable tasks; and sequencing and logic skills for designing inquiries. Drawing from so many of these higher order skills, and employing group work and question-and-discovery as the method of inquiry, data bases help to keep the energy level high and the student's interest focused (see Vignette 8-1).

Using a Data Base with Handicapped Students

Designing activities for handicapped students using data base software can cover a wide range, based on the specific instructional needs of the student. Each of the activities suggested in this section may have a variety of uses, and should be used as a model for other related ideas, or modified for other functional levels.

Creating Content Data Bases

A data base is an excellent device for storing information. Students who are pursuing a content area, either academic or vocational, can use the

---

VIGNETTE 8-1
Teaching Banking Skills with dBaseIII

Learning to manage personal finances is a major focus of teaching daily living skills to disabled students. One of the more difficult skills to teach is the use of a bank for personal financial management. Ms. Brown, a high school special education teacher in Michigan, has developed a simulated bank account instructional unit using *dBaseIII*. The data base modules include input forms for deposits, account summaries, writing checks, and making deposits. Each student is assigned an account when he or she enters the class, and is instructed on how to access it. Each student is paid a wage (simulated) for completing assignments, class attendance, extramural participation, special projects, and meeting instructional objectives of the IEP. Students are paid on a weekly basis with a paycheck generated by *dBaseIII*, and are required to deposit these wages in their accounts. Students may write checks to purchase free time, special activities, time on the computer, and special tangible goods. Each student is provided a monthly statement and is required to balance the statement with their personal records. When the statement is acceptable to the student, they must turn both statement and their own ledger into the teacher for credit. In addition, the data base has been used to expand instruction in the use of the automatic teller machines (ATM) by simulating the screen of the ATM that issues cash, takes deposits, and can report the status of the students' accounts.

data base for compiling the information necessary to obtain functional competency. For example, a data base of the jobs an auto mechanic must be able to perform, together with a list of tools, a flat rate schedule, diagnosis procedures, and shop manual references, can be critical for a student with long-term memory deficits (see Figure 8-6).

For a student who needs to categorize the words that describe household items, a data base could be used to store information about where the item is found, its use, and how much it costs (see Figure 8-7).

Filing Personal Information

Many students at all levels of functioning have trouble with the organization of personal information. Take, for example, a physically handicapped student who cannot write his address or phone number. A data base can provide the student with a programmed search routine that allows him or her to strike one function key to make the address appear, or another preprogrammed key to display or print his or her name, address and phone number. For a mildly handicapped student who cannot remember her class assignments, a data base can be created that allows her to enter assignments, and retrieve them by date or by class or provide a schedule for a week at a time (see Figure 8-8).

Task: Change sparkplugs

Tools: Ratchet, sparkplug socket, feeler gauage

Time (flat rate): 45 minutes

Diagnosis: Rough idle, missing under load

References: Chilton's pages 34-35

FIGURE 8-6. *Auto mechanics job data base.*

Item: Laundry soap

Location: Bathroom chest

Use: Wash clothes

Amount: 1/2 cup per tub

FIGURE 8-7. *Household items.*

Date: 7–1–87

Assignment: Survey three employers

Due: 7–5–87

Class: Career exploration

FIGURE 8–8. *Class work schedule.*

Preparing for a Vocational Future

All students who are preparing for living and working in the community need career information, and many will also prepare for the future through vocational education. As the world of business and industry becomes increasingly complex, many handicapped students will need the assistance of a data base to cope with the extensive information needed in the workplace. In many cases, the data base could be appended to an already existing computer in the vocational training area to provide assistance with particularly complex calculations, descriptions, and specifications or names of parts or products. In addition, complex procedures could be established to allow a student to complete a task and then search the data base for the next task by referencing a step number or previous task description.

Using a Data Base for Educational Management

The use of data bases for student instructional use is exciting, but for many professionals who are buried in IEPs, reports, and other data gathering and information distribution, the data base can perform other desperately needed functions. These management functions are described here as lesson planning, materials file, student observations, activities file and performance evaluations.

Individual Education Plans

The information needed to meet the IEP requirements for Public Law 94-142 makes the use of data bases desirable for school divisions to assist them in developing and monitoring reports. However, two different levels of IEP data base systems have emerged: one that meets system needs, and one that meets teacher needs. Many commercially available IEP data bases are geared toward administrators rather than teachers and tend to be more rigid, meeting system needs rather than teacher and child needs. More information can be found in a recent review of commercially available IEP data base programs completed for the state of Missouri (O'Donnell & Marshall, 1986), which discusses many of the advantages and disadvantages of specific systems.

Some IEP data base packages are more flexible than others and can be customized to meet specific school system needs. One such system is the *Modularized Student Management System (MSMS)* by Education Turnkey in Falls Church, Virginia. This system has the capacity to be user-defined, that is, users can customize the content (goals, objectives, etc.) of the data base to meet local needs, formatting reports and communications, and the ability to edit individual goals and objectives written in the IEP.

An example of a teacher-oriented IEP data base system is the *Comprehensive Learner Adapted Scope and Sequence (CLASS)* by Technical Perspectives in Garland, Texas. This program does not even attempt to meet school system data base needs; rather, it is designed to meet the needs of teachers in developing and implementing relevant IEPs. *CLASS* uses a data base to provide teachers of handicapped children with a core curriculum that is referenced to regular education programs of study. The system suggests minimum competencies, annual goals, and sequenced objectives to achieve those goals. Most importantly, the data base system provides commercially available resources such as texts and kits which have been validated as effective materials for teaching the specific skill.

Lesson Plans

Data bases are a natural for establishing a format for lesson plans so that a teacher can simply fill in the blanks, and does not have to develop a customized page for each day. In many cases, a coding system can be developed so that, by simply entering a code, an entire phrase or objective can be inserted into the plan. Figure 8–9 depicts a sample lesson plan format developed with data base software.

Inventory of Instructional Materials

The ability to locate appropriate instructional materials is essential to instructional planning. Using a data base, instructional materials can be organized with a variety of descriptors that are useful to the instructor for locating and retrieving instructional resources. Materials can be selected according to students' instructional needs, content, age appropriateness, type of media, and activity. Figure 8–10 depicts a sample data base record inventory of instructional materials.

Date:

Objective:

Select an activity from the list below: (These items are displayed
   automatically after selecting an objective)

Enter names of participating students:

Modifications to be made:

          Name of Student   Modification Required

FIGURE 8-9. *Sample lesson plan format using data base software.*

Record No: 1

Instructional Material Name: Making sense of relationships

Publisher: Macro Press

Date: 1986

Instructional Content: Social skills

Target Audience: Adolescent mildly handicapped

Cost: $49.95

Availability: Resource room

FIGURE 8-10. *Inventory of instructional materials.*

Student Note Cards/Observations

The ability to observe a student's performance, and to retrieve a record
of his or her performance for periodic analysis is essential to effective teaching for students who are experiencing learning problems. These observations may range from simple frequency counts of disruptive behavior to a
more in-depth analysis of a student's verbal and social interactions. Figure
8-11 depicts a sample of a student observation format constructed with a
data base software package.

Date: 8-1-87

Name: Holmes

Behaviors: Moaned loudly while doing math problems.

FIGURE 8-11. Student observation.

Activities File

In conjunction with a data base of instructional materials, an activities file can be created to catalog instructional activities that are useful across settings and/or with a variety of instructional materials. These activities can be identified by fields such as subjects, most appropriate audience, objective, and alternative activities. Figure 8-12 depicts a typical activities record.

Performance Evaluations

Using a data base to collect performance evaluation data for students provides an easy way to store and analyze data related in individual daily assessment. The teacher can easily observe and record data into a file, which can then be used to compare a student on a variety of attributes, using a descriptive analysis, summary data, or to provide the basis for transferring to a data analysis format like SAS, SPSS or a spreadsheet like 123 (Lotus) or Filing Assistant (IBM).

SPREADSHEETS

Spreadsheets are, in their simplest form, electronic ledgers that have been used primarily for accounting purposes. Most spreadsheets are organ-

Activity: Printing award certificate

Subject: Language

Appropriate For: Ted, Susan, Perry

Reaction: Good activity, fairly time consuming, can be used for independent activity by Susan

FIGURE 8-12. Activities record.

ized in rows and columns across the page, allowing for neat, organized entry of numerical (or sometimes textual) information. With spreadsheets, the emphasis shifts from the process of calculating to the meaning of the information. Forecasting, projecting consequences of a change in a variable, "guesstimating," and making comparisons, are all easily within the reach of a wide variety of students through the use of spreadsheets.

Correction of mistakes, or changes to any number in the spreadsheet, will automatically update any other number in the spreadsheet that is affected by the change (called recalculation). Not only can you enter numbers and text on the spreadsheet, you can also enter formulas that can rapidly calculate values entered from one or more other locations. In addition to the ease of entry and modification, spreadsheets can be infinitely large, with rows and columns numbering in the hundreds, and provide users with the ability to move easily to any place in the spreadsheet.

Using a Spreadsheet

The use of a spreadsheet involves several steps that are relatively consistent, regardless of the application software that is selected. These steps include setting up a format, entering data, manipulating data, and retrieving data. Figure 8–13 defines commonly used spreadsheet terminology.

Cell: The intersection between a specific row (usually numbered) and a specific column (usually letters). For example, A1, B3 or AA102.

Row: The horizontal axis of the spreadsheet, generally indicated by a letter, or letters, of the alphabet.

Column: The vertical axis of the spreadsheet, generally indicated by a number.

Range: A group of cells, indicated by a pair of coordinates (such as A1 to B75 or C3 to C55).

Template: The format of the spreadsheet, including the column and row names, and forumlas.

Formula: A mathematic formula that uses numerals, operators and cell locations.

Window: The portion of the spreadsheet visible on the computer screen.

FIGURE 8–13. *Spreadsheet terminology.*

Setting Up a Spreadsheet Format

In the development of a spreadsheet, most of the time is spent in setting it up, or designing the layout of the rows and columns. Each format usually has labels for each row and column, descriptive information such as title and file name and formulas to provide calculation and recalculation of the numerical data entered (see Figure 8–14). For more advanced applications, formulas and macros can be included that allow information to be selected from another file and used in the spreadsheet.

Entering Data

Once the format has been established, data can be entered into any blank cell, or new data can be superimposed on old data in that cell. The data can be either numeric or alphanumeric.

Manipulating Data

Once data has been entered, some of the usefulness of the spreadsheet comes into play, with the ability to create "what if?" scenarios. These scenarios are created by modifying data to determine questions such as, What would happen if a student could earn three more points a day for appropri-

	A	B	C	D	E	F	G
01							
02	My Personal Budget						
03							
04	Food	Rent	Util	Transp	Enter	Insur	Total
05							
06	100	400	85	35	35	15	665
07							
08							
09							
10							

FIGURE 8–14. Typical spreadsheet.

ate behavior? Using such an application, a child can determine the number of points needed to earn a field trip at the end of the month. If the child has a bad day, he or she can recalculate the new number of points needed each day. An almost infinite number of other "what if" questions can be formulated, and new formulas or data entered into the spreadsheet in order to forecast results.

Retrieving Information

All the information that is entered can be retrieved either on the screen, printed out on a printer, or transported to another software package (like a word processor or data base) for use in preparing reports. This information can be printed in the standard row/column format that was used for entry; some software packages offer the option of retrieving information in the form of graphs. Figure 8–15 illustrates a report with the data reported in a graph format.

Using Spreadsheets in Instruction

Although the primary use of spreadsheets has been in the management of business, the use of spreadsheets for instruction has been increasing, partly due to the increased sophistication of the software that allows for easy

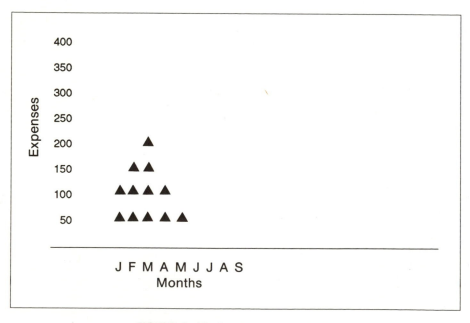

FIGURE 8–15. *Report in graph form.*

learning and use. Recently, several publishers have offered spreadsheets in basic versions or offered instructional packages designed for classroom use (Allen, 1985). These enhanced versions provide instruction in the use of the package and, in some cases, provide instructional lessons for use by elementary or secondary level students. Spreadsheets can help students with learning difficulties, for whom manipulation of numbers may not be easy, become more independent and less frustrated. Tasks such as budgeting, balancing a checkbook, and paying bills, are all practical applications of spreadsheet technology. In prevocational and vocational settings, spreadsheets are also extremely useful. Defining goals, gathering and analyzing data about professional options, identifying job placement opportunities, and experimenting with salary increases, are all potential uses.

Many applications are immediately apparent when the manipulation of numbers is automated. Story problems and statistical or probability data in mathematics, chemical reactions in science, taxes and expenditures in social studies, are all easily completed without sophisticated knowledge of mathematics.

Procedures for Teaching Use of a Spreadsheet

In order to teach students to use a spreadsheet, the first step is to create a simple spreadsheet to allow students to begin entering data. Like data bases, spreadsheets are actually easier to use than to explain, and this is generally how they are introduced to the classroom. Working with a prepared format, students learn the terminology of spreadsheets (row, column, cell, range, formula), the design of a particular spreadsheet software, including commands for entering, deleting, changing, moving around in the spreadsheet, displaying the content, and the procedures for printing out results of a search.

Generally, an introduction to spreadsheets begins by asking a student to find the answer to a factual question. The answer is retrieved by locating the intersection of the correct row and column. For example, students might search for the amount of the utility bill for March, 1987 (where the row is a description of household expenses and the columns are months of the year). Given the chance to explore and become familiar with the row/column/cell format and command structures, students can begin to manipulate the spreadsheet. By supplying a complete spreadsheet screen (see Figure 8–16), students are asked to research a "what if" question as in the following example: If your base hourly rate is $3.75 and you think that you will get a 5 percent increase each year, what will your hourly rate be in five years? Using a formula of $3.75 in cell A3, then cell B3 = (A3 × .05) + A3. This formula can then be copied across cells D3 through F3 to predict yearly increases.

After students are comfortable with basic entry and moving around in the spreadsheet, they can be assigned to work in small groups which students research and enter the new data they will use. Analytical skills are re-

	A	B	C	D	E	F
01						
02	Salary Increases					
03						
04	Base	Year 1	Year 2	Year 3	Year 4	Year 5
05						
06	3.75	3.94	4.13	4.34	4.56	4.78
07						

FIGURE 8-16. *Projecting changes to salary.*

fined at this stage as students attempt to explore variations of existing information. They can learn comprehension skills in order to avoid duplication of information they gather, and categorizing and synthesizing skills while identifying common traits of data they have developed. And they can begin to use problem-solving skills while extracting information in the spreadsheets variations they create. Of all the operations in a spreadsheet program, one of the more difficult is the development of formulas for individual cells. These formulas are used for summing a row or column, finding an average for a row/column, multiplying a cell or cells by a constant number, copying numbers from another location (cell), and an almost infinite variation of logical operations such as percentages, square roots, logs and other higher order calculations. For most practical applications, the ability to create a formula for summing rows/columns, or a variation of that, is the most important. Figure 8-17 shows some examples of formulas that can be used to sum row/columns or cells, and some examples of sums for partial rows or cells.

	A	B	C	D	E	F
03	35	35	35	35	40	sum (a3..e3)

which will be also displayed as:

	A	B	C	D	E	F
03	35	35	35	35	40	180

FIGURE 8-17. *Sample formulas for sums.*

As a culminating exercise in learning to use spreadsheets, students often design their own spreadsheets. Given a topic, they build on their earlier experiences with the system, agreeing on the content and format of the spreadsheet. They correct their own errors as they work with the data. Decision-making and consensus-building skills can be developed during these exercises. Evaluating and refining the usefulness of content and structure can be encouraged.

Use of a spreadsheet includes the use of planning and researching skills for identifying and gathering data; problem solving, analysis and decision-making skills for breaking down a given problem into functional categories; and sequencing and logic skills for designing inquiries. Drawing from so many of these higher order skills, and employing group work and question-and-discovery as the method for inquiry, spreadsheets help to keep the energy level high and the student's interest focused.

Spreadsheet Applications for Students

Any mathematical calculations that would ordinarily be done with paper and pencil or a hand calculator can be completed on a spreadsheet. More important than its function as a calculator is the power of the computer to allow a change to the base data or the formulas that show the comparative calculations. For example:

■ Calculating prices of produce at different prices per pound
■ Finding the area of a rectangle as the length of one side changes
■ Determining the number of chickens produced as the number of hens increases
■ Determining the "mystery" formula used to calculate a result when the base is known
■ Calculating distance, time, and velocity ratios
■ Determining points needed for desired grade in class
■ Determining statistics and scores of sports teams

Probably more important than the strictly academic skills obtained by using spreadsheets is the functional use that students with difficulty completing mathematical relationships can make of this as a decision-making resource. They can, for instance, calculate volumes and areas, chart a diet or exercise program, set up a family budget, and keep track of household expenses and utilities.

VOCATIONAL APPLICATION. Related to practical and functional applications are vocational applications. Spreadsheets are being used in a wide variety of sales and service applications, agri-business, and manufacturing. The ability to interpret a spreadsheet is becoming a high priority work-related skill for many jobs. For example, a spreadsheet is often used for inventory control when the student is required to stock shelves or replaced perishable goods.

Keeping track of working hours is an important function for both the employee and the employer. A spreadsheet provides a simple way to record daily hours and even sum and multiply by rate to produce a pay amount. It is not uncommon for an employee to have to computer this amount for the employer, or to check the accuracy of payroll services.

Work schedules are also easily developed and maintained for employees, and can include a running total of the time being earned towards accrued personal leave.

Many of the vocational opportunities for disabled youth are found in retail sales. Sales of consumer goods may be easily recorded on a spreadsheet that continues to update personnel.

Keeping track of expenses in seeking employment and job leads, and comparisons of salary and fringe packages are also easily handled through a spreadsheet.

Using a Spreadsheet for Educational Management

In addition to student use of spreadsheets, many management tasks required of special education personnel can be accomplished with greater efficiency through the use of this software. In fact, it is probably these uses that first introduced spreadsheets into schools. One of the most functional uses is an electronic gradebook, or use of spreadsheets to record and calculate student performance. Figure 8–18 depicts a typical spreadsheet used for recording student performance. Formulas can give different weights to as-

	A	B	C	D	E	F	G
01							
02	Functional Math Skills I					Mrs. Smith	
03							
04	Name	Pretest	Test 1	Test 2	Test 3	Midterm	etc.
05							
06	Adams	13	9	7	7	13	
07							

FIGURE 8–18. *Student electronic gradebook.*

signments and thus the spreadsheet can calculate grades using only raw score data rather than percentages or average scores.

Statistics and Demographics

Developing and keeping statistical information on students provides excellent information to the teacher on how to redesign or modify instruction, and how to provide more individualized services to handicapped students. The factors that influence students' behavior and academic performance can be analyzed through the ability of a spreadsheet to keep anecdotal records and statistics such as the number of students who complete specific tasks (i.e., change sparkplugs or spell a group of words).

Budgets and Material Allowance

Using a spreadsheet to keep track of class and program budgets provides an accurate and easy way to handle these responsibilities. A properly set up spreadsheet will keep a running total of expenditures and the amount remaining, and allow a teacher to input theoretical expenditures to determine budgetary impact. The spreadsheet in Figure 8–19 depicts a typical classroom budget.

The uses of a spreadsheet for both instruction and educational management are limited only by the creativity of the individual teachers as they attempt to be more efficient in their instructional activities.

	A	B	C	D	E	F	G	H	I	J
01										
02	Annual Budget School Year 87–88									
03										
04	Date	Item			Category of Expenditure					
05			Books	Instr Supp		Field Trips		Equip	Total	
06										
07	9-8-88	IBM-PC						1,200	1,200	
08										

FIGURE 8–19. *Typical classroom budget.*

SUMMARY

The use of data bases for the delivery of services for students who are disabled offers a wide latitude of options for instruction, direct student use, and the management of instruction. With the expansion of available data base software options to a wide variety of sophistication levels, data bases are finding increased popularity with instructional staff. The various sophistication levels provide options for the beginning instructor who feels only moderately comfortable with data bases and spreadsheets and the advanced instructor who has experience with software that offer more advanced instructional options. The differing levels of software also offer options to students who vary in sophistication levels of operation or need.

REFERENCES AND SUGGESTED READINGS

Allen, V. (1985, April). Software: Side by side. *Electronic Learning,* pp. 52–53.

Bitter, G. G. (1986). *Computer literacy.* Menlo Park, CA: Addison–Wesley.

Cameron, C. T. (1987). *Guide for use of general software with students who have special learning needs.* Silver Springs, MD: Macro Systems.

Hummel, J. W., & Balcom, F. W. (1984). Microcomputers: Not just a place for practice. *Journal of Learning Disabilities, 17*(7), 432–434.

Hunter, B. (1985, May). Problem solving with data bases. *The Computing Teacher,* 20–27.

O'Donnell, L., & Marshall, V. (1986). *Computerized administrative software programs for special education.* Unpublished manuscript, Missouri Technology Center for Special Education, Kansas City, MO.

Russell, S. J., Mokros, J., Corvin, R., & Kapisovsky, P. (1987). *Beyond drill and practice: Using learner-centered software in special education.* Boston, MA: Technical Assistance Resource Center.

Underwood, J. D. (1986). Cognitive demand and CAL (Computer assisted learning). In I. Reid & J. Rushton (Eds.), *Teachers, computers and the classroom.* Manchester University Press.

Wheeler, F. (1987). Questions to consider before purchasing a data base. *Classroom Computer Learning, 7*(6).

CHAPTER 9

Keys to the World: Microcomputer Technology and Telecommunications

ROBERT S. GALL

In the network environment rewards come by empowering others, not climbing over them.
— John Naisbitt, *Megatrends*

Microcomputers can enhance both oral and written communication, provide intellectually stimulating content that improves motivation, provide a means of expression for students previously unable to show talent due either to personality or physical restriction, and allow a greater measure of personal control over the learning environment. They can also provide recreation, reinforce systematic thinking processes, and assist both academic achievement and gainful employment.

CURRENT APPLICATIONS OF COMPUTER TECHNOLOGY IN SPECIAL EDUCATION

The introduction and application of computer technology has dominated both regular and special education during this decade. Nonetheless, many questions concerning the effective use of this technology remain as we approach the 1990s.

Computer assisted instruction (CAI) and computer managed instruction (CMI) have attracted much attention. CAI and CMI are well documented as powerful instructional and life-support tools that can enhance the learning processes of individuals with widely varying needs.

The recent avalanche of publications serves as a primary index of the firm foothold that microcomputer utilization has gained in the field of special education. Closing the Gap, an influential technology advocacy group, releases numerous publications and delivers state-of-the-art conferences, directed toward increasing the use of microcomputers in special education. Journals such as *BYTE, Exceptional Children,* and *Special Services in the Schools* have published special issues on the topic. Journals targeted toward special interest groups, such as the *Journal of Special Education Technology,* are now dedicated to the issue. Primary references are now appearing, of which *Handbook of Microcomputers in Special Education* (Behrmann, 1984), *Microcomputer Resource Book for Special Education* (Hagen, 1984), and *Microcomputers in Special Education* (Taber, 1983) serve as exemplars.

When interfaced with advanced conceptions of how individuals learn, advanced computer technology will provide a fresh insight into the disadvantaged learner. Ideally, such an individual might come to be seen as a remarkable learner, as educational research leads to effective designs of general methodology and a sharpened focus on how the individual acquires new learning. At a minimum we can realistically expect such an individual to demonstrate enhanced competency and self-esteem as technology facilitates the growth of independence.

Determining Applicability of Telecommunication Implementation

The decision to use telecommunications for a particular application requires a careful review of need relative to other communication options. Educators should examine their level of general commitment to microcomputer technology, their access to adequate funding, and their motivation to complete the necessary "homework" that will enable judicious purchases. Attitude and lifstyle are primary factors in determining the utility of telecommunications as an appropriate add-on to present microcomputer holdings.

Speaking to the issues that plague effective bulletin board implementation, Southern (1985) presented his view of key difficulties which, if left unchecked, will eventually destroy their utility. These issues, expanded by the author, include:

- Novelty effect, in which an initial flurry of interest and activity is soon replaced by apathy
- The time-delay factor, in which board managers do not keep the information current and response-effective

- The issue of limited access by students and other legitimate users whose time is usurped by others higher on the bureaucratic totem pole
- The "kids will break it" syndrome, in which adults restrict student use due to fears
- The fear of committing ideas, principles, and the like to a medium where criticism might later be directed by more knowledgeable individuals
- "Wetware" problems (the human brain and applied intelligence are the "wetware" working in harmony or disharmony with hardware and software components).

In other words, a myriad of problems can arise due to inappropriate consideration of the psychosocial impact a new form of communications imposes on a social environment without a clearly defined hierarchy of traditional communication rules. If Southern and many others are correct, technological innovation requires maximum consideration of human resistance to change.

It is simplistic to select a strategy that seeks the appropriate new methodology and implements it. Innovation of any type represents widespread changes for people within an organization. It is essential to consider the technology implementation and associated methodologies within the context of three transition phases involved in any change process: adoption, implementation, and continuation. Knowing what to implement and then successfully implementing it are two distinct problems requiring unique solutions. People determine the utility of successful technical feasibility and people are, at best, not technologically consistent. Innovators must present their expertise and knowledge in the context of understanding and dealing with the sociopsychological environment, which either plagues or facilitates successful adoption and implementation.

An information system, itself, is not a social system, but exists within one. The tangible components such as data elements and software products must be aligned with the intangible, unpredictable human components associated with the environment such as user expertise and user resistance.

While the information age necessitates better access to information systems and technology makes such systems possible, sociopsychological theories of change must guide the implementation.

TELECOMMUNICATIONS: AN INTRODUCTION — THE *INTRAPERSONAL* COMPUTER BECOMES *INTER*PERSONAL

Perhaps the most exciting next step in technology's march into schools is telecomputing. With the advent of the modem ... teachers and students will be able to use their computer to search data bases and retrieve up-to-date topical information, send and receive electronic mail including educational software, participate in both private and public conferences . . . or just chat with others who have similar interests. (Dyril, 1985, p. 74)

In *Megatrends*, John Naisbitt (1984) postulated that society has undergone a subtle, yet explosive shift from an industrial based society to an information based society. "In an industrial society, the strategic resource is capital . . . But in our new society, the strategic resource is information. Not the only resource, but the most important" (p. 6). The management of information through its collection, control, organization, and dissemination has become a primary objective in all facets of contemporary society, and therefore should receive priority attention from the educational community.

Telecommunication systems (including local area networking products, modems, communications software, and autodialers) comprise one of the most promising technological families for education. The visionary objective of a school without walls is now possible, enabled by the application of computer-generated, telephone-delivered instruction from a knowledgeable source to populations previously isolated by age, severity of handicap, and physical distance.

Traditional print media have served for some 5,000 years to bring knowledge to an information-hungry world. Contemporary examples range from the colloquial-practical knowledge extended through newspring to the scientific journals of a myriad of research communities, all bringing information to specialized target populations.

Today, futurists discuss the emergence of the "global village" in which electronic highways usurp the information dissemination role of traditional communication systems. Even today, communication media thought visionary in the mid-twentieth century are a pragamatic reality, facilitated by applications such as microwave transmission, fiber-optic relays, videotex/teletext, satellite broadcasting, and cable exchange. Information utilities and computer subscription services are now commonplace as a result, although multinational business and military applications currently dominate these communications services.

Nonetheless, even relatively unsophisticated computer users are able to participate in the global village through the use of modems, other specific peripheral devices, and communications software packages. The powerful stand-alone capacity of a microcomputer is incrementally enhanced by enabling it to share and to interact.

The 1980s have seen the emergence of data processing information management and telecommunication (via telephone, radio, and television) as both independent and interactive entities. Computer-based information manipulation strategies have blended with telecommunications processes. Telecommunications is brought to the computer world by networking technologies that permit control and management of information across dispersed locations.

A new term, "telematics," (Brennan & Sniggs, 1984) has recently emerged to describe the hardware, software, network, and content comonents involved in this exciting process. Telecommunications and networking appear to have gained a slot for future academic investigation, and new concepts such as image grammar, mediatrics, and telematics may become colloquial expressions in the near future.

Networking: A Primary Definition

Behrmann (1984) defines networking as "a computer-controlled system for managing information across locations" (p. 253). Networking permits the sharing of peripheral devices and software, leading to greater participation by all in applications such as teleconferencing and electronic publication. Behrmann (1984) comments:

> The concept of networking is a major step toward breaking down barriers to the education of handicapped children. Networking fosters professional development, professional communication, accessibility, and integration of information and human resources, and direct individualized interactive student instruction regardless of possible geographic or physical limitations. Finally, it offers the opportunity to extend school services to the home environment and facilitates parent-school communication and interaction. (p. 253)

Telecommunication processes managed by network systems offer a powerful potential educational service that could revolutionize concepts of schooling and education for all children. For example, electronic bulletin boards currently give many teachers and parents the ability to directly and inexpensively access and retrieve qualitative curriculum strategies. Information utilities such as SpecialNet allow subscribers access to large specialized libraries of educational information.

Local Area Networks

Local area networks (LANs) are communication systems that are generally "hard-wired" and therefore limited to single building or campus-based environments. They provide powerful communications and multi-task features for computers and peripherals located in relatively close proximity to each other, and allow educational institutions to customize networks for every conceivable use.

Highly beneficial in the educational environment, LANs allow stand-alone microcomputers to exchange data with one another and to share expensive peripherals such as hard disks, modems, and printers. Therefore, they can improve instructional management by linking each student's work station to a teacher's central processor, linking micros to minicomputers or mainframes to upload and download files, and allowing shared access to centralized data bases and spreadsheets.

Telephone-based Networks

Telephone-based systems, which can also be enhanced with numerous service configurations, use standard telephone equipment and services, which can tap the services of the global telephone network.

Telecommunications processes have extended our communication neighborhood from relative "back-fence chatter" to global interaction in less than a decade. The lives of all persons living in isolated communities, including special needs individuals, can be radically improved through vigorous individual, collective, and corporate advocacy in bringing these developments to their service. To illustrate, INTELSAT (International Tele-communications Satellite), the 109-country cooperative organization that owns and operates a global system for international telecommunications, has operated Project SHARE since 1984. INTELSAT and the International Institute of Communications have operated a wide range of telecommunication technologies to serve the health and education fields.

Project SHARE primarily sought to investigate improved service to rural and isolated parts of the world. Audio-video communication modalities, microcomputer-to-mainframe interactive data links, and simultaneous two-way voice transmission developed by the project became tools for educators and medical specialists.

The acquisition of hardware (e.g., modems, acoustic couplers) and appropriate communications software enable the "intrapersonal" computer to become "interpersonal." Acquiring and disseminating information can become a universal opportunity, provided that advocates for the handicapped demand equity in the distribution and utilization of the requisite technology.

Thus, "interpersonal" microcomputers, accessing information banks, and communicating (electronically but not necessarily impersonally), should generate excitement in the special education community, if not elsewhere in public education.

COMMON FEATURES OF TELECOMMUNICATIONS SYSTEMS

Telecommunication systems offer several basic services: dispatch and receipt of electronic mail through the long distance access of larger computers by smaller access computers, electronic conferencing, special-interest group information collections on bulletin boards, and information access through special purpose data bases.

Three pieces of equipment are required: a telephone or dedicated telephone line, a terminal or microcomputer (brand is irrelevant), and a modem (see Figure 9–1). (The microcomputer must be enhanced with special software to convert it into "terminal mode," features that will be discussed in detail later.)

One must also subscribe to an information system (with or without cost) and obtain a password to protect confidentiality. Once this is completed, normal post office services are presented to the electronic mail user (e.g., registered mail and bulk mail). Electronic mail offers the advantage of the capacity to send one letter to an unlimited list of addresses, and the corresponding ability to solicit instantaneous responses.

A typical electronic mail system enables one to send memoranda, letters, and other textual material to other subscribers in the same system. These communiques are "posted" immediately and the addressee reads them at will when "signing on" to the system.

Electronic bulletin boards are identical in function to the wall-mounted versions where notices can be posted and read. There is a tendency for electronic boards to proliferate, however, and as they do so to become specialized and less informal. Such "closed" boards generally limit access to special subscribers, while "open" boards allow any user to read what has been posted.

A third function involves conferencing. Electronic "chatting" (keyboard-to-keyboard conversation) resembles live telex communication at much greater speed and at minimal cost. Online data bases are the fourth major feature of telecommunication systems. There are three types of data bases: full text, which carries exact transcriptions of content such as news-

FIGURE 9–1. *A portable computer with an internal modem facilitates use of telecommunications.*

paper collections; bibliographic, which provides retrieval through key descriptors; and nonbibliographic collections, such as statistical data.

One of the most efficient ways to pinpoint and gain access to a special data base is through a data base vendor. The following list will provide access to most of the common online data bases:

- BRS — (800) 833-4707
- CompuServe — (800) 848-8990
- Dialog — (800) 227-1927
- NewsNet — (800) 345-1301
- Pergamon International InfoLine — (703) 442-0900
- The Source — (800) 336-3366
- TechCentral — (202) 466-4780.

Data base searches can be accomplished in either a technical or a plebeian fashion. Individual search modes usually require the use of more complex search strategies taught to those with technical proficiency. Data base search software enables average users to accomplish their own objectives, and employ software (such as IN-SEARCH by Menlo Corporation) to search, for example, the Dialog data bases. SEARCH HELPER (Information Access Company), to cite another example, is also considered very user-friendly.

WHY USE TELECOMMUNICATIONS FOR SPECIAL-NEEDS INDIVIDUALS?

> For the first time, the handicapped will have equal access to information ... an equality of opportunity never before available. The blind will never be restricted to someone else's choice of literature, the hearing impaired will be able to communicate with anyone over great distances, and the physically handicapped will have access to any information they choose from their wheelchair. Telecommunication via the microcomputer will, for the first time, give the handicapped equal opportunity in society. (Hagen, 1984, p. 9)

In rehabilitation literature, an impairment is any disturbance or interference of normal body functioning, a disability is a loss of functional ability, and a handicap is the consequent disadvantage imposed by these in the sociopsychological environment. Dramatic examples of technological support to allay or diminish the effects of impairments and disabilities have emerged in the past decade, and the specialized field of rehabilitation engineering has emerged to promote further achievements. Even more dramatic have been the technical achievements made in the area of enhanced communication processes enabling the impaired and the disabled to be minimally handicapped.

Gregg Vanderheiden (1982) in his article "Computers Can Play a Dual Role for Disabled Individuals" suggested:

the immediate future promises to be an extremely exciting and productive period, which will see rapid advances in the development of both special function programs and new strategies to ensure the complete access to disabled individuals to the world of microcomputers.

If this access can be assured, then the functional disabilities currently experienced by these individuals should decrease markedly as our society moves more and more into the electronic information age. If we *fail* to ensure access to our computer and information-processing systems for disabled individuals, our progress into the electronic information age will instead only present new barriers. (p. 66–67)

Freedom Through Effective Technology

Taber (1984) identified five significant freedoms that would accrue to advocates and individuals with special needs through the effective use of technology. These include the efficient and effective use of time, the enhancement of learning processes and outcomes, greater environmental independence, and meaningful involvement in gainful employment. Such primary achievements can be expected from the judicious applications of technology on behalf of those with special needs, and each relates directly to the enhancement of communication, Taber's fifth freedom.

The most important potential freedom achieved through technological intervention is the freedom to communicate. Effective communication processes provide a vehicle for information sharing, and also enhanced self-esteem, given the priority assigned to communication skills in our society.

Communication is one of civilization's most significant processes, primarily because it enhances the capacity and extension of intelligent social interchange. Inefficient, ineffective, or nonexistent communication skills isolate and restrict the power of intellect. Further, the interpersonal exchange of intrapersonal thought can both enhance social affiliation and catalyze the learning process by providing a medium for the embellishment of concepts.

This dual interface between information exchange and social interaction is outlined by Heward and Orlansky (1988):

Communication, in its broadest sense, is any interaction that transmits information . . . for true communication to exist, there must be both a sender and a receiver. (p. 213)

To illustrate, the physically handicapped individual has specific needs in the areas of communication, computer access, environmental control, and mobility. Of these needs, Romich and Vagnini (1984) state:

communication is by far the most important . . . the level of achievement reached is closely tied to the ability to communicate. The transition to an information based society is a boon to people with physical handicaps . . . who now can process, and communicate information. Today, no person should be provided with a communication system, environmental control, or powered wheelchair without consideration for access to computers. (pp. 71–72)

Enhancing Microcomputers with Peripherals

Microcomputers enhanced by peripherals such as modems and speech synthesizers enable the handicapped to share thought even if they are limited to a single physical space.

Recent developments in peripheral technology, such as *Autospeak* (a text-to-speech synthesizer that allows a speech-impaired person to pre-enter as many as 32 sentences and direct these at will to a speech synthesizer), and the *Cacti Communication Program* (which enables the printing of words and phrases on the screen or printer with a minimum number of key presses) serve as examples of liberating technology. These facilitative devices, when linked together through a telecommunications network, greatly enhance communication freedom because the boundaries of space and time can be overcome.

For many disabled students the addition of a simple, inexpensive "shelf item" peripheral device may be all that is required to permit full access to the computer and the telecommunications network. When access is established, many such students will be able to participate fully in many "normal" school activities.

Vanderheiden (1981) has identified two broad categories of input and access devices: direct selection and scanning. A common example of direct selection, where the user physically contacts a keyboard or alternate display, is provided by normal keyboarding. Adaptive enhancements to normal keyboarding activities include keyguards, headsticks, and expanded (larger key) keyboards. Scanning, or indirect pointing, is made possible by on-off microswitches and can be activated by a single physical movement which moves a cursor across a grid. Microcomputer input is now possible for almost all handicapped individuals in increasingly efficient and cost-effective modes (McWilliams, 1984).

As a result of these types of technical applications, immediate benefits have been activated for physically and sensorily handicapped individuals. In the near future all special-needs populations are projected to benefit from this technological catalyst promoting their independence. To achieve this, however, the educational social service, business, and technical communities must be motivated to advocate vigilantly on their behalf. As was suggested by Cunningham and Gose (1985).

Non-verbal physically handicapped students can communicate via modem as well as you and I. Telecommunications and all its benefits are just as applicable to the physically handicapped user ... getting on-line is easy, and enjoyable when you use software equipment or addition of peripherals such as switches or electronic communications boards. (p. 1)

Vignette 9–1 provides an example of the enabling power of telecommunications software and peripherals for multiply handicapped users. It is now widely accepted that the full utility of established technological achievements for special needs populations is restricted only by the limits of our imaginations and creativity. Powerful interpersonal advocacy is required if we are to ensure the equitable distribution of the requisite technology to these individuals.

THE RURAL SPECIAL EDUCATION ENVIRONMENT: FERTILE SOIL FOR TECHNOLOGY

Rural-based special educators universally share frustration and disenchantment as they wrestle with urban-oriented service models that assume large population bases and homogeneous target service populations.

VIGNETTE 9–1
Georgia Griffith: Disabilities Disappear Through Telecommunications

One of the most moving expressions of the power of "liberating technology" was encountered by the author recently at a meeting of the Advisory Board of the Center for Special Education Technology in Reston, Virginia. Fully participating in that meeting was Georgia Griffith, an information specialist resident of Lancaster, Ohio, who had been blind from birth and deaf since the age of 38.

In spite of her dual sensory handicaps, Ms. Griffith has achieved some remarkable personal and professional milestones. The first blind student to graduate from Capital University in 1954, she has consulted with the Library of Congress and served it and the National Braille Association as a braille music proofreader. She is self-taught in a dozen foreign languages. From the perspective of this chapter, however, her most noteworthy accomplishment is her position as manager for the National Issues Forum on the CompuServe Information Services, as well as originating and managing CompuServe's Handicapped Users Data Base. This feat is accomplished with a Versabrailler and a number of adaptive peripheral devices that enable her to access the telecommunication utility. Ms. Griffith thus can originate and receive electronic mail and participate in electronic conferences.

Readers wishing to contact Ms. Griffith are urged to do so by mail or through CompuServe at the CompuServe address located elsewhere in this chapter.

The typical rural human service reality is a complex one, as variables such as small size, geographic isolation, and minimal financial, technical, and professional supports challenge even the most competent administrators and advocates. The impact and effectiveness of many special education undertakings in rural settings demand an inordinate amount of human energy and financial support and therefore often significantly increase the interpersonal tensions of those involved.

As Helge (1980) reported, the post-1975 environment in the United States marked a major turning point in educational service provision for rural-based, special-needs populations, with major improvements in the quantitative impact of all services provided. However, qualitative service delivery in rural areas will forever challenge the innovativeness of educational leaders because all resources will be taxed maximally. The rural special education environment provides fertile soil in which to implant cost-effective and time and energy-enhancing technological aids (see Vignette 9–2).

Overcoming Isolation

Isolation in its physical, interpersonal, and intrapersonal dimensions is the primary obstacle to overcome if the rural handicapped are to achieve meaningful standards of normalization and integration.

VIGNETTE 9-2
Project Special, Kentucky's Special Education Network

Project Special uses telecommunications in a pilot test of a computer network linking educational agencies and the Kentucky Office of Education for Exceptional Children (OEEC) based in Frankfort. The host computer, an IBM AT, is located at the OEEC office. The host computer software, BBS-PC, was obtained from Micro-Systems Software (Boca Raton, Florida). The project has provided telecommunications process training to special education administrators and their designates. Districts and special education cooperatives participating in the project use a variety of computers, including Apple II+, IIe, IIc; TRS-80; and IBM PC.

Project Special offers both bulletin boards and electronic mail features to its users. Information for the 15 bulletin boards that reside on the host computer at last count comes from the OEEC staff, SpecialNet, journals and publications such as *Closing The Gap*, and a variety of other sources.

The Kentucky Network operates an in-state WATTS line with callers paying for their connect time based on actual WATTS line charge. The project also publishes a newsletter on activities of the Kentucky Network.

To illustrate, using 1984 as the base year and the Northwest Territories of Canada as the venue, more than 49,000 inhabitants were spread over 3.3 million square kilometers (1.3 million square miles). Visualize approximately one inhabitant for every 70 square kilometers of relatively harsh terrain. Visualize further an ethnically diverse population in which handicapped individuals are disproportionately affected by climatically induced factors (e.g., chronic otitis media) and socially-induced factors (e.g., fetal alcohol syndrome). With today's value system, traditional service models based on institutionalization and consequent severance from family and community ties are inappropriate. Such a population requires ingenious and bold innovation if the ideal of individualized service is to be attained in the home community.

Special Challenges of Rural Environments

In commenting on the need for careful ecological analysis appropriate to the environment in which technology is implanted, Helge (1983) noted that rural areas present special challenges that go beyond technological limitations, fiscal inadequacies, and staff development issues:

Rural communities value tradition and direct personal contact. Technology is often perceived as an alien influence. Gaining parent and community acceptance is essential ... when strategies include improvement of parent-educator communication, or parent involvement via technology. (p. 11)

These issues, brought to the surface by technological innovation, must be addressed by the educational community at large if a significant redesign of human potential is sought as a major object in this global village. Rural-based handicapped populations universally will benefit greatly from the application of technology, and telecommunications technology is perhaps the most significant application. As Helge (1983) concluded:

Rural schools have generally had less accessibility to most forms of educational technology ... The smallest and most isolated rural schools can potentially gain the most from the current technological flurry. (p. 1)

In further elaborating these concerns, Helge (1983) identified four problem areas that act to restrict technological effectiveness in the rural special education environment. These include the relatively immature state of the art of applied technology, the fiscal inadequacies in providing for appropriate staff training as well as hardware and software acquisition, the pressing problem of appropriate staff development and support, and the potential rejection of technology by parents and others in the community who see it as dehumanizing.

It is obvious that the sociopsychological environment must be carefully considered if the promise of techology is to be sustained.

ACQUIRING HARDWARE AND SOFTWARE COMPONENTS TO INITIATE TELECOMMUNICATIONS

Careful selection of tools to support the application must be made. A few hardware items (specifically, a microcomputer and modem; ideally, also a printer) are necessary. Information about the communication parameters they employ must be obtained. Appropriate terminal or communications software, a telephone line, and access to information utilities must be acquired.

There are several publications available that provide advice on the selection of tools and processes for telecommunications. An appropriate start could be made by consulting *The Complete Handbook of Personal Computer Communication: Everything You Need to Know to Go Online with the World* (Glossbrenner, 1983).

Whereas some microcomputers have specific advantages for accommodating disabling conditions (e.g., the Apple's eight internal slots readily accommodate cards for specialized peripheral devices), most microcomputers can facilitate the telecommunication process. The microcomputer's impressive functional ability can be extended dramatically, as relatively limited stand-alone units become "smart" interactive terminals.

Computer-to-Computer Communications: A Simplified Overview

In order to allow computers to communicate with each other, three elements are necessary:

1. A *communications circuit* must exist between the two computers. For short distances, this can be a simple twisted pair of wires to "hard wire" the units together; for longer distances, telephone circuits can be used.

2. A *method of translating and retranslating* computer-originated data to electronically transferrable signals carried by the communications circuit must be acquired. Modems are the devices that allow this translation and communication along a telephone circuit. They are connected with the telephone circuit via a direct connection to the telephone jack, or by "acoustic coupling" (a speaker and a microphone converts electronic signals to and from audible tones generated by the telephone handset).

3. A *communications protocol* that allows the two computers to "handshake" or communicate effectively must be implemented. Any one computer controls the data transfer, preventing both from "talking" at the same time.

There are essentially three levels of communications protocol. At the "dumb terminal" level, the host computer is always controlling the flow of data to and from the second "dumb" computer, which only responds to commands. At the "intelligent terminal" level, the host computer controls the flow of data to and from the second, which is assumed to have some processing capability, such as the ability to transfer files, edit, and preprocess data. Finally, at the "system architecture" level, control of the flow of data is shared between computers, allowing each to maintain some part of the total data base.

Hardware and Software Units

Communications Software: Overview

The communications software, as the information choreographer, is simply the set of computer instructions (i.e., program) that determines how the microcomputer should process the information it receives or transmits. It is a very critical component in the effective use of a microcomputer as a telecommunications device.

Communications software turns the microcomputer into an intelligent communicating terminal. Functions such as communications protocols, data transfers, and command operations are controlled by software. Some software allows microcomputers to automatically save information on disk when the buffer becomes full during a transmission.

Efficient communications software also supports the autodial and autoanswer capabilities of many modems. This feature automatically dials numbers from a memory directory, or permits night dialing when rates are lower.

Software choice directly affects communications flexibility, just as different telephone formats (e.g., regular, memory-phone, cordless, radio-telephone) permit customization of standard audio communications.

An inexpensive program that transforms the computer into a "dumb" terminal — one that sends and receives information — is adequate for infrequent users. "Smart" terminal programs that save and send information are obviously more expensive, but offer many conveniences.

Newstand journals, such as *Creative Computer* and *PC Magazine*, regularly review the qualities of popular communications packages. Given the wide range and confusing array of choices offered the potential buyer, it is judicious to investigate this area thoroughly.

Communication Software: Expanded Description

"Smart" software functions allow transfer of information to and from a storage medium such as a diskette; thus, information sources can be captured for future reference. The most common information transfer, the retrieval of text files, can thus be accessed and modified using a text word processor such as *Applewriter* or *Screenwriter*. Messages may also be prepared in advance using a word processor, and then transferred to another computer.

This capture-to-disk and send-from-disk feature allows information to be transferred at the maximum rate that the computer can transfer. The important consequence of this feature is the reduction in telephone connection time and associated charges, as the message is formatted off-line at the user's convenient speed and style.

Another feature that assists efficiency is the macro comand function. A "macro" is a command or string of commands that may be issued with a single or mimimal number of keystrokes. (e.g., the command "Check Exchange; Scan Since February 20; read from Counterpoint" can be given using essentially one keystroke).

Automatic dialing allows the software to take control of the computer, executing the composed macro list (including the appropriate telephone number and log-on procedures of computer identification, names, and passwords). This feature is most helpful where the complexity of the system inhibits user access or where a specific disabilitiy reduces keyboard efficiency.

Further, "front-end search software" can be used to permit convenient off-line search entries, and permit automatic searching, downloading, and logging exits. Examples of software that accomplishes this include *In-search* (Menlo Corporation) and *Search Helper* (Information Access Company).

Finally, "gateway" systems such as Easynet (Lisanti, 1984) have major potential use for the handicapped because they provide user-friendly, menu-driven systems to access data bases such as Dialog. Minimum computer skill proficiency is required (e.g., Easynet is accessed via a U.S. toll-free number that permits immediate data base search once the user's credit card number is approved).

In summary, effective communication packages allow these features: storage of data either in memory or to a disk; peripheral "toggling" (e.g., turning printer on and off with the touch of a key); the creation of macros or "script files," which eliminate log-on direct activities; and receipt of information while the computer is unattended.

Telecommunications Search Software and Data Base Subsets

There is an alternative to accessing data bases online. Search software and subsets of some data bases can be purchased on floppy disks. Two examples are *ERIC MICROsearch*, and *MIND* (Microcomputers Index on Disk).

ERIC MICROsearch, produced by the ERIC Clearninghouse on Information Resources (Syracuse University, Syracuse, NY 13210), provides subsets of selected portions of the ERIC data base. With one subscription option, each quarter, ERIC mails floppy disks including about 300 new ERIC citations. Subscribers may choose between citations on educational technology or library and information science. A small initial subscription fee includes the *MICROsearch* program, one data disk, and a user's manual. In addition, there is a small quarterly subscription fee per disk.

MICROsearch runs on Apple II+ and IIe computers, and at the time of printing, an IBM PC version was planned. Libraries are using *MICROsearch* as a simulation system to teach simple search strategy and online searching skills. It is a low-cost teaching aid to be used before allowing students access to the online data bases.

MIND (Data Base Services, P.O. Box 50545, Palo Alto, CA, also available online via Dialog) indexes approximately 65 popular microcomputer journals, including *Popular Computing, Personal Computing, BYTE,* and *Creative Computing.* A subset of *MIND* can be purchased with a search program called *MicroAccess.*

The Modem

An appropriate modem must also be selected. The word "modem" is condensed from two words that describe its function: *m*odulator and *dem*odulator. The modem is the electronic circuitry that acts as a translator between the computer and the telephone network. The telephone network was designed to transmit audibly recognizable analog sounds, whereas the computer uses a code of digital electrical impulses. The modem simply translates the computer's codes into audible tones, which can be sent over the telephone. A receiving modem retranslates these tones into computer code interpretable by the receiving computer. Sending text is referred to as "uploading," while receiving text is called "downloading."

Those who plan to use modems where outmoded telephone exchanges may still be in operation are advised to discuss potential transmission difficulties with telephone utility representatives and the modem distributor. Rural users should note that modems should not be connected to party lines, as the computer link is disturbed if another person on the line picks up the telephone. Even contemporary telephone convenience features such as call waiting and forwarding can produce an audible tone that may interfere with computer links. It may be necessary to disconnect these features.

Computer users who travel may not be able to connect the modem directly to the phone lines, and often carry acoustic modems with cups to provide a less reliable but necessary substitute.

MODEM SPEED (BAUD RATE). Modem speed, measured in bits per second, is commonly referred to as the "baud rate." While 300 to 1200 baud rates are commonplace, 2400 baud and even 9600 baud rates are now commonly advertised in upscale modems when access to a mainframe computer is desirable. At present, standard telephone lines are unable to carry reliable transmission at rates above 2400 baud, but this is being changed as high quality fiber-optic lines become commonplace.

Readers contemplating regular transmission of long files should consider the 1200 baud feature as a time and dollar economizer; a file of 10,000 words can be sent in six minutes at 1200 baud, but would require almost 25 minutes at 300 baud. Novice, irregular, or informal users with more casual needs will find the 300 baud modem acceptable, even though this transmission speed requires over a minute to fill a screen of 80 columns by 24 lines. However, modems at each end of the line must be operating compatibly at equal speeds, and it is very important to determine the transmission rate of the network to be accessed.

Modems have numerous and different applications in education; educators must carefully consider the potential uses of modems before making a purchase. Most educational modems are voiceband modems, which means that they operate at speeds that can be transmitted over the telephone's voice channel. Large installations with massive data transmission requirements may require dedicated or leased lines to send data.

MODEM TYPES. A modem protocol specifies details such as which audio frequencies carry information. All 300 baud modems use the Bell 103 protocol, the AT&T communication standard. Similarly, most modern 1200 baud modems use the Bell 212A protocol. Bell Laboratories originally set the standards and gave the protocols their names, and these are ratified by the International Telegraph and Telephone Consultative Committee.

A modem that can transmit data in two directions at once is called a full-duplex modem. A modem operating in half-duplex is either sending or receiving. Many modems allow users to select either mode.

An important distinction is also made between synchronous and asynchronous modems. Asynchronous modems utilize a start-stop data transfer method that sends digital signals one character at a time. The big configuration of a standard *ASCII* character includes a start bit and one or more stop bits, seven binary information bits, and a parity bit.

Synchronous communications (generally used for micro–mainframe communications) involve block mode data transfer, or characters that are transmitted in groups. The "synchronous" designation comes from the use of synchronization characters that are put at the beginning and end of each data block, negating the need for asynchronous start and stop bits.

Modems are available in various hardware configurations. The first modems for microcomputers were acoustic modems, which have rubber couplers that hold the phone receiver. Acoustic modems send tones through the mouthpiece of the telephone and receive them through the earpiece, but also collect unwanted extraneous noise and voltage shifts from adjacent devices.

Today, the more popular method is the "direct-connect" modem, which avoids the phone receiver by interfacing the microcomputer directly into the phone line. However, they are also more expensive and are incompatible with older telephone systems.

Direct-connect modems may be external or internal. External modems connect to the computer via a cable either to an RS-232 serial interface or to a modem card. Internal modems are completely self-contained on cards that fit into expansion slots in the chassis of a microcomputer or on a rack of a larger computer. (Built-in RS-232 interfaces that convert characters into signals that can be read by modems are now common on many microcomputers.)

Modems are available as part of a telecommunications package (including software, cables, and serial circuit boards) from companies such as Apple, Atari, Commodore, IBM, and Radio Shack. Package deals are convenient for the user who may have limited funds or be physically isolated from appropriate technological advice. The industry standard at the time of writing remains Hayes Microcomputer Products (Norcress, Georgia). Competitive units are also sold by Anchor Automation, Cermetek, and Novation.

GETTING ONLINE: STEPS IN THE TELECOMMUNICATIONS PROCESS

The modem is connected to the computer and to a telephone jack, according to the instructions in the modem manual. The communications program disk should then be inserted into the disk drive. Although specific set-up instructions vary among communication programs, the general set-up procedures are very similar.

MacTerminal, An Example

The appropriate baud rate, character width, parity, and other handshake parameters should be selected. These primary and secondary parameters are explained in the modem manual. When first communicating with an information service, eight data bits, no parity, XON/XOFF handshake is the most commonly encountered basic communication protocol format.

The terminal type is then entered; if unknown the user may start with TTY or VT52. A wrong choice leads to problems only if the other computer expects full-screen editing or other more exotic features.

When the pararmeters have been selected, the telephone number is entered in the dialog box. If the phone line used requires dialing of nine for an outside line, a comma should follow the nine, inserting a two-second pause in the automatic dialing sequence; for longer delays, more commas should be used. (The modem ignores hyphens.)

If the dialing process needs to be started through an operator, the phone number is dialed manually, using operator assistance to arrange for a collect or credit-card call. Once the connection is completed, it is arranged with the other party to switch to data mode, and the calling computer is concurrently switched to data mode.

When making a credit-card call using touch-tone dialing services, a zero must be dialed first, followed by the complete long distance number. When the tone sounds, the credit-card number may be dialed.

Connection Achieved

Modems with speakers broadcast the modem dial tones and also the shrill answering tone from the other modem. Data mode has now been changed from voice mode and the transmission is prepared. At this point, the calling modem operates on "originate" frequencies and the receiving modem on "answer" frequencies without interference. If two 1200 baud automatic answering modems are employed, the following sequence ensues: One modem dials the other modem, which answers the line with a 300 baud answer tone, eliciting a 1200 baud phase-modulated originate tone from the first modem. This elicits another 1200 baud answer tone. The originating modem switches to data mode, and disconnects its speaker. If the originating modem's 1200 baud originate tone is answered by a 300 baud unit, the first modem switches back to 300 baud.

It is possible to use a second phone line to converse with the person operating the other computer while parameters are set. Once a link is established, all parameters should be stored. When communication is concluded, the program must be instructed to hang up.

INFORMATION UTILITIES

Once the appropriate hardware and software acquisitions have been made, the microcomputer user can access the global village. That village contains an ever-expanding array of information bases to tap, each commercially available at costs that depend on subscription fees and connect time.

These information services can all be reached independently, should the user be prepared to incur the long distance telephone charges involved. Of special interest as a cost-saving procedure is the provision of inexpensive digital transmission through packet switched networks made available by telephone consortiums. For example Telenet, Tymnet, and Uninet in the

United States and Datapack in Canada can be accessed through one of many PADs (packet assembler-disassemblers) that are usually located in larger urban communities. Local telephone utilities, as well as computer dealers, will be able to provide the appropriate numbers to call for 300 and 1200 baud transmissions.

What Is a Packet Switched Network?

Packet switched networks take advantage of the fact that a single dedicated telecommunications circuit can transfer very large volumes of digital communications between two points. Most computer communications use only a very small proportion of the available capacity and thus many digital communications can occur simultaneously between major cities.

In order to capitalize on these facts, systems that allow several digital conversations to share the dedicated high speed telecommunications circuit by packaging and transferring data from one major center to another have been developed. Smaller computers called packet-assembler-dissasemblers (PADs) facilitate the exchange of data between local telephone circuits and the larger network.

The PAD takes in data from a local telephone line connected to a computer or terminal, "packetizes" it by accepting the data until it gets an end-of-line character, adds an "address," and ships the resulting data string to the nearest switch. The switch reads the address and ships it via the network to the addressed switch, which transfers it to the appropriate PAD. Finally, the data is transmitted to the appropriate local telecommunications circuit to the requested computer.

The results of this process are transparent but significant. Subscribers are able to reduce expenses by unobtrusively sharing otherwise prohibitively expensive digital telecommunications circuits. (Rural users will still incur a small long distance charge to connect to the nearest PAD.)

Generic Information Utilities

Many electronic information services, such as Delphi, CompuServe, and The Source, are general interest networks, and are set up to allow the general public to participate in the electronic information world with maximum ease. Unlike a bulletin board system (BBS), which can usually accept only one caller at a time, networks can take many simultaneous callers. Network subscribers sign on by making a local call through Telenet, Datapac, or Tymnet.

A network has several advantages over more traditional forms of communication. It links the user with a large number of people who share interests or concerns. It allows messages to be forwarded and received immediately. Considering the spiraling cost of long-distance telephone calls and postage, electronic communication systems are cost-effective if used judiciously.

The subscriber is provided with a wealth of information through data bases, information resources, and human resources available through the networks, which provide a wide range of services. One of the most versatile is online conferencing, which permits users to communicate and converse with each other in real time. Individual comments appear on the monitors of all who join the conference, thereby allowing spontaneous reaction. Ongoing discussions over a period of time are possible using such forums. Subscribers scroll through the messages at their convenience, and add their comments at any point.

Most networks are linked by a host system (e.g., Telenet or Datapac) that provides and charges for the necessary computer capabilities. Therefore, the costs of joining a network differ depending on the organization and the host system. Subscription rates, connect charges, and storage costs are the usual costs incurred. Subscription rates and connect charges (based on connect time with the computer, charged by the minute) vary widely from network to network. Storage charges (based on the amount of information stored in the host computer's memory) are normally very small.

Almost 350 data repositories containing over 2,400 files are currently accessible by a microcomputer and modem (Lisanti, 1984). While commenting that present subscription rates vary from $35 to thousands of dollars, Lisanti notes that online searches are becoming progressively less expensive as major information utilities introduce low cost subscription to the most utilized bases.

Readers interested in acquiring constantly updated information on bulletin board systems in the United States can access the *Online Computers Telephone Directory,* (published quarterly by J. A. Cambron Co. Inc., P.O. Box 10005, Kansas City, MO 64111).

Several information services provide access to data bases of direct benefit to educators (see Vignette 9–3). Generally, the data bases operate on a user fee system (the charge is a standard connect fee depending on the time of day and the number of minutes of use). Most services accept payment through a major credit card. Some of the more readily recognized information utilities include, Dialog, BRS, CompuServe, and The Source. (See Appendix B for more specific data on information utilities.)

THE ALTERED HUMAN LANDSCAPE: PROBLEMS ASSOCIATED WITH MICROCOMPUTER TELECOMMUNICATING

Defects are always more tolerable than the change necessary for their removal.

— Descartes

VIGNETTE 9-3
CompuServe in the Classroom

Richard Riedl (1986) described an exciting telecommunications project that he initiated in Fairbanks, Alaska. He and three colleagues employed at the Tanana Junior High School used CompuServe as the information source for a student-generated news magazine. Although the teachers controlled log-on security in order to discourage unauthorized use, students were allowed to explore the many *CompuServe* data bases at will. As Riedl described:

> The types of information used from CompuServe varied a great deal. Some students did simple data base searches on what kind of computer software was available for certain purposes or for information on particular celebrities. Others used information collected by some of the Forums (special interest groups) located on CompuServe. Still others made contact with individuals in other parts of the country who had information or interest in the topic being researched. One of the most exciting experiences was when one student made contact with a man who was riding his bicycle across the United States and using a lap-top computer and a modem to send his stories and experiences to his publisher. His goal was to write a book about the people he encountered on his travels. I am not even sure how the original contact with this individual was made, but a lively exchange of electronic mail followed, which captured the interest of many students for some time.

Riedl, in describing the student-teacher online costs, maintenance costs (monitoring), and material costs, calculated an overall expense of $300 for this exciting project. However, he concluded with the following judicious advice:

> This type of project is not to be jumped into lightly. The world of computer communications is not yet a user-friendly one. The search for the right combination of hardware, software, and information utility can be time consuming and confusing to the beginner. The planning of a project that will fit the curricular objectives of the classes involved and still keep the online costs in line takes much thought, experimentation, and planning. Yet, even with such problems confronting the teacher, I encourage interested teachers to forge ahead. The results can be tremendously rewarding.

A somewhat utopian vision of the practical and humanitarian aspects of communication via microcomputer has been presented thus far. Perhaps illustrative of this enthusiasm is the following testimonial from Cunningham and Grose (1985):

The benefits of telecommunications to physically handicapped students are enormous. As stated previously, this is one and maybe the only sphere in their lives where they're on the equal basis with able-bodied persons ... physically handicapped students using telecommunications are looked up to as "experts" by other able-bodied students. It has greatly enhanced their mainsteaming and social opportunities. Roles are reversed when the able-bodied student is dependent on the disabled student for assistance within this area. (p. 4)

It is valuable to consider some of the factors that have the potential to reduce the phenomenal potential for human empowerment noted in the above quotation and throughout this chapter.

Accessing Knowledge Equitably

Several dystopian phenomena might emerge as segments of the population gaining relatively unlimited access to knowledge. We are currently at a major turning point in history, in which individuals with complex combinations of special needs stand to gain much through the application of technology. Such individuals have not received an equitable share of educational resources under traditional service structures. Being handicapped has been synonymous with being disadvantaged, and has resulted in reduced power and control in the human as well as physical environment. Will the expanded understanding and application of technology, now more equitably distributed to the handicapped, lead to a greater latitude of choice in making life decisions? Will the handicapped actually be empowered and politically emancipated through technology? What sociopolitical changes might accrue as a result of expanded access to information by this subgroup?

Wolfensberger (1972) has argued that both physical and mental abuse have long accompanied the lives of the handicapped, many of whom are devalued and seen as deviant in the dominant culture. In his view, a handicapped individual is stigmatized because external manifestations of the handicapping condition lead to a rejected deviant status.

Many of Wolfensberger's writings have identified the specific limitations imposed on the lives of the handicapped as a result of denigration. He also suggested that some individuals and groups benefit, directly or indirectly, from keeping handicapped individuals in positions of dependency. If this premise is correct, what new social inventions in the global village will develop to extend such control over the lives of others in the future?

Those who advocate for technological extensions to the handicapped population must be prepared to argue vehemently for equity of acccess. According to Romich and Vagnini (1984):

With all of this exciting technological progress, however, new problems are being created. Now that functional technical aids are available, we must address the task of getting them to the people for whom they have been created. The first aspect of this is that of awareness building. People who need, or who have clients who need, technical aids must become familiar with the capabilities that these systems offer. At the next level, those rehabilitation professionals who select and apply technical aid systems must learn how to do so in a manner that best serves the interests of the client. Finally, funding for technical aids and the necessary corresponding services must become more straightforward. In all of these areas we are making progress, but more work is needed. (p. 77)

Technology proponents must remember that technology is not universally seen as a panacea. Some view it with fear, to the point that the term "technophobia" is applied. Advocates for individuals with special needs know well the cycle of rejection that many face, and arming such individuals with technological hardware may act to create even further social distance from those who feel alienated from both.

Effecting Change in Public Education

This potential malaise may be even more acute in the domain of public education, where innovation in both attitudes and methodology is not commonplace. Lindsley (1984) pointed out that many powerful technologies were resisted by the educational community until the eleventh hour. These included moving pictures (1911), the typewriter (1920), overhead projector (1944), television (1962), programmed instruction (1955–1968), and microcomputers (1977). Even today, the mass presence of microcomputers in schools is not a guarantee of their appropriate utilization or equitable distribution to children.

It is widely accepted that the educational community prefers to make haste slowly. For example, a study commissioned by the National Science Foundation in 1973 reported a time lag of two decades between discovery and implementation of 10 major technical inventions (Illbach & Hargen, 1984).

The dominant response to novel approaches in public education has been to directly resist their implementation or, more effectively, to assign them to the eternal limbo of careful study, as Illbach and Harger (1984) have recommended.

For schools to fully determine the applicability of microcomputers to the educational problems of special needs children, a planned change approach to microcomputer implementation must be taken. A critical element of this planned change approach involves the assessment of a range of organiational factors which may be predictive of the effectiveness of a special services microcomputer program. (p. 92)

These authors then provide an evaluation plan that includes an analysis strategy of eight educational organization factors: ability, values, information, circumstances, timing, obligation, resistance, and yield, each of which must be identified and encountered.

It is hard to argue with the wisdom of such an approach, and Illbach and Hargen's plan deserves special scrutiny. At the same time, to wait a decade or two to apply and enhance technology that can enrich the communication options of the handicapped today is to deny the population a multitude of life-supporting experiences. Catholic theologians would call this a "sin of omission" because society thus denies opportunity for personal growth.

Microcomputers have already demonstrated their ability to support improved initial learning and transfer of knowledge organized and delivered by competent teachers. Microcomputer-based telecommunications can widely expand that potential if we are prepared to examine a new set of human relationships occasioned by significantly altered modes of communication. Chorover (1984) pointed out importance of considering the human element:

> It would be very serious error to look only at the technical aspects ... It is only in the context of a supportive educational community — a human environment conducive to learning — that the hazards ... can be avoided.
>
> We must take it as our goal to draw people into an intimate and creative human context. The people who are on the receiving end of the innovations have to be involved in the transition. (p. 266)

SUMMARY

This chapter disucssed the application of telecommunications processes and systems as supports for improved learning environments for all students. Simply defined, microcomputer telecommunications involves computer-to-computer information transfer over telephone lines. The discussion focused on "networked"/interactive systems linking microcomputers through a larger host computer to share text, data files, and electronic messages. Supportive information was provided on the hardware, software, and adaptive peripheral devices required.

The primary focus, however, was on the facilitative role such systems have played in producing greater equity in both educational and vocational settings for those with special life challenges. Such individuals are able to access these systems in a variety of "invisible" modes. Consequently, value-free alternative communication systems are provided for both handicapped and nonhandicapped sectors of society. The implications of this emerging tool were raised in the context of both historical and contemporary sociopsychological phenomena.

REFERENCES AND SUGGESTED READINGS

Behrmann, M. (1984). *Handbook of microcomputers in special education.* San Diego, CA: College-Hill Press.

Bowen, B. (1985). *Business/rural education partnerships.* Unpublished manuscript, Apple Corporation, Cuptertino, CA.

Brennan, M., & Spriggs, D. (1984). *Reflexive communication.* Unpublished manuscript, Protestant School Board of Greater Montreal.

Cartier, M., & Cartwright, G. (1984). *The computer and education: Reflections on a development plan.* Unpublished manuscript. McGill University, Montreal, Canada.

Chorover, S. (1984). Cautions on computers in education. *BYTE, 9*(6), 223–226.

Cunningham, P., & Gose, J. (1985). *Telecommunications for the physically handicapped.* Unpublished monograph. Mesa, AZ: Mesa Public Schools.

Dyril, O. E. (1985). Modems: The school's link to the world. *Classroom Computer Learning, 10*(1), 74–75.

Glossbrenner, A. (1983). *The complete handbook of personal computer communications.* New York: St. Martin's Press.

Hagen, D. (1984). *Microcomputer resource book for special education.* Reston, VA: Reston Publishing.

Helge, D. (1980). *A national comparative study regarding rural special education delivery systems before and after passage of P.L. 94-142.* Murray, KY: Murray State University.

Helge, D. (1983). *Technologies as rural special education problem solvers: A status report and successful strategies* (pp. 1, 11). Bellingham, WA: National Rural Development Institute.

Heward, W. L., & Orlansky, M. D. (1988). *Exceptional children* (3rd Edition). Columbus, OH: Merrill Publishing Co.

Illbach, R. J., & Hargen, L. (1984). Assessing and facilitating school readiness for microcomputers. *Special Services in the Schools, 1*(1), 91–105.

Lindsley, O. (1984). *Innovations resisted by educators.* Unpublished manuscript, University of Kansas, Lawrence.

Lisanti, S. (1984). The on-line search. *BYTE, 9*(13), 215–230.

McWilliams, P. (1984). *Personal computers and the disabled.* New York: Quantum Press.

Naisbitt, J. (1982). Megatrends. *Ten new directions transforming our lives.* New York: Warner.

Romich, B., & Vagnini, C. (1984). Integrating communication, computer access, environmental control, and mobility. In M. Gergen & D. Hagen (Eds.), *Computer technology for the handicapped.* (pp. 71–72). Henderson, MN: Closing the Gap.

Snodgrass, G., & Campbell, R. (1982). The application of electronic communication in special education. In J. Domingues & A. Walstein (Eds.), *Educational applications in electronic technology.* Monmonth, OR: Westar.

Southern, T. (1985). Informal comments. Presented at the First National Rural Teacher Education Conference, Billingham, WA.

Taber, F. (1983). *Microcomputers in special education.* Reston, VA: Council for Exceptional Children.

Taber, F.(1984). Micros — a place in the wide open spaces. In M. Gergen & D. Hagen (Eds.), *Compuer technology for the handicapped.* Henderson, MN: Closing the Gap.

Tawney, J., Aeschleman, S. R., Deaton, S. L., & Donaldson, R. M. (1979). Using tele-communications technology to instruct rural severely handicapped children. *Exceptional Children, 46,* 118–125.

Vanderheiden, G. (1982, September). Computers can play a dual role for disabled individuals. *BYTE, 7,* 13.

Vanderheiden, G. (1983). The practical uses of microcomputers in rehabilitation. *Rehabilitation Literature, 44*(3–4), 66–70.

Wolfensberger, W. (1972). *The principle of normalization in human services.* Toronto: National Institute on Mental Retardation.

APPENDIX 9-1: NETWORK CHECKLIST

Features to Consider

■ Electronic mail
- ☐ has mail options
- ☐ has urgent mail
- ☐ has registered mail
- ☐ has private mail
- ☐ has timed delivery
- ☐ has broadcast list
- ☐ can scan mail
- ☐ can automatically inform user of new mail
- ☐ gives summary of new mail
- ☐ has multiple commands on one line
- ☐ has overnight hard-copy delivery
- ☐ provides listing of subscribers

■ Telex Interface
- ☐ has inbound/outbound telex interface
- ☐ has interface with voice mailboxes (turns voice into data and data into voice messages)

■ Bulletin Boards
- ☐ notifiers user of unread information
- ☐ can scan bulletin boards
- ☐ can search by number of message
- ☐ can search by date
- ☐ can search by sender
- ☐ can search by subject
- ☐ has national-level information and network capacity
- ☐ has state-level information and network capacity
- ☐ has key-word search on subject line
- ☐ automatically informs user of monitored bulletin boards
- ☐ is menu driven
- ☐ is command driven

■ Speed of Transmission
- ☐ works at 300 baud
- ☐ works at 1200 baud
- ☐ works at 1200 baud with no premium charges
- ☐ works at 2400 baud

■ Security
- ☐ Uses invisible password (not shown on screen)
- ☐ Has individual passwords within user account (private ID)
- ☐ User is able to change password

■ Equipment Compatibility
   □ compatible with diverse equipment and languages
   □ requires standard telephone line
   □ requires RS-232C port on microcomputer
   □ requires asynchronous communications capabilities
   □ requires a full duplex
   □ uses *ASCII,* 8 bit, no parity

■ Location Independent
   □ operates nationally
   □ operates internationally
   □ has toll-free access

■ Connect-time Rates
   □ prime time 300 baud, $ _____ / hour
   □ prime time 1200 baud, $ _____ / hour
   □ off-peak hours 300 baud, $ _____ / hour
   □ off-peak hours 1200 baud, $ _____ / hour
   □ night hours 300 baud, $ _____ / hour
   □ night hours 1200 baud, $ _____ / hour

■ Telephone Access
   □ via Telenet/Datapac?
   □ via other carriers: which _____ ?

■ Connect-time Estimates
   □ _____ monthly average, $ _____
   □ _____ annual average, $ _____

■ Volume-charge Estimates
   _____ / $ _____ per year

■ Subscription Price
   _____ / $ _____ per year

■ Gateway Capacity with other Data Bases
   □ access to other data bases
   □ access to news services
   □ access to private data bases
   □ access to public data bases

APPENDIX A

Glossary

Access. Used either as a noun or verb to indicate either gaining control of a system or the acquisition of data from a storage device of peripheral unit.

Acoustic coupler. A data communications device that converts computer data into audible tones for communication over telephone lines. (The part of the modem that transmits data to the handset of a common telephone, but not the modem itself. The telephone handset fits into special rubber cups for transmissions of data.)

Alphanumeric. Data that consist of letters and numbers.

Articial intelligence. An area of study aimed at developing machines that "think" like humans.

ASCII. Acronym for American Standard Code for Information Interchange. It is an international standard that defines how characters are represented in a computer's storage.

Asynchronous. Participants in a computer network do not need to be present at the same time to interact. The store and forward features of the computer permit users to access information and messages at their convenience.

Baud. A measurement of communications speed between devices. Baud can be roughly translated into characters by dividing by 10: 1200 baud is 120 characters a second.

Bit. A contraction of binary digit (1 or 0). A bit is the smallest unit of information in a digital computer.

Buffer. A temporary storage area for holding computer data until they are processed by another device. It is needed because the data can flow at different rates between computer and its peripherals.

Bulletin boards. Systems on computer networks where computer users can deposit and read messages.

Bug. A set of electrical circuits into which other circuits boards can be plugged.

Byte. A unit of computer memory, made up of a series of bits. One byte will store one number, letter, character, or space. Bytes are normally measured in groups of 1,024, which are designated by a "K." The more "K" (bytes) a computer has, the more memory it has.

CAI (Computer assisted instruction). International materials and tutorial programs presented via a computer. The application usually involves a dialogue between the student and a computer program that informs the student of mistakes as they are made.

Carrier services. Communication services available on the networks of authorized common carriers (that is, telephone company network services).

Compatibility. The ability of two devices to work together. In addition, if a program can be run successfully without alteration on two different computers, then the computers are generally said to be compatible.

CPU (Central processing unit). The part of the computer containing the circuits that interpret and execute instructions.

Cross talk. In telecommunications, the unwanted transfer of energy from one circuit to another.

Data base. A store of interrelated data on files, for use in an information retrieval system.

Data base management system. A collection of software that handles the storage, retrieval, and updating of records in a data base. A data base management system controls redundancy of records and provides the security, integrity, and data independence of a data base.

Data communications. The transfer or exchange of information between computers, requiring the transmission of digital signals.

Disk (disk drive). A disk is a circular object coated with magnetic material on both sides to store information. For data retrieval, it is rotated inside a disk drive. It can be floppy (flexible) or hard.

Disk operating system (DOS). A computer program responsible for the housekeeping and communications functions needed to get the disk storage system and main computing unit to work together. DOS also handles communications with other peripheral devices.

Download. To transfer data or programs from a remote location into a computer.

Dumb terminal. A terminal with no independent processing capability of its own. It only works when connected to a computer. A smart (or intelligent) terminal can be used for local processing without connection to a central unit.

Duplex (full duplex). The ability of two devices to transmit simultaneously and separately along the same communications channel. Half-duplex designates the ability of devices to transmit in both directions, but not at the same time.

Electronic mail. A general term for the electronic distribution of messages that can be stored for reception or reading at a later time.

Emulation program. An emulation program permits a computer to imitate another brand or type.

End user. The user who ultimately receives computer service or information.

Expert system. A development of artificial intelligence. The effort to have a computer contain specialized knowledge and mimic the thinking of a human expert.

File. A collection of similar data, or a group of related records, treated as a unit.

Gateway. A point in a communication network that has a high density of use and equipment and that provides a link between two or more networks. Telephone companies also provide gateway services so that users can access different data bases with one access code and terminal.

Hard copy. Text and graphics printed out on paper.

Hard disk. A disk made of rigid, ceramic-like material with a magnetic coating.

Hardware. The physical components of a computer system.

Information. The collection of technologies involved in handling information by computer.

Information center. A large computer that serves data processing needs, as well as the main memory and controller of decentralized terminals and smaller computers in a network.

Information provider. An individual or organization that provides information for a data base.

Integrated software. A collection of computer programs that are interactive. For example, data can be transferred from one to be used in another.

Interactive The use of a computer, or other device, in such a way that the operator is in control of its activity. An interactive system may also be conversational, implying continous dialogue between the user and the system.

Interconnect. Organizations other than regulated telephone utilities that supply telephone terminal equipment. The term also refers to the regulatory decision permitting customer ownership of telephones.

Local area network (LAN). A communications system that allows several information processing devices to link with one another for a limited distance, such as within a college campus.

Microcomputer. A desktop computer of that uses a single chip, the microprocessor, as the central processing unit.

Minicomputer. A computer of intermediate size and computing power, between mainframe and microcomputer.

Modem. A contraction of modulator-demodulator, a device that translates computer data into pulses that can be transmitted over telephone lines or optical cables.

Multi-tasking. The computer's ability to do more than one job or program at the same time.

Network. A system consisting of a computer and its connected terminals and devices. Computers can also "network" with each other.

Noise. The unwanted electronic signals in telecommunications.

On line. Refers to equipment that can interact directly with a computer's central processor.

On-line services. Usually a term to describe a computer that provides information searching services for a fee, available over telephone lines to a computer.

Operation systems. The set of programs that make it easier to operate the computer. It acts as a kind of traffic cop, directing tasks such as input and output between the computer and its peripherals, or accepting and interpreting information entered through a keyboard.

PABX (PBX). Private automatic branch exchange. A switching system within a company that also has access to the public telephone network. If it is operated manually, it is a PBX.

Packet switching. A method of data communications in which the message is split up into smaller units, transmitted, and reassembled at the other end. Each packet may be sent by a different route.

Peripheral device. A device that attaches to the computer, such as a disk drive, terminal, or printer.

Protocol. A format of communications for information exchange.

RAM. An acronym for random-access memory, also known as internal memory. It is memory that can be altered by writing over previous contents. RAM is volatile and the contents will be destroyed if power is lost.

ROM. An acronym for read-only memory. ROM is a form of internal memory or chip on which the commonly used programs are permanently placed to be read by the computer.

RS-232. An interface standard for asynchronous data communications between any two devices.

Software. The collections of instructions or programs that direct a computer's operations.

Stand-alone. A device that is self-contained, not dependent on another unit for memory or processing.

Teleconferencing. A general term for conferencing that involves telecommunications links. It includes full-frame videoconferencing, where people can see and hear participants at other locations; audio teleconferencing; slow scan; and freeze-frame image transmission.

Teletext. A one-way, non-interactive system that transmits information through regular or cable television broadcast signals or through FM radio signals to an adapted television set.

Upload. The electronic transfer of files from a microcomputer environment to a mainframe computer environment.

Videotex. A two-way information system that uses television sets or special terminals. Information is displayed with text and graphics.

APPENDIX B

Networks

INFORMATION SERVICES

DIALOG Information Services
Pala Alto, CA
(800) 227-1927

One of the largest information utilities of interest to those in the educational community is DIALOG's Knowledge Index, a subsidary of Lockheed Corporation. Some of the educational data bases included in DIALOG are:

- ERIC (Educational Resources Information Center, Bethesda, MD), which has more 1/2 million entries and offers a rich resource for special education searches of numerous kinds
- ETSF (Educational Testing Service Test Collection, Princeton, NJ), which describes more than 5,000 test materials and evaluation tools of all kinds
- ECER (Exceptional Child Education Resources, Reston, VA), which lists journal articles, curriculum materials, texts, program descriptions, conference papers, and dissertation citations of interest to any area of exceptionality

DIALOG Information Services has approximately 700 data bases, referencing more than 80 million journals, articles, reports, conference papers, and the like. DIALOG has Knowledge Index, a scaled down version of the parent system (containing 24 of the 700 data bases) designed for the home user.

BRS and BRS/After Dark
Latham, NY
(518) 783-1161

BRS has a special plan for formal instructional programs at all grade levels. For a relatively small charge ($15 per hour at printing), BRS Instructor provides access to almost all of the BRS data bases: ERIC, Medline, Peterson's Guide, the Academic American Encyclopedia, Magazine Index, and National Newspaper Index are all available, as well as nearly 100 other data bases.

Some data bases of special interest to educators are available only on BRS. Resources In Computer Education (RICE) contains information on school applications of microcomputers and specific information about software. School Practices Information File contains descriptions of all types of educational programs.

BRS After Dark, a menu-driven system, offers a subset of the BRS data bases directed to home computer user. It is available only after 6 p.m. and on weekends. After Dark charges range from $6 to $25 per hour with a monthly minimum of $12 at the time of printing. For menu-driven access during the day, users can choose BRS/BRKTHRU. BRKTHRU provides access to all of the BRS data bases with no monthly minimum charge after a $75 start-up fee.

CompuServe, CompuServe Information Services
Columbus, OH
(800) 848-8199

CompuServe, a subsidiary of H & R Block Company, offers a wide collection of information through knowledge categories such as financial, electronic encyclopedia, shopping, banking, and text editing. CompuServe also offers a sophisticated statistical package with numerous educational applications. MECC (Minnesota Educational Computing Consortium) software catalogs, as well as the last five years' acquisitions of ERIC can be accessed through CompuServe. CompuServe has an educational software data base called "EPIE on-line," which provides on-line access to approximately 5,000 software programs listed in The Educational Software Selector (TESS) (Teachers' College Press). Information can be searched by fields such as computer manufacturer, subject, grade, title, and area of educational applications.

The Source, Telecomputing Source
McLean, VA
(800) 336-3366

The Source offers more than 700 programs in an easily accessed menu-driven format that includes news, business services, entertainment, travel, word processing, and the like. It has a very reputable sophisticated electronic mail system.

Telecomputing SOURCE is another information utility frequently accessed. It offers a very sophisticated electronic mail system, information on stocks and commodities, news and business information, teleconferencing, communications programs, and games.

SpecialNet, North America's Largest Utility
Washington, DC
(202) 296-1800

Of special interest is SpecialNet, which offers electronic mail, bulletin boards, and data collection and information management services targeted specifically to those involved in all aspects of special education. At the time of writing SpecialNet had over 2,000 individual and agency subscribers, and while the great majority reside in the United States, this service is now attracting international attention. It is the largest computer-based communication network oriented toward educational concerns in the U.S.

Developed by the National Association of State Directors of Special Education (NASDSE), SpecialNet had 43 boards or information bases at the time of writing. These include technology areas (e.g., computer, software, television), program areas (e.g., early childhood, deaf), special education management (e.g., litigation), and special purpose boards (e.g., CHAIN, a parent-oriented information base). Eighteen boards are designed to appeal to a general audience, while the remaining have a focused objective.

SpecialNet is easy to use and requires no special expertise. It can be accessed on any computer or terminal, either of which must be equipped with a modem. The connection to SpecialNet is available through a local or toll-free 800 number anywhere (in the United States via the GTE Telenet, or its Datapac Canadian equivalent) through which SpecialNet information is transmitted and stored.

SpecialNet offers numerous information access and communication potentials for those interested in special education, and further details regarding its potential can be obtained from its originator, Gary Snodgrass (2021 K Street, Washington, DC 20006; 202 296–1800). SpecialNet's format for designating competent individuals or agencies to act as board managers provides a model for small board management. To illustrate, the Center for Special Education Technology (which is sponsored by the U.S. Department of Education but located at the Council for Exceptional Children headquarters in Reston, VA) shares its board mandate through news releases, monographs and academic publications. It also manages two electronic bulletin boards on SpecialNet, Tech Line (a "closed" board), and Tech Talk (an "open" board) sharing both specialized and general knowledge on technological applications. Other individuals or agencies manage specific boards. To illustrate: Education Turnkey Systems in Virginia manages the "Computer" board, while the "Voced" board is managed by the University of Missouri.

Of special interest to rural-based readers is the ACRES (American Council on Rural Special Education) "Rural" Electronic Bulletin Board, which lists relevant publications, events, and miscellaneous information geared to the special problems encountered in rural special education settings.

ACRES is one of the affiliated projects of the National Rural Development Institute based at Western Washington University (Bellingham, WA). At the time of printing, SpecialNet charged a $200 annual subscription fee, and additional computer connect rates ranging from $4 (night hours, 9 p.m.–7 a.m.), $7 (off-peak, 6–9 p.m.), and $13 (business hours, 7 a.m.–6 p.m.). Standard electronic services are reinforced by consultation, systems tailoring, and training, which makes the fees a "good value."

It can be seen that most information utilities offer a broad catalog of specialized data bases that cater to unique but multiple needs presented by subscribers. As the quantity and quality of services increase, and as educators begin to realize their potential, direct extension to the unique demands of special needs populations can be expected. The cost/benefit ratio has to be considered carefully, as each utility charges unique combinations of subscription and connect-time costs that prove burdensome over time.

KendallNET Access, Telecommunications for Educators of the Hearing Impaired
Washington, DC
(202) 651–5260

KendallNET is an electronic communication system established by Kendall Demonstration Elementary School at Gallaudet College in Washington, DC, to facilitate communication between programs for the hearing impaired across the United States and in Canada. It supports both personal mail and bulletin boards (public and private).

Kendall School houses the host computer system. This system is composed of an IBS Ultraframe connected to a DEC multiplexor, which is tied into Telenet. The IBS is also connected to Kendall's LAN (local area network) which is composed of Corvus hard disks with a number of IBM PC and Apple IIe microcomputers networked to them. The software controlling both systems is the Magus Electronic Mail system created by Software Sorcery in Vienna, VA.

In addition to Kendall's central system and its LAN, KendallNET is connected to 10 satellite centers. These centers are located at:

- St. Mary's School for the Deaf, Buffalo, NY
- Atlanta Area School for the Deaf, Atlanta, GA
- Oregon School for the Deaf, Portland, OR
- California School for the Deaf, Fremont, CA
- California School for the Deaf, Riverside, CA
- Wisconsin School for the Deaf, Delavan, WI
- Sir James Whitney School for the Deaf, Belleville, Ontario, Canada
- Louisiana School for the Deaf, Baton Rouge, LA
- Model Secondary School for the Deaf, Washington, DC
- Texas School for the Deaf, Austin, TX

Each satellite center has its own LAN composed of Apple or IBM microcomputers networked to a Corvus hard disk. Each is responsible for demonstrating KendallNET and for providing access to remote users who wish to phone directly into their site.

Remote users (i.e., other programs for the hearing impaired wishing to join in this communication network but not having the hardware and software to function as satellite centers) can then call up the closet satellite center to read or write personal mail to any user at any of the sites or to read or write information in the public bulletin board. A second option will be to call into KendallNET Central in Washington, DC, via a Telenet number. A minimal charge is made for these services.

For more information on accessing KendallNET or on becoming a satellite center, contact Phil Mackall, CMES Project Leader, Kendall Demonstration Elementary School, 800 Florida Avenue, NE, Washington, DC 20002 (202 651–5260, voice or TTD).

TELECOMMUNICATIONS SERVICES DESIGNED TO ASSIST SPECIAL NEEDS INDIVIDUALS

Of interest to the reader are the following selected special data based focused on the concerns of the handicapped. These include ABLEDATA, C-CAD, HEX, ERIC, NIGSEM, NISH, REHABDATA, and TRACE.

ABLEDATA, National Rehabilitation Information Center
Washington, DC
(202) 635–6090

The ABLEDATA system offers a national computerized data bank with information about rehabilitation products, and a network of information brokers. It provides access to the national data bank, and develops supplemental local information resources. Information on product data from the national data bank to meet rehabilitation product information needs is provided.

The ABLEDATA system is a service of the National Rehabilitation Information Center, supported by the National Institute of Handicapped Research (NIHR), United States Department of Education.

C-CAD, The Center for Computer Assistance of the Disabled
Arlington, TX
(817) 429–9729

C-CAD is a newly formed, non-profit corporation organized to create, discover, modify and train the disabled in marketable computer skills. A resource list of manufacturers, software companies, and a bibliography of articles and books of interest to the disabled have been collected. The bulletin board is available to all persons interested in finding or sharing information on computer applications for the physically and mentally disabled. The system operates 7 p.m. to 9 a.m. daily, and all day on weekends. The access number (714) 783–7548.

HEX, Handicapped Educational Exchange
Silver Spring, MD
(301) 593–7033

HEX is a clearinghouse for information on the use of modern technology, such as computers, to aid the disabled. It lists sources of hardware and computer software, as well as conferences communications and seminars dealing with handicaps and special education. The bulletin board is available 24 hours a day. It is primarily intended as a free service to those involved in the education of the handicapped.

HEX is operated by AMRAD, the Amateur Radio Research and Development Corporation. They have also developed adaptive devices that will allow a variety of microcomputers to transmit and receive in Baudot, a code used in telecommunications for the deaf.

Other Special Needs Bulletin Board Systems

The remaining services are more briefly described.

Center for Special Education Technology (Technology Information Exchange, Reston, VA) provides two electronic bulletin boards focusing on special education technology.

CONFER (Blissymbolics Communications Institute, Toronto, Canada) utilizes a computer conferencing network that enables users to establish and employ electronic forums for the disabled.

ERIC (Eric Clearinghouse, The Council of Exceptional Children) distributes school-based information on the handicapped.

LINC Resources (Columbus, OH) offers a computerized data base of special education software.

NIGSEM/MINIS (National Information Center for Special Education Materials, University of Southern California, Los Angeles, CA) provides media and devices for use with handicapped children in the school system.

NISH (National Information Sources on the Handicapped, Clearinghouse on the Handicapped U.S. Department of Education) lists all resources and organizations assisting handicapped persons.

REHABDATA (Catholic University of America, Washington DC) is an electronic source for information in computer applications for the handicapped.

TRACE (Trace Center University of Wisconsin, Madison, WI) lists many of the available computer communications and rehabilitation aids in its International Software/Hardware registry.

UNIVERSITY-BASED NETWORKS

CONFER and *MERIT NETWORK*
University of Michigan, Professional Development Office
Ann Arbor, MI

MERIT is jointly supported by four major Michigan Universities: Michigan, Michigan State, Western Michigan, and Wayne State. It serves as an excellent example of a specific purpose system that has expanded to meet emerging needs.

Utilizing the CONFER software package, users are able to access data on microcomputers generated by the Center for Research on Learning and Teaching. Unlike SpecialNet systems, systems such as CONFER are free to eligible users who qualify for academic access by the sponsoring institutions.

SPEEDNET
Center for Multisensory Learning, Lawrence Hall of Science, University of California
Berkley, CA

SPEEDNET (SPEcial EDucation NETwork) provides an opportunity to examine academics advocating on behalf of special needs individuals. SPEEDNET seeks to positively offset the educational difficulties of physically disabled and visually impaired students by organizing and monitoring a telecommunications network (including the adaptive hardware and software, the operating system, the location of the system, and the content carried to the students by the system).

The project employed 20 Apple computer stations in the schools or homes of participating blind, visually impaired, and orthopedically disabled youngsters. Each station included appropriate adaptive devices to ensure that each student using the station had access to the computer. The SPEEDNET project provided training for parents and teachers, with primary focus on involvement in a telecommunications network. Participating students were to be selected on the basis of geographic inaccessibility requiring a telecommunications network. The Disabled Children Computer Group of the San Francisco Bay Area, coordinated this project.

University-based conference systems are expected to grow exponentially in the near future, and to expand to link specific campuses to the larger world network of academic institutions. One example of this catalytic effect is provided by NETNORTH, which originated at the University of Guelph and soon expanded to six other Ontario universities and community colleges, McGill University in Montreal, and the National Research Council in Ottawa. In 1984, IBM provided the funding to permit NETNORTH to establish a three-year liaison with Cornell University and thereby access to an American-based university network identified as BITNET. At the time of writing NETNORTH was being extended throughout Canada, and will eventually permit a North America/Europe/Israel affiliation.

CORPORATE SPONSORED NETWORKS

Commodore Corporation's Educational Resource Center
West Chapter, PA

For some time now, internally focused local area networks have served the corporate and organizational information needs of major corporations: examples include ETHERNET (Xerox Corporation) and WANGNET (Wang Laboratories).

Unique telecommunications systems, developed as a service to large scale purchasers of hardware designed by computer companies, are also now in existence, one of the most extensive being Commodore's Educational Resource Center (with over 500 participants at the time of writing).

Commodore provides participant schools and agencies with requisite facilitative devices (a VICMODEM telecommunications access device), a specialized conference/bulletin board facility (COMED, the special interest group on the CompuServe Information Service), and free or nominal-cost subscriptions to CompuServe. They are thereby able to share information regarding innovative microcomputer users, resources, and technical assistance.

Details on the Commodore program can be obtained through their education division, 1200 Wilson Drive, West Chester, PA 19380.

Apple Corporation
Cupterino, CA

Apple Corporation, through its Apple Education Affairs Grants originated in 1983, has supported several projects involving microcomputer telecommunications, including:

- A computer network for gifted science students in rural Appalachia, administered by Western Carolina University
- An electronic network of rural writing teachers in five states, administered by Middlebury College in Vermont
- An intercultural network sharing international news and socio-cultural surveys, administered by the University of California, San Diego, but linking students in Alaska, California, Israel, Japan, and Mexico (Bowen, 1985).

Apple now sponsors a special bulletin board on SpecialNet, and has developed a communications system serving its dealer network, both of which cater to the unique hardware and software configurations required by special needs populations.

It is obvious that corporate support of telecommunications networks can be expected to expand in the future, and advocates for special needs populations should piggyback on these efforts developed to serve the broader educational community.

ADVOCACY-ORIGINATED NETWORKS

The Disabled Children's Computer Group
P.O. Box 186
El Cerrito, CA 94530-0186
(415) 528-3224

Microcomputer-based telecommunications systems can benefit any who have made the requisite equipment purchases and who wish to advocate on behalf of special needs populations. One of the most exciting groups is the Disabled Children's Computer Group based at the Lawrence Hall of Science (University of California, Berkeley).

The Disabled Children's Computer Group was formed in November 1983 by a group of parents of disabled children, and now includes parents, teachers, and professionals in the field of education, social services, and computer technology.

The DCCG provides a forum for the sharing of information and experiences about computer applications for all categories of disabled children. They have established a "lending library" of computer hardware for disabled children, providing parents an opportunity to try out a system before investing. They also operate a Demonstration Center, which serves as a focal point for hardware modification and software development and for parent, teacher, and student training.

More recently, the DCCG has established a local computer network to share resources and needs, with an electronic bulletin board as part of this network.

Advocacy-originated electronic network, such as that sponsored by the DCCG can be expected to grow if motivated individuals are prepared to dedicate the human and technical resources such systems require.

RESEARCH-ORIENTED NETWORKS

DEAFNET Project
New York University

Recently, the School of Education of New York University's Deafness Rehabilitation Program received a short-term grant from the National Institute of Handicapped Research to investigate innovative pedogical strategies in the area of language arts and literacy skills for deaf young adults.

Of interest is the project's use of an interactive telecommunications system, made possible by General Telephone and Electronic's donation of ten communications terminals and a DEAFNET subscription access. Thirty deaf students ranging in age from 16 to 21 years work at terminals that link five cooperating schools (in the Albany, Boston, New York City, Northampton, and Washington, DC, areas). Electronically conveyed concurrent messages are generated and modified by participants who improve their language arts facilities.

Reflexive Communication Project
McGill University

An interesting Canadian application of telecommunications is provided by an ongoing experiment with gifted children in Montreal entitled "reflexive communication" (Brennan & Spriggs, 1984). In an attempt to motivate gifted students to acquire computer-based skills and to share ideas, this project enabled them to develop joint science projects concurrently over distance as computers linked by modems share the same program. Using Radio Shack Duofone telephone amplifiers (which enable hands-free voice contact) to supplement the data exchange on the computer, these students actively edit and modify documents of their own design. Of special interest is the fact that the hardware system required is readily available: two computer stations, each with an Apple IIe (or II+ compatible) computer, monitor, at least one disk drive, and a modem. The software required is equally common and relatively inexpensive: a communications program permitting transfer of any DOS file (DFX-II), a word processor program (Bank Street Writer), and additional software permitting presentation of experimental data (Visicalc) and graphic data (Visiplot).

While this project is presently limited to gifted students, the process it identifies has a wide generic application to many special needs students.

It can be expected that microcomputer telecommunications will become a major research tool in the near future, as university and agency representatives are drawn to the portability and use of access these processes permit. Researchers desiring to access general information sources and to search bibliographic data from field sites and less exotic university applications will be supported in their efforts.

Such research projects, where electronic communications systems facilitate the application and generalizability of research projects, should also generate more vital information of benefit to all individuals unable to physically interact directly.

SERVICE-ORIENTED NETWORKS

DCI DEAFNET
SIR International
Menlo Park, CA
(415) 859-2236

DCI DEAFNET is a non-profit organization that serves deaf users, schools serving the hearing impaired, and hearing people who advocate within the deaf community.

DCI DEAFNET, a nationwide electronic mail service for the deaf, makes use of Telemail, a commercial electronic mail service owned by TELENET, a division of GTE (General Telephone and Electronic Corporation).

Users require a computer terminal that uses the ASCII code (which has both upper and lower case letters) and not the older Baudot code used by the TDDs (telecommunication devices for deaf people), and a Bell-compatible modem, either 300 baud or 1,200 baud. A specially designed TTD that has a 300 baud modem designed for use with modem computers can also be employed.

Prairie Post
University of Lethbridge
Alberta, Canada

The Rural Special Education Outreach Project of the Faculty of Education at the University of Lethbridge was established in 1981 on a grant from the Department of Advanced Education and Manpower (Government of Alberta).

A small electronic bulletin board system called "Prairie Post" was developed to enable a cost-effective alternate communication system for selected regional participants. The Prairie Post had these primary objectives:

- Develop a physical network of hardware units in the service region, and to establish a communications network between them
- Share these units between selected representations of the teaching and administrative components of the targeted school systems
- "Broker" information services available on information utilities (such as SpecialNet and BRS-After Dark) on behalf of the participants, and establish appropriate subscription contacts with these utilities
- Encourage the development of a variety of telecommunications applications through the RSEOP network, (including electronic mail, internal and external consultation services, and electronic conferencing between system participants).

Prairie Post had the following hardware configuration. A bulletin board program developed by Micro-data Products (Aurora, CO) was purchased to run continuously on the Apple IIe master unit. An Apple Super Serial Card acted as the modem interface, and a Hayes Smartmodem 1200 served as the modem, accepting calls at either 300 or 1,200 baud rates on a dedicated line (403 329-2738).

The board used two software packages to permit data-capturing capability. *Transend* enabled auto-dial interactions between bulletin board users and the network. *Datacapture IIe* provided software enabling message format and transmission.

A Percom hard disk system (10 megabyte winchester drive) enabled the board to incorporate storage that is the equivalent of 19 floppy disks (2,000 pages of single-spaced documentation).

Incoming and outgoing transactions were monitored by the Thunderware "Thunderclock" time card, which collated and reported the frequency and duration of all calls, a monitoring function that considered critical to all cost-sharing projects.

Inquiries regarding developments associated with the Prairie Post can be made by writing the SYSOP, Prairie Post, c/o Faculty of Education, University of Lethbridge, Lethbridge, Alberta, Canada TIK 3M4.

REFERENCES

Bowen. (1985). Business/rural education partnerships. Cuppertino, CA: Apple Corp. Unpublished manuscript.

Brennan, M., & Spriggs, D., (1984). *Reflexive communication.* Protestant School Board of Greater Montreal. Unpublished manuscript.

Subject Index

ABELDATA, National Rehabilitation
    Information Center, 52, 271
Access, definition of, 261
Acoustic coupler, 261
Activities file, using data base for, 221
Adaptive devices
  input, 31–34
    keyboard emulators, 33–34
    switches, 31–32
    video pointing, 32–33
    voice recognition, 34
  other adaptive devices, 38–39
  output devices, 34–37
    audio systems, 35–37
    other devices, 37
    printers, 35
    telecommunications, 37
    video screens, 34–35
Adaptive Firmware Card, 32, 33, 49, 182
*Addons: The Ultimate Guide to
    Peripherals for Blind Computer
    Use,* 184
Advocacy-originated networks, 274
Aimstar, 75, 76, 150
Alien Addition, 110
Alphanumeric, definition of, 261
American Standard Code for
    Information Interchange (ASC

II), 16, 23, 25, 26, 30, 248
  definition of, 261
Apple computers, 9
  Apple II, 3, 4, 5, 15, 19, 21, 32, 35,
    36, 63
  MacIntosh, 3, 4
Apple Corporation, 273–274
Appleworks, 181, 193, 195, 196, 197,
    198, 199
  classroom materials on use of,
    197–199
Applewriter, 246
Applications software, 17
Arithmetic logic unit (ALU), 3
Articulation Error Analysis, 42
Artificial intelligence, definition of, 261
ASC II. *See* American Standard Code
    of Information Interchange
ASC II Express, 245
Assembler language, 16
ASSIST (Authoring system
    supplementing instruction
    selected by teachers), 125
Assistant Series, 193
Asynchronous, definition of, 261
Asynchronous communication,
    description of, 26
Audio computer parts, 20–21

Key: (*App*) indicates Appendix, (*f*) indicates figure, (*t*) indicates table.

Audio systems, as adaptive output
    devices, 35–37
Authoring, use of to individualize
    instruction
    evaluation, selection and use of
        authoring systems and language
          selection, 132–133
        minisystems, selection and use,
          132
        process, 130–132
        products, 129–130
        utilities, selection and use,
          133–134
    languages, 126–128
        for educators, 127
        other, 127–128
    mini-authoring systems, 109–113
        game formats, 110
        other formats, 110–113
    software systems, comparisons of,
        104–109
        individualizing programs,
          108–109
        limitations of, 106–107
        teacher and, 107–109
    summary of, 134
Authoring systems
    blocks, 113–114
    HELPmate system, 122–123, 124 (*f*)
    MACS, 114
        creating lessons with, 114-115,
          118
        features of, 118–119
        teaching and applied research
          applications, 119–120
    regular education systems, 123–125
        ASSIST, 125
        EAZYLEARN, 125
        Ghostwriters, 125
        McGraw-Hill Courseware,
          125–126
        SKILLCORP/AIDS, 123, 125
        Super Sofcrates, 126
    SPE.ED system, 121–122
    utilities, 128–129
Authoring system checklists, 130 (*t*),
    131 (*t*)

Autospeak, 240
Avoider (robot), 90

Bank Street School Filer, 181
Bank Street Writer, 45, 181, 182
Banking, teaching with dBase III, 216
BASIC computer language, 4, 16, 17,
        33, 88, 104, 126
Baud, definition of, 261
Baud rate (modern spread), 247–248
Beginners All Purpose Symbolic
        Instruction Code. *See* BASIC
Big Trak, 87
Bit, definition of, 261
Blocks authoring system, 113–114
Braille-Talk, 185
BRS and BRS/After Dark, 267–268,
    282
Budgets, using spreadsheet for, 229
Buffer, definition of, 261
Bug, definition of, 261
Bulletin boards, definition of, 261.
BYTE, 232, 247
    definition of, 262

Cabbage Patch Talking Kids, 83
Cacti Communication Program, 240
CAI. *See* Computer-assisted instruction
Carrier services, definition of, 262
C-CAD, The Center for Computer
        Assistance of the Disabled, 271
Cell, definition of, 222
*Center for Special Education
    Technology,* 271–272
Central Processing Unit (CPU), 3–4, 5, 6
    definition of, 262
Centralized data analysis, 65–67
Choice Maker II, 47
Choosing Educational Software, 160
Circular (robot), 90
Classifying, definition of, 213
Classroom activities from toy robots, 85
Classroom, use of CAI in, 166–170
    assessing suitable instructional use,
        169–170

complementing curriculum goals, 167–168

determining instructional plan, 168–169

Classroom testing, computer in
   advantages of, 60–62
   computerized testing applications, 62–76
      centralized data analysis, 65–67
      computer adaptive testing, 72–75
      decentralized, 67–69
      guidelines for evaluating test, scoring software, 70–72
      for instructional decision making, 75, 76
      present, 63
      as storer and retriever of test information, for instructional decision making, 75–76
      as test data collector scorer and reporter, 64
      as test developer and administrator, 72
   summary of, 76–77
   teacher use of, 59–60

COBOL, 16

Column, definition of, 222

Commodore Amiga Computer, 3, 4, 21, 63

Commodore Coporation's Educational Resource Center, 273

Common Business Oriented Language (COBOL), 16

COMMON PILOT, 127

Communication training, computer programs for, 45–48

Compatibility, definition of, 262

Comprehensive Learner Adapted Scope & Sequence (CLASS), 219

Compurobot, 87

Compuserve, 37, 251, 252
   in the classroom, 253
   compuserve information center, 268

Computer adaptive testing, 72–75

Computer-assisted instruction (CAI), 39–41, 75, 129
   definition of, 262

effects of feedback provided by, 119–120

games, 157–159
   types of, 158–159

overview of, 146
   recent trends, 147
   special education, transforming nature of, 146–147

software evaluation, 159–164
   evaluating reviews, 163–164
   using forms for evaluation, 160–163

software of generalized learning, 153–156
   problem-solving, 153–154
   simulation program, 154–156

sources of further information on, 175–178 (*App*)

summary of, 170

types of programs, 148–153
   drill and practice, 148–149
   tutorial program, 149–153

using, 164–170
   planning for classroom use, 166–170

writing program, 156–157

Computer Assisted Speech Tool, 42

Computer Disk Read Only Memory (CDROM), 8–9

Computer Equipment and Aids for the Blind and Visually Impaired, 184

The Computer Phone Books, 252

Computer-managed instruction (CMI), 39–41

Computer systems, institutional versus individual ownership of, 53–54

Computers
   hardware
      peripheral devices, 6–14
      system unit, 3–5
   intercommunication with, 17
      hardware: cables and interfaces, 18–25
      software, 25–27
   software, 14–17
      applications, 17

Computers *(continued)*
  software
    operating systems, 15
    programming, 15–17
    summary of, 27–28
    types of, 1–2
Computers in the Classroom, 160
Computers in Special Education, 232
Computers in Today's World, 1
Confer, 271
Contained Reading Series, 108
Control Programs for Microcomputers, 15
Coporate sponsored networks, 273–274
Creative Computer, 245
Cross Talk, definition of, 262
Curriculum
  areas of
    communication training, 45–48
    daily living skills instruction, 50–51
    language development, 44–45
    motor training, 44
    recreational uses, 49–50
    therapeutic applications, 51–52
    vocational training, 48–49
  integrating computers into, 39–41

Daily living skills instruction, computer programs for, 50–51
Daisywheel printers, 13, 14, 24
Data base, definition of, 207, 262
Data base management system, definition of, 262
Data bases, 208–221
  use of for educational management, 218–221
  using with handicapped students, 216–218
  using in instruction, 212–215
  record example, 210 *(f)*
  teaching with, procedure for, 215–216
  terminology, 210 *(f)*
Data bases, hardware resources, 52–53
Data capture, 276

DataCaputer, 245
Data collection for tests, computer uses for, 64–69
Data communication, definition of, 262
Data communication equipment (DCE), 25
Data item, definition of, 210
DATA Program, 75
Data terminal equipment (DTE), 25
dBase III, 208–209
  teaching banking with, 216
DCI DEAFNET, 275–276
DEAFNET Project, 274–275
Decentralized data analysis, 67–69
Decision making using data bases, 214
Decisions Software, 156
Delphi, 251
Desktop publishing, 194
Developing Reading Power, 151
Developmentally disabled children, word processing with, 182–183
Dialog, 252
DIALOG Information Services, 267
Digital indexing system, 49
Digitalker, 36
The Disabled Children's Computer Group, 274
Disk (disk drive), definition of, 262
Disk drives, 7
Disk operating system (DOS), definition of, 262
Displaywriter, 195
Distributors of software, 177
Dot matrix printer, 13, 14, 24
Double Touch, 46, 184
Download, definition of, 262
Dr. Peet's Talk/Writer, 184
Drill and Practice, as CAI program, 148–149
  ease of use, 149
Dumb terminal, definition of, 262
Duplex (full duplex), definition of, 262

E2 authoring system, 25, 125
EAZYLEARN, 125

Easynet, 246
ECHO speech synthesizer, 118
Echo/Cricket speech synthesizer, 36
Educational management using data base for, 218–221
Educational Products Information Exchange (EPIE), 167
The Educational Software Selector (TESS), 160
Educational toys, 80–81
Electronic mail, definition of, 263
Electronic Musical Soft Tunes, 80
Electronic toys
  educational, 80–81
  interactional, 81–82
Elementary Vocabulary/Spelling, 128–129
Emulation program, definition of, 263
End user, definition of, 263
ERIC MICROsearch, 246–247
ETHERNET, 273
Evaluation of authoring programs, 129–134
Exceptional Children, 232
Exploratory Play, 45
Exploratory Play and Representational Play, 33
Expert system, definition of, 263
E-Z Learner, 110, 111
E-Z Pilot, 127

The Factory, 154
Fastrack Quizzer, 128
Field, definition of, 210
File
  creating a data base, 211
  definition of, 210, 263
File transfer protocols, 27
Filing Assistant (IBM), 221
Filing personal information, with data bases, 217
First Categories, 44, 108
First Words, 44, 108
Formula, definition of, 222
Forth language, 16
Frame, 105

Game computer ports, 19
Game formats, 110
Game Frame, 109
The Game Show, 110
Games, CAI, 157–159
  types of, 158–159
Gateway, definition of, 263
Ghostwriter authoring system, 125
Glossary, 261–264
Graphics tablet, 118

Handbook of Microcomputers in Special Education, 232
Hard copy, definition of, 263
Hard disk, definition of, 263
Hard or fixed disks, 8
Hardware. *See also* Adaptive devices
  definition of, 263
  hardware resource data bases, 52–53
Hardware: cables and interfaces, 18–19
Hardware components for microcomputers, acquiring, 244–245, 246–247
Hardware for computers
  peripheral devices, 6–14
    computer-to-computer input/ output, 9–14
    data storage/retrieval, 7–9
  system unit, 3–5
    intercommunication in, 4–5
Hawaiian Developmental Disabilities Council, 182
Hearing impaired children, word processing with, 185–186
HELPmate authoring system, 122–123, 124 (f)
HEX, Handicapped Educational Exchange, 271
  language, 16
High-level computer languages, 16–17
Homework, 181
Hypothesis testing using data bases, 213–214

IBM, 4, 6, 9, 21, 23, 63
  PC, 5, 32, 33, 36, 43, 127, 128
  8088 (Intel) series computers, 3
  Token Ring, 9
Individual Education Plan (IEPs), 148, 197
  data bank system, 218–219
Individual versus institutional ownership of computer system, 53–54
Information center, definition of, 263
Information, definition of, 263
Information provider, definition of, 263
Information services networks, 267–270
Information utilities, 250–252
  generic, 251–252
  packet switched network, 251
Ink jet printer, 13, 14, 24
Input adaptive services, 31–34
  keyboard emulators, 33–34
  switches, 31–32
  video pointing, 32–33
  voice recognition devices, 34
Input devices, computer-to-computer, 9–11
Input/Output (IO), 6
IN-SEARCH, 238
Instruction, computer-assisted. See Computer-assisted instruction
Instruction, individualizing. See Authoring, use of to individualize instruction
Instruction, using spreadsheets in, 224–229
  budgets and materials allowances, 229
  using for educational management, 228
  procedures for teaching, 225–227
  spreadsheet for students, 227
  statistics and demographics, 229
  vocational application, 227–228
Instructional materials, inventory with data base, 219–220
Integrated Learning Systems (ILS), 150
Integrated packages, definition of, 207
Integrated software, definition of, 263

INTELSAT, 236
Interactive, definition of, 263
Interconnect, definition of, 263
Institutional versus individual ownership of computer systems, 53–54
Intex Talker, 36
Intro Voice II, 34

K-8 Math Worksheet Generator, 129
KendallNET Access, Telecommunications for Educators of the Learning Impaired, 269–270
Keyboarding, teaching of, 187–188
Keyguard, use of for handicapped, 38
Keytalk, 45
Kidwriter, 45
KidWord, 45
King Keyboard (TASH), 33
Kits, robot, 88–91
Koala Pad, 33, 49, 118
Kurtzwell Readers, 11

LAN. See Local Area Nework
Language assessments, remediation and screening, 42
Language for authoring, 126
  for educators, 127
  other, 127–128
Language development, computer programs for, 44–45
Laser printers, 13, 14, 24
LEGO, 90
Lesson plans, use of data base for, 219
Lessons, creation with MACS, 114–118
Library, 193, 194
Light Talker, 34
Line Tracer II (robot), 90
Listen to Learn, 180
Listening to Learn, 46
Local Area Networks (LANs), 9, 235
  definition of, 263
Logo language, 16, 17
  programming language, 87, 88, 90

123 Lotus spreadsheet, 221
Low-level computer language, 16

MacIntosh computer (Apple), 3, 4
MACS. *See* Multisensory Authoring
      Computer System
Magic Slate, 45, 181, 184
Magic Want Speaking Reader, 80
Mailbag, 193–194
Mainframe computer, 2
Math Competency Series, 108
Math Power Program, 108
Mathematic binary system as basic
      computer language, 4
McGraw-Hill Courseware authoring
      system, 125–126
Medusa (robot), 89
Memocon Crawler (robot), 90
MERIT NETWORK, 272
Micro Access, 247
Micro II E2 Authoring System,
      120–121
Microcomputer, definition of, 263
Microcomputer Information
      Coordination Center (MICC), 160
*Microcomputer Resource for Special
      Education,* 232
Microcomputer, use of in school
      testing, 60–62
Microcomputer technology and
      telecommunications
   acquiring hardware and software
      components for, 224–249
   common features of, 236–238
   current applications of in special
      education, 231–233
   determining applicability of,
      232–233
   getting online, steps in, 249–250
   information utilities, 250–255
   networking
      local area, 235–236
      telephone-based, 236
   problems associated with, 252–255
   public education, change effecting,
      255–256

rural special education environment,
      241–244
   overcoming isolation, 242–243
   special challenges of, 243–244
   use of for special needs individuals,
      238–241
   summary of, 256
   telecommunications, introduction to,
      233–235
Microcomputers, major components of,
      2, 3
   peripheral devices, 6–14
   system units, 3–5
Micro-LADS, 108
Microsoft DOS, 15
Microtutor II EZ authoring system,
      123–125
Mid-level computer languages, 16
The Milliken Word Processor, 181
MIND, 246, 247
Mini Keyboard (TASH), 34
Mini-authoring systems, 109–113
   commercially available,
      137–143 (*App*)
   game formats, 110
   other formats, 110–113
   publishers of, 114 (*App*)
Minicomputer, 2
   definition of, 263
Mockingbird speech synthesizer, 36
Modem
   definition of, 247, 264
   speed, 247–248
   types, 248–249
*Modularized Student Management
      Systems (MSMS),* 219
Monitors, 12–13
Monkey (robot), 90
Moptown, 154
Morsewriter, 182
Motor training on computer, programs
      for, 44
Motor training games, 44
Mr. Bootsman (robot), 90
Multiple Choice File, 128
Multipurpose Authoring Language
      (MPAL), 128

Multisensory Authoring Computer
    System (MACS), 114–121
  creating lessons with, 114–115, 118
  features of, 118–119
  teaching and applied research
    applications, 119–121
Multi-tasking, definition of, 264
Muppet Learning Keys, 33

National Council of Teachers of
    Mathematics (NCTM), 160
National Education Association (NEA),
    160
National Service Robot Associations,
    96
Navius (robot), 90
NCR Sentry 3000, 63, 64 (*f*)
Network checklist, features to
    consider, 259–260
Network, definition of, 264
Networking, 235–236
  local area, 235–236
  telephone-based, 236
Networks
  advocacy-originated, 274
  corporate-sponsored, 273–274
  information services, 267–270
  research-oriented, 274–275
  service-oriented, 275–276
  special needs bulletin board system,
    271–272
  telecommunications service designed
    to assist special needs
    individuals, 270–272
  university-based networks, 272–273
Newsroom, 194
Noise, definition of, 264
Note cards, student, using data base
    for, 220

Occupational therapy evaluations, use
    of computer for, 43
Omnibox, 51–52
Online Computer Telephone Directory,
    252

On-line, definition of, 264
On-line services, definition of, 264
"Open architectures" of computers, 5
Operating system software, 15
Operation Frog, 155
Operation system, definition of, 264
Optical storage of data, 8–9
Opticon tracking guide for CRT
    displays, 49
Output adaptive services, 34–37
  audio systems, 35–37
  other, 37
  printers, 35
  telecommunications, 37
  video screens, 34–35
Output devices, computer-to-computer,
    9, 11–14
  monitors, 12–13
  printers, 13–14

PABX (PBX), definition of, 264
Packet-assembler disassemblers (PADS),
    251
Packet switched networks, 251
Packet switching, definition of, 264
Paint With Words, 49
Parallel computer parts, 21, 23
Parent communication, use of word
    processing as tool for, 195–196
Parenting Reporting, 129
Pascal language, 16, 17, 104, 126
PC-1 Powerline, 37
Peppy (robot), 89
Peripheral computer devices, 6–14
  computer-to-computer input/output
    device, 9–14
    input, 9–11
    output, 11–14
  data storage and retrieval devices, 7–9
Peripheral device, definition of, 264
Personal Computing, 247
PFS File, 209
Physical therapists, use of biofeedback
    for, 52
Physical therapy evaluations, use of
    computer for, 43

Pic-Man, 49
Picture Communication, 46
Pilot language, 16, 17, 104
Piper Mouse (robot), 90
Plain Vanilla, 110
Planner software package, 193
Plato, 150
Play, the value of, 79
Plotter printers, 13, 14
The Pond, 154
Popular Computing, 247
Ports for computers, major, 17–24
  audio, 20–21
  game, 19
  parallel, 21, 23
  serial ports, 24
  video, 19–20
Power Pad, 118
Prairie Post, 276
Print Shop, 49
Printshop, 194
Printers, as adaptive output devices, 34–37
Printers for computers, types of, 13–14
Problem-solving using data bases, 214–215
Productivity tools, 205–208
  breaking code for, 207–208
  rationale for use with handicapped students, 208
  technology explosion and, 207
  terminology, 207 (*f*)
Productivity tools, definition of, 207
Programming software, 15–17
Programs for Cognitive Rehabilitation, 52
Programs for Early Acquisition of Language (PEAL), 45
Project Special, Kentucky's Special education network, 242
Prosthetics, robotic arms as, 95–96
Public education, effecting change in, 255–256
Public Law 94-142, 218
Publishers, software, 175
Publishing, desktop, 194
Puzzles and Posters, 129

Quill, word processing package, 193
Quizmaster, 128, 199

The Rabbit Scanner, 47
RAM. *See* Random-access memory
Random access memory (RAM), 3–4, 5, 6, 9
  definition of, 264
Range, definition of, 222
RB5X (robot), 93, 95
Read and Spell, 80
Read only memory (ROM), 3–4, 5, 13, 14
  definition of, 264
Reading Tutor, 110, 111
Record, definition of, 210
Recreational users of computers, 49–50
Reflexive Communication Project, 275
Rehabilitation Project in Data Processing to train disabled students, 48
Relational Data Base, definition of, 210
Representational Play, 45
Research-oriented networks, 274–275
Retrieval of test information on computer, 75–76
Robot kits, 88–91
Robotic toys. *See* Toys, robotic
Robotics Industries of America (RIA), 96
Robots
  arms as prosthetics, 95–96
  evolution of, 82
  future of, 96
  kits, 88–91
  personal services, 91–95
    application of, 92, 93
    availability of, 91–92
    characteristics of, 92–93
    evolution of, 93–95
    in future, 94–95
  robotic toys, 82–83
  summary of, 97
  toy robots, 83–88
    activities with, 87 (*t*)

Robots *(continued)*
    toy robots
        use of in classroom, 83
        classroom activities, 85
        function of, 84–85
        teaching with, 86
        types of, 85–88
Robots, sources of information on,
        99–102 *(App)*
ROM. *See* Read only memory
Romeo Brailler, 35
Row, definition of, 222
RS-232, definition of, 264
Rural special education environment,
        241–244
    overcoming isolation, 242–243
    special challenges of, 243–244

SAAVY programming language, 95
Scanning with Language Arts, 110, 111
Scanning with Math, 110, 111
ScanWriter, 34
Scan-WRITER (Zygo), 37
S-Cargo (robot), 90
School testing, computer in
    advantages of, 60–62
    applications of, 62–76
        data analysis, centralized, 65–67
        data analysis, decentralized, 67–69
        guidelines for evaluation, 70–72
    summary of, 76–77
    teacher use of, 59–60
Screening Test of Syntactic Abilities,
        43
Screenwriter, 246
SEARCH HELPER, 238
Search helper, 246
Sensible Speller, 193
Sequenced Inventory of
        Communication Development
        (SICD), 42
Sequencing, definition of, 213
Serial computer parts, 24
Service-oriented networks, 275–276
Service robots, personal, 91–95
    applications of, 92–93

availability of, 91–92
    characteristics of, 92
    evolution of, 93–95
Shadow/VET, 34
Simple Corn I, 47
Simulation programs, 154–156
    advantages of, 155
    elements of effective programs, 156
The Single Switch Assessment, 44
SKILLCORP/AIDS (Assisted
        Instructional Development
        System), 123–125
    microtutor II EZ authoring system,
        123–125
    voice-based learning system (VBLS),
        123
Sofcrates-The Courseware Creator, 125
Softerm, 245
Software, authoring, comparing
        systems of, 104–109
Software of CAI, for generalized
        learning, 153–164
    evaluation
        using forms for, 160–163
        knowledge of marketplace,
            159–160
        reviews, 163–164
        problem-solving, 153–154
Software, definition of, 164
Software: Communication between
        devices, 25–27
Software components for
        microcomputer, acquiring, 244,
        245–247
Software for computers, 14–17
    applications, 17
    operating system, 15
    programming, 15–17
        high-level languages, 16
        low-level languages, 16
        mid-level languages, 16
Software planning preview form, 160,
        161–162 *(f)*
Software systems for authoring,
        comparisons of, 104–109
Software test scoring, evaluating,
        70–72

The Source, 37, 251–252
The Source, Telecomputing source, 268
Speak and Spell, 80
Special education software information sources for, 177–178
Special Education Technology, 232
Special education, transforming nature of, 146–147
Special needs bulletin boards systems, 271–272
Special Services, 232
Special Skills Builder, 108
SpecialNet, North America's largest utility, 37, 268
Speech and Language assessments, software programs available for , 42–43
Speech-language pathologists
  use of computers by, 41
  use of microcomputer for, 51
SpeechPac (ACS), 34
SPE.ED authoring system, 121–122
SPEEDNET (Special EDucation NETwork), 272–273
Spell and Define, 110, 111
Spelling Machine, 111
Spreadsheet, definition of, 207
Spreadsheets, 221–229
  using in instruction, 224–229
  terminology for, 222 (*f*)
  using, 222–224
Stand-alone, definition of, 264
Statistic package for the social sciences, 65
Statistics and demographics, using spreadsheets for, 229
Stickeybear Printer, 49
Storing and retrieving test information, 75–76
Story Machine, 45
Students, feedback to on teaching writing, 192–193
Study Quiz Files, 128
Super Sofcrates, 126, 127
SuperPILOT, 127
Supertalker, 36

Sweettalker II, 36
Switches, use of as adaptive input devices, 31–32
Switchmaster, 44
Synchronous communication, description of, 26
System unit of the computer, 3–4
  internal communication in, 4

Talking BlissApple, 47
Talking Screen Test Writer, 180
Talking Screen Textwriter, 46
Talking Wheelchair, 46
Talk/Writer, 46
Tandy Color Computer, 128
Tape memory, 7–8
Tasman Turtle, 87
Teacher use of test information, 59–60
Teacher's Helper, 128
Teachers of word processing, applications for, 194–195, 198
Teacher-student conferences on teaching writing, 191–192
Teaching
  and applied research applications with MACS, 119–121
  with a data base, 215–216
  with toy robots, 86
  word processing
    formatting for printed text, 189
    keyboarding, 187–188
    writing and editing, 188–189
    writing with methods of, 189–192
Technology in the Curriculum, 163
Telecommunications
  common features of systems, 236–238
  determining applicability of, 232–233
  introduction to, 233–235
  networking, 235–236
    local areas, 235–236
    telephone-based, 236
  process of, 249–250
  use of for special needs individuals, 238–241

Telecommunications, as adaptive output devices, 34–37
Telecommunications services designed to assist special needs individuals, 270–272
Teleconferencing, definition of, 264–265
Telephone-based networking, 236
Teletext, definition of, 265
Template, definition of, 207, 222
TenCORE Authoring System, 127
Test Made Easy, 128
Test making software, 199–200
Test applications, computerized, 62–76. See also Classroom testing
  computer adaptive testing, 72–75
  data collecting, 64, 65
    centralized analysis, 65–67
    decentralized analysis, 67–69
  present, 63
  scoring guidelines, 64, 70–72
  storing, 75–76
TetraSam (Zygo), 32, 34
Text, formatting of printed, 189
Therapeutic applications of computers
  areas of, 51–52
  evaluation, 41–43
    physical occupational therapy, 43
    speech and language assessments, 42–43
Thermal printers, 13, 14
TIC TAC SHOW, 105, 113
Touch and tell, 80
Touch Talker, 34, 47 (f)
Touch Windows, 33, 47, 49
Toy Assessor, 44
Toy Scanner, 44
Toys, electronic
  educational, 80–81
  enabling active interaction, 81–82
  robotic, 82–88
    activities with, 87 (f)
    classroom activities, 85
    use of in classroom, 83–84
    function of, 84–85
    teaching with, 86
    types of, 85–88

Traffic Service Position System for long distance operators, 49
The Trine System, 182
Turn Backer (robot), 90
Tutor, 104
Tutorial programs, 149–153
  application of various levels of instruction, 151–152
  courseware, 149–150
  evaluating student performance, 150–151
  teaching skills versus concepts, 152–153

Ufonic Voice Speech synthesizer, 36
Unex II Exercise system, 43
Unicorn Expanded Keyboard, 33
Universal Laboratory Training and Research Aid (ULTRA), 36
University-based networks, 272–273
UNIX systems, 9
Upload, definition of, 265
Use of Computers in Education, 186
Utilities for authoring, 128–129

VersaBrailler, 35
Video computer parts, 19–20
Video painting, use of as adaptive input device, 33–34
Video screens as adaptive output devices, 34–35
Videotext, definition of, 265
Visual Perceptual Diagnostic Testing, 52
Visual Perceptual Diagnostic Testing and Training, 43
Visually impaired children, word processing with, 183–185
Vocabulary Machine, 111
Vocational application, using spreadsheets for, 227–228
Vocational training, computer programs for, 48–49
Voice Input Module (VIM), 34
Voice recognition devices, use of as adaptive input, 34

Voice synthesizers, 40
Voice therapy, microcomputer-based
    biofeedback device for, 51–52
Voice-based learning system (VBLS),
    123
Votrax Type 'N Talk, 36
The Voyages of the Mini, 156
VP speech system, 36

Walk-in Scoring Center, test scoring
    for classroom teachers and,
    73–74
WANGNET, 273
Watchwords, 111
Window, definition of, 222
Wireless Data Transmission System,
    37
Word Attack, 105, 150
Word Handler, 197
Word processing in special education
  applications for teachers, 194–195
  classroom materials, creating,
    197–200
  IEPs, 197
  parent communication, 195–196
  summary of, 201
  testing, 199–200
Word processing with handicapped
    children
  developmentally disabled, 182–183
  hearing impaired, 185–186

mildly handicapped, 180–182
physically handicapped, 182–183
skills, need for, 186
training in computer skills need for,
    186
visually impaired, 183–185
Word Processors to facilitate writing
  additional applications of
    desktop publishing, 194
    integrated packages, 193–194
  methods of teaching, 188–193
    assessment, 190
    feedback to students, 192–193
    modeling, 190
    prewriting, 190–191
    teacher-student conferences, 191
  teaching, 187–189
    formatting for printed text, 189
    keyboarding, 187–188
    writing and editing, 188–189
  writing, nature of, 186–187
Word talk, 184, 185
Wordisk Maker, 111
Wordfind/Crossword Magic, 128
Wordstar, 195
Write Once Read Only Memory
    (WOROM), 8–9
Writer's Assistant, 193
Writing CAI programs, 156–157
Writing, teaching of, 188–189
Writing with word processors,
    teaching, 189–192

Notes

Notes

Notes

Notes

Notes

Notes

Notes

Notes

Notes